The Constantinos Karamanlis Institute for Democracy Series on European and International Affairs

Series Editors:
Constantine Arvanitopoulos
Nikolaos Tzifakis

The Constantinos Karamanlis Institute for Democracy
Vas. Sofias Ave. 10
10674 Athens
Greece
info@idkaramanlis.gr

The Constantinos Karamanlis Institute for Democracy Series on European and International Affairs consists of edited multi-author works dealing with contemporary political and socio-economic issues of European and international concern. It attempts to offer comprehensive and up-to-date accounts of the relevant debates currently taking place within the discipline of International Relations. The series is addressed to a wide audience: undergraduate and postgraduate students, scholars, think tanks and decision-makers.

Constantine Arvanitopoulos
Editor

Turkey's Accession to the European Union

An Unusual Candidacy

Professor Constantine Arvanitopoulos
Constantinos Karamanlis Institute for Democracy
Vas. Sofias Ave. 10
10674 Athens
Greece
arvanito@idkaramanlis.gr

This is a joint publication of the Centre for European Studies and the Constantinos Karamanlis Institute for Democracy. This publication receives funding from the Community and the European Parliament.

ISSN 1866-1270

ISBN 978-3-540-88196-4 e-ISBN 978-3-540-88197-1

The Constantinos Karamanlis Institute for Democracy Series on European and International Affairs

Library of Congress Control Number: 2008939142

Springer is a part of Springer Science+Business Media

springer.com

Published by Springer-Verlag Berlin Heidelberg 2009

Cover-design: WMX Design GmbH, Heidelberg

9 8 7 6 5 4 3 2 1 0

Printed on acid-free paper

Acknowledgements

For the publication of this edited multi-authored volume there are several people whose assistance has been needed and is very much appreciated. First of all, I express my gratitude to the Centre for European Studies for our excellent track record of cooperation in making this joint venture come to fruition. In addition, many thanks to our friends at Springer for believing in this new book series and showing particular interest in this first volume.

I also gratefully acknowledge the kind assistance of the Fundación para el Análisis y los Estudios Sociales (FAES), the Hanns Seidel Foundation (HSS) and the Fondation pour l'innovation Politique for suggesting the participation of certain authors whose valuable insights enrich the book. Also, special thanks to Marvin DuBois and his team for their invaluable copy-editing work.

At the Constantinos Karamanlis Institute for Democracy, I thank both the present and past staff members of the Department of International Co-operation – namely, Pantelis Sklias, Nikolaos Tzifakis, Christianna Papageorgaki and Evangelia Sofroni – for their constant support and ready involvement.

Finally, I am profoundly indebted to the scholars whose work is included in this volume for their participation and contribution.

September 2008 Constantine Arvanitopoulos

The Editor

Constantine Arvanitopoulos is Professor of International Relations and Chair of the Department of International and European Studies at Panteion University, Athens. He is a graduate of Panteion University and holds an MA and a PhD in International Relations from the School of International Service, American University, Washington, DC.

He has been a Lecturer of International Relations and Comparative Politics in the School of International Service at the American University (1987–1989), post-doctoral Fellow at the Center for European Studies at Harvard University (1990–1992) and Assistant Professor of Government and European Politics in the Department of Public and International Affairs at George Mason University (1992–1995).

His research interests are in International Relations theory, specifically the study of regime change, European politics and US foreign policy analysis. He has taught courses on theory and methodology of International Relations, European politics and comparative politics.

He has published articles on the EU, the non-aligned movement, Greek–Turkish relations, the study of leadership and authoritarian regimes. He has written books on the transitions from authoritarianism to democracy, on transatlantic relations, on US foreign policy and a textbook on international relations.

He has been the Director General of the Constantinos Karamanlis Institute for Democracy since June 2000. His latest appointments include the following: Representative of the New Democracy Party (ND) to the National Council of Foreign Policy, Member of the Academic Council of the Centre for European Studies (CES) and Member of the Board of Directors of UNESCO–Greece. Constantine Arvanitopoulos was also the spokesperson for the New Democracy Party during the last national elections (September 2007).

Contents

List of Tables

Contributors

Mustafa Akyol is a Turkish journalist who has written extensively on Islam and the modern world. He has degrees in political science and history from Istanbul's Bosphorus University. He is currently the opinion editor and a columnist for *Turkish Daily News*, Turkey's oldest English-language daily. He also writes a regular column for the Turkish national daily, *Star*. Akyol's opinion pieces have also appeared in publications such as *The Washington Post*, *The Wall Street Journal*, *International Herald Tribune*, *Newsweek*, *Der Spiegel*, *The American Interest*, *First Things*, *The Weekly Standard* and others. He is the author of a Turkish-language book entitled *Rethinking the Kurdish Question: What Went Wrong? What Next?* (2006).

Ali Ihsan Aydin is Associated Researcher at the French think tank Fondation pour l'innovation politique in Paris. A graduate of Boğaziçi University in Istanbul and of l'Institut d'études politiques de Strasbourg in France, he is now a PhD candidate in political science at the Centre d'études européennes of Science Po de Paris (Institut d'études politiques de Paris), studying the religious and cultural factors in the construction of Europe. He is the Paris correspondent of the Turkish daily *Zaman*.

Can Buharalı is a Graduate of Lycée de Galatasaray and Boğaziçi University (International Relations and Political Science). He holds a post-graduate degree in European administrative studies from the Collège d'Europe, Bruges, Belgium. Mr Buharalı worked for the Turkish Ministry of Foreign Affairs as a Career Diplomat between 1993 and 2001 in Ankara, Brussels and Tehran. He started his consultancy practice in 2001 and is currently a managing partner of Istanbul Economics Consultancy. Between 2002 and 2004 he lectured at Boğaziçi University on 'Economic Integration and the European Union'. Buharalı is also a Member of the Executive Board of the think tank EDAM (Center for Economics and Foreign Policy Studies) based in Istanbul.

Thanos Dokos received his PhD in International Relations from the University of Cambridge and has held research posts at the Hessische Stiftung Friedens- und Konfliktforschung (1989–1990) in Frankfurt, and the Center for Science and International Affairs at Harvard University (1990–1991). He served as the Director for Research, Strategic Studies Division, Hellenic Ministry of National Defence

(1996–1998) and as an Adviser on NATO issues to the Ministry of Foreign Affairs (1998–1999). He is currently the Director-General of ELIAMEP and a visiting lecturer at the University of Athens (Department of Turkish and Modern Asia Studies). His research interests are in the areas of international security, Greek–Turkish relations and Turkish security policy, arms control and Mediterranean security. His recent publications include 'The Case of Greece', in Karin Von Hippel (Ed.), *European Responses to Terrorism* (Oxford University Press, 2005) and *Countering the Proliferation of Weapons of Mass Destruction* (Taylor & Francis, 2007). He is the editor of *Security Sector Reform in Southeastern Europe and the Middle East* (Kluwer Academic Publishers, 2007).

Özgür Ünal Eriş (Assistant Professor) holds a BA in Political Science and International Relations from Bosphorus University in Istanbul, Turkey, an MA in European Studies from the University of Exeter in the UK and a PhD from the Department of Government of the University of Essex. While her PhD was on 'German Foreign Policy's Influence on Turkey's Wish to Become a Member of the European Union', she later specialised in the concept of new security threats, specifically, illegal migration and energy security. She has also done research in and published articles on the European Neighbourhood Policy and the EU's role in the solution for Kosovo, topics also related to the EU's security policies. Currently, she works in the Department of European Union Studies of the University of Bahcesehir, Istanbul.

Ranier Fsadni is Adviser to the Prime Minister of Malta on Mediterranean and Maritime Affairs. He is the Chairperson of the Academy for the Development of a Democratic Environment (AZAD), a Euro-Mediterranean think tank based in Malta, and teaches social and cultural anthropology at the University of Malta. He is a weekly columnist for *The Times of Malta*.

Diba Nigar Göksel joined the European Stability Initiative (ESI) in 2004, where she is the Senior Analyst and Caucasus Coordinator. Since 2003, Nigar has also been the Editor-in-Chief of the policy journal *Turkish Policy Quarterly* (TPQ). She has a weekly column in *Turkish Daily News* and is the author of the Freedom House report 'Turkey in Transit' covering 2006 and 2007. Prior to joining the ESI she worked for leading Turkish NGOs including the Turkish Industrialists' and Businessmen's Association (TUSIAD), the Turkish Economic and Social Studies Foundation (TESEV) and the ARI Movement. She spent a few years prior to 2000 in Washington, DC, working for the Azerbaijan Embassy.

Kostas Ifantis is Associate Professor of International Relations in the Department of Political Science, University of Athens. His papers have appeared in edited books and in periodicals such as *Democratization*, *International Journal*, *Southeast European and Black Sea Studies*, *Journal of Southern Europe and the Balkans*, *Turkish Studies*, etc. His publications include *NATO and the New Security Paradigm* (Frank Cass, 2002), *Theory and Reform in the European Union* (Manchester University Press, 2002) and *Turkish–Greek Relations* (Routledge, 2004); and he has co-edited *Multilateralism and Security Institutions in an Era of Globalization* (Routledge, 2008).

Dimitris Keridis is Associate Professor of International Politics in the Department of Balkan, Slavic and Oriental Studies, University of Macedonia, Greece, and the Deputy Director of the Karamanlis Foundation in Athens. His research interests include south-eastern European politics, European security and theories of international relations, nationalism and democracy. His latest book is *The US Foreign Policy and the Conservative Counterrevolution*. Dr Keridis has served as the Constantine Karamanlis Associate Professor in Hellenic and South-Eastern European Studies at the Fletcher School, Tufts University (2005–2007), as the Director of the Kokkalis Foundation in Athens (2001–2005), and of the Kokkalis Program on Southeastern and East-Central Europe at the John F. Kennedy School of Government, Harvard University (1997–2001), and as a Lecturer of Balkan Studies at the John F. Kennedy School of Government (1998–2001). Since 1995, he has been a Research Associate at the Institute for Foreign Policy Analysis (IFPA), Cambridge, MA, and since 2001, he has been the Director of the Olympia Balkan Studies Summer Seminars. Professor Keridis is a graduate of the Fletcher School of Law and Diplomacy (PhD 1998, MALD 1994).

Julio Crespo MacLennan, MA D.Phil. (Oxon) is a historian, international analyst and writer. He was the founding director of the Instituto Cervantes in Istanbul and cultural attaché of the Spanish Embassy in Turkey (2001–2002) and in Ireland (2002–2005). He has held academic positions at San Pablo-CEU University and Instituto de Empresa business school in Madrid. At present, he is a visiting professor at Tufts University (US). He is a member of the editorial board of the Spanish daily *ABC* and writes regularly on European affairs for the press. His books include *Spain and the Process of European Integration* (Macmillan, 2000), *España en Europa, del ostracismo a la modernidad* (Marcial Pons, 2004) and *Europe Makers: Great Europeanists and Eurosceptics in the Twentieth Century* (forthcoming).

Thomas Silberhorn, born on 12 November 1968, has been a member of the German Bundestag for the constituency Bamberg-Forchheim since 2002. He is the spokesperson on European and foreign affairs, defence, development cooperation and human rights for the group of CSU parliamentarians in the German Bundestag. After studying law from 1987 to 1992 at the universities of Erlangen, Munich and Bayreuth and completing his compulsory period of practical legal training from 1992 to 1994, part of which was spent in Paris and Brussels, Silberhorn was an Assistant Professor in the field of public law specialising in public international law and European law at the University of Bayreuth. Admitted to the bar in 2001, Silberhorn is a member of the party executive of the Christian Social Union.

Pantelis Sklias is Associate Professor of International Political Economy in the Department of Political Science and International Relations, University of Peloponnese. His main research interests include the issues and agents of international political economy, the economic ties of the developing world with the EU, societies and economies in transition as well as the role of civil society in sustainable development. He has written both in Greece and abroad on the political economy of the Balkans (e.g., the consequences of war in Kosovo and the Former Yugoslav Republic of Macedonia, the transition and the accession process of Croatia), EU relations with the countries of the former Soviet Union, the international trade regime in Ecuador and the Commonwealth of Dominica, etc. Between 2004 and 2007, he was the Head of the International Cooperation Department of Constantinos Karamanlis Institute of Democracy, and is still a member of its Advisory Board.

Panayotis J. Tsakonas is Associate Professor of International Relations and Security at the Department of Mediterranean Studies, University of the Aegean, Rhodes, Greece. He has held research posts at NATO and Harvard University, and he was a Fulbright Visiting Scholar at Yale University. He served as Special Adviser at the Hellenic Ministry of National Defense (1996–1998) and at the Ministry of Foreign Affairs (1999–2003). He is co-editor of *Études Helléniques/Hellenic Studies* and his articles have appeared in professional journals (including *Turkish Studies*, *The Hague Journal of Diplomacy*, *Politics*, *Journal of Southeast Europe and Black Sea Studies*, *Journal of Modern Hellenism*, *Security Dialogue*, etc.). His latest publications include *National Security Strategy: Building the Greek Model for the Twenty-First Century* (Papazissis, 2005), *Multilateralism and Security Institutions in an Era of Globalization* (Routledge, 2007) and *The Incomplete Breakthrough in Greek–Turkish Relations: Grasping Greece's Socialization Strategy* (Palgrave-Macmillan, forthcoming).

Aristotle Tziampiris is Assistant Professor of International Relations in the Department of International and European Studies of the University of Piraeus, a member of the Scientific Board (and former member of the Board of Directors) of the Institute of Defense Analyses (IAA-Athens, Greece) and Research Associate at the Hellenic Foundation for European and Foreign Policy (ELIAMEP-Athens, Greece). He is the author of *Greece, European Political Cooperation and the Macedonian Question* (Ashgate Press, 2000), *International Relations and the Macedonian Question* (ELIAMEP, 2003; in Greek) and *Kosovo's Endgame: Sovereignty and Stability in the Western Balkans* (IAA, 2006). Dr Tziampiris has also published a series of essays primarily on international relations and Greek foreign policy in the Balkans. He holds a PhD from the London School of Economics and Political Science.

Nikolaos Tzifakis (PhD, Lancaster University, 2002) is head of the International Cooperation Department of the Constantinos Karamanlis Institute for Democracy and Research Fellow at the Centre for Political Research and Documentation (KEPET) of the University of Crete. He has been a Visiting Lecturer of International Relations in the Department of Political Science of the University of Crete and the Department of Geography of the Harokopion University of Athens. He has research interests in contemporary developments in the Balkans, EU external policies and International Relations theory. His recent publications include, inter alia, articles in *Ethnopolitics*, *European Foreign Affairs Review*, *European View*, *International Journal*, *Journal of Political and Military Sociology*, *Journal of Southern Europe and the Balkans*, *Perspectives: The Central European Review of International Affairs* and *Southeast European Politics*. He has published two monographs and a co-edited volume dealing with aspects of contemporary security problems in the Balkans.

Eugenia Vathakou has a PhD in International Conflict Analysis (University of Kent, 2003). She has been a Visiting Lecturer of International Relations in the Department of Mediterranean Studies of the University of the Aegean and Director of Networking and Development of European Perspective, a non-governmental development organisation. She has lived in Turkey for four years, there she worked as correspondent for the Athens News Agency and, at the same time, did research on Greek–Turkish crises and peace processes. Eugenia Vathakou has extensive experience in dialogue processes involving members of different minorities in FYROM and Kosovo. She has worked there as a practitioner (facilitator and trainer) in the framework of projects funded by the EAR, UNDP and European Commission.

Hakan Yılmaz is Professor in the Department of Political Science and International Relations, Boğaziçi University, Istanbul. He received his MA (1991) and PhD (1996) degrees from the Political Science Department of Columbia University in the New York City. He has taught courses and published in the areas of contemporary Turkish politics, European–Turkish cultural perceptions and external-internal linkages in the processes of democratisation. Dr Yilmaz has conducted research projects on Euroscepticism (2004), conservatism (2006) and the middle classes (2007) in Turkey. Several of his recent articles are 'Turkish Conservatism and the Idea of Europe' (in Paul Sant Cassia and Thierry Fabre (Eds.) *Between Europe and the Mediterranean: The Challenges and the Fears*, pp. 137–161. New York: Palgrave MacMillan, 2007), and 'Turkish Identity on the Road to the EU: Basic Elements of French and German Oppositional Discourses' (*Journal of Southern Europe and the Balkans*, *9*(3): 293–305).

Abbreviations

ACE	Allied Command Europe
AKP	Adalet ve Kalkinma Partisi, Justice and Development Party
ANAP	Anavatan Partisi, Motherland Party (of Turkey)
CEECs	Central and Eastern European countries
CFSP	Common Foreign and Security Policy
CHP	Cumhuriyet Halk Partisi, Republican People's Party
COMECE	Commission of the Bishops' Conferences of the European Community
CSU	Christlich-Soziale Union, Christian Social Union
DSP	Demokratik Sol Parti, Democratic Left Party
DTP	Demokratik Toplum Partisi, Democratic Society Party
DYP	Doğru Yol Partisi, True Path Party
EDA	European Defense Agency
EDAM	Center for Economics and Foreign Policy Studies
EEC	European Economic Community
EKD	Evangelistische Kirche in Deutschland
ELIAMEP	Hellenic Foundation for European and Foreign Policy
ENP	European Neighbourhood Policy
ESDP	European Security and Defence Policy
ESI	European Stability Initiative
EU	European Union
EUPM	EU Police Mission in Bosnia-Herzegovina
FCO	Foreign and Commonwealth Office
FYROM	Former Yugoslav Republic of Macedonia
HCA	Helsinki Citizens Assembly
ICJ	International Court of Justice
ICMPD	International Center for Migration Policy Development
IHS	Imam-Hatip Schools
IMF	International Monetary Fund
IOM	International Organisation for Migration
ISAF	International Security Assistance Force in Afghanistan
JHA	Justice and Home Affairs
KADEK	Kongreya Azadi u Demokrasiya Kurdistan, Kurdistan Freedom and Democracy Congress

KEK	Conference of European churches (Konferenz Europäischer Kirchen)
KFOR	Kosovo Force
MHP	Milliyetçi Hareket Partisi, Nationalist Action Party
MSP	Milli Selamet Partisi, National Salvation Party
NAC	North Atlantic Council
NPAA	National Program for the Adoption of the Acquis
OECD	Organisation for Economic Co-operation and Development
OLAF	Office Européen de Lutte Antifraude/European Commission: European Anti-fraud Office
PAG	Political Analysis Group
PASOK	Panhellenic Socialist Movement
PKK	Partiya Karkerên Kurdistan, Kurdistan Workers' Party
PRIO	Peace Research Institute of Oslo
PSC	Political and Security Committee
PSW	Problem-solving workshops
RP	Refah Partisi, Welfare Party
RUSI	Royal United Services Institute for Defence Studies, UK
SFOR	Stabilisation Force in Bosnia-Herzegovina
TIPH	Temporary International Presence in Hebron
UNHCR	United Nations High Commissioner for Refugees
UNIFIL	United Nations Interim Force in Lebanon
WEU	Western European Union
WMD	Weapons of mass destruction
WEF	World Economic Forum
WW I	First World War
WW II	Second World War
YTP	Yeni Türkiye Partisi, New Turkey Party

Introduction

Constantine Arvanitopoulos and Nikolaos Tzifakis

Turkey's accession to the European Union (EU) is in every respect an extraordinary process. Its integration is not merely about the entry of another state into European structures. Turkey's European membership is expected to profoundly affect both the material and ideational components of the Union. This is why it is commonly assumed that Turkey's European integration will not be decided solely on the basis of the candidate's success in meeting the Copenhagen membership criteria. As one analyst put it, Turkey's EU membership will be determined by at least three additional criteria: the material benefits and costs of its accession, the perceptions of its Europeanness and the internal dynamics in the EU (Müftüler-Baç, 2008, pp. 204–205).

Utility-based and value-based considerations have certainly come into play in previous rounds of enlargement (Sjursen, 2002; Sjursen & Smith, 2005). Yet the extent to which the question of Turkey's EU accession has been intermingled with debates on Europe's borders, the content of European identity and the capacity of the Union to integrate more members is definitely without precedent. Indeed, the European Commission's Negotiating Framework (for Turkey) includes stipulations that have not been part of previous negotiations with other applicants. To illustrate, the Commission (2005, p. 5) stated that it may consider the inclusion of 'permanent safeguard clauses' in areas such as the free movement of persons, structural policies or agriculture. More importantly, the negotiations have, for the first time, been described as 'an open-ended process, the outcome of which cannot be guaranteed beforehand' (2005, p. 1). Not only has the Union reserved the formal right to reduce the cost of Turkey's membership but also has maintained the option of giving up altogether the accession process (Nugent, 2007, pp. 494–495).

The current context of EU politics without doubt adds to the uncertainty regarding the prospect of Turkish accession. The negative national referenda in France and the Netherlands on the ratification of the European Constitutional Treaty have plunged the Union into a period of introversion. What the Commission and the European Parliament initially described as mere 'hiccups' (Sedelmeier & Young, 2006, p. 3), turned out to be an enduring crisis following the rejection of the Treaty of Lisbon by the Irish people. The Union's deepening process has come to a standstill and this, in turn, has also brought the widening process to a halt. Although the 'No' votes in the European national referenda cannot be attributed to any single cause (Font, 2008), one cannot overlook entirely the role that public discontent with enlargement actually

C. Arvanitopoulos (Ed.), *Turkey's Accession to the European Union*

did play in the French and Dutch votes (Qvortrup, 2006, p. 92; Whitman, 2007, p. 228). It is worth noting here the uncommonly low level of support among European citizens with respect precisely to Turkey's EU membership prospects.

Turkey's accession to the Union is also complicated by its own insufficient progress towards meeting the Copenhagen criteria. The latest annual Commission evaluation report of Turkey inter alia underscored the absence of progress in ensuring full civilian supervision over the military, parliamentary oversight of defence expenditures, cultural diversity and respect for and protection of minorities in accordance with European standards (European Commission, 2007, pp. 9, 22). More importantly, political assassinations, occasional threats by the military to intervene (to defend secularism) and the two cases that were brought before the country's Constitutional Court, aiming at banning the governing Justice and Development Party (Adalet ve Kalkinma Partisi, AKP) and the pro-Kurdish Democratic Society Party (Demokratik Toplum Partisi, DTP) – that together represent over 50% of the Turkish people – have recently manifested how volatile Turkey's democracy is (ESI, 2008). Some analysts claim that the EU has lost the ability to persuade the country to adopt EU norms and goals owing to its growing scepticism about Turkey's membership. One possible result is, as Sahin Alpay (2008, p. 12) states, that '[t]he narrowly avoided crisis will hopefully contribute to increased awareness in Brussels that politics in Turkey may take a very ugly turn if the EU fails to provide credible and strong support for Turkish accession'.

Others have for some time pointed precisely to Turkey's sui generis democracy in order to assert that there is a real danger that the accession negotiations might fail. To avoid, in the words of German Chancellor Angela Merkel, 'failure or catastrophe', it is claimed that the Union should be ready to make an alternative offer such as a 'privileged partnership' (cited in İçener, 2007, p. 423).

European views on Turkey's accession to the Union have indeed been split between those in support of its full integration, on the one hand, and those advocating a privileged partnership, on the other. To the extent that many of the latter proposals imply the applicant's partial (or restricted) European integration in certain areas, the question of Turkey's accession is probably not about 'if', but about 'how much' integration into the Union's structures. The purpose of this book is not to offer a definitive response to this question. The book aims instead to examine the complexity of the issues pertaining to Turkey's prospective EU membership by presenting several often-divergent accounts of the political, security and socio-economic dimensions of the entire process. In this regard, the book aspires to be informative of the relevant debate. It provides a forum for an exchange of views among distinguished scholars and researchers from different national backgrounds in order to make a contribution to the ongoing public discussion of Turkey's accession.

The book is divided into three parts. The first part (Chaps. 1–6) discusses institutional dimensions of Turkey's European integration. It is here that the question of whether the candidate should eventually be granted (or seek) full membership is more intensively debated. The second part of the book (Chaps. 7–12) deals with the security implications of Turkey's accession to European structures. It analyses Turkey's potential contribution to the European Security and Defence Policy (ESDP) and European policies against illegal migration; the overall impact of the accession process on the Greek–Turkish conflict is also assessed. Finally, the third part (Chaps. 13–17) presents socio-economic perspectives, placing particular emphasis on questions of identity as well as the political economy of Turkey's EU membership.

The first chapter provides an overall account of why the EU has increasingly utilised enlargement for the attainment of foreign policy objectives. Arvanitopoulos and Tzifakis propose that enlargement functions as a form of governance potentially influencing not only the immediate policies of third countries but also their long-term attitudes. The authors argue that enlargement has nevertheless become the victim of its own success. The debate on the EU's absorption capacity has demonstrated that the EU has generated expectations of membership among third states (such as Turkey) that the Union was not genuinely intending or ready to pursue. The chapter concludes that the EU should honour all of its actual commitments and cease using enlargement instrumentally where other means of external policy seem to be failing.

In the second chapter, Julio Crespo MacLennan points to the fact that many Europeans and Turks have fears with respect to Turkey's integration into the Union's structures. References to historical analogies such as the siege of Vienna and the conquest of Constantinople are definitely unfortunate but they suggest something about the content of these fears. The author argues, however, that the candidate's accession to the EU will be advantageous for both parties. A possible breakdown in negotiations is described as disastrous. MacLennan argues that it is necessary that the EU and Turkey overcome prejudices and continue the negotiations, which are bound to take a very long time but which should culminate in a mutually beneficial agreement.

The third chapter underscores the need for predictability in EU–Turkish relations. Diba Nigar Göksel recalls that support for the country's European perspective brought about in Turkey the formation of a loose heterogeneous coalition of social forces that was able to implement essential reforms. The visibly growing opposition in recent years in Europe to Turkey's EU membership as well as the rise of nationalism in the country have, nonetheless, undermined the work of this coalition. Göksel argues that the EU accession process should be rejuvenated to become again the cause that would energise the pro-reform coalition, which, in turn, would lead to the enactment of much-needed reforms.

Thomas Silberhorn asserts in the fourth chapter that alternatives to full Turkish membership in the EU should be developed. This is so because there are important factional disputes in both the EU and Turkey that render uncertain the outcome of the accession negotiations. Silberhorn claims, moreover, that the two parties do not sufficiently share a common identity (in terms of history and culture), which is indispensable for the eventual attainment of a political union in Europe. Hence the author suggests that the exact content of the Union's relationship with Turkey should be largely determined by the extent to which Turkey will consent to surrender sovereignty in order to be partially integrated into EU structures.

In the fifth chapter, Hakan Yilmaz researches an often-ignored theme in the EU–Turkish relationship, that is, to say, the existence in the candidate country of a sizeable Eurosceptic trend. Yilmaz's contribution offers a historical account of the evolution of this trend from the late 1950s till the present; he remarks that its recent growth is due to the revival of the so-called 'Sèvres syndrome', denoting a fear of the country's dismemberment with the complicity of the West. Yilmaz notes the simultaneous rise in Europe of Turco-scepticism and claims that the concurrence of these two trends can endanger the efforts of AKP (Adalet ve Kalkinma Partisi, the Justice and Development Party), to Europeanise the country's public sphere and accommodate public displays of Islamic identity.

Aristotle Tziampiris remarks that the aspiration of third countries to become EU members increases the capacity of the Union to project soft power, that is, its ability to make them desire the same outcome that the EU desires. However, if Turkey eventually fulfils the Copenhagen criteria and is not admitted to the Union, owing to widespread opposition to its membership, then, the author suggests, additional identitarian criteria will have been at work. The chapter elaborates on the content of these criteria that are behind much of the scepticism about the Turkish candidacy and argues that it would be ironic if cultural concerns determine the limits of the EU's soft power, which is largely culturally based.

The chapter by Thanos Dokos undertakes a thorough assessment of what Turkey could contribute to the European Security and Defence Policy (ESDP). The author goes through the threat perceptions and the strategic culture of both parties as well as their perspectives on developments in proximate regions of mutual interest (e.g., the Balkans, the Caucasus and the Middle East) in order to question the existence of common ground for joint action. Dokos concludes that the Union's own vision of its international role (which has not yet crystallised) will eventually determine the extent to which Turkey's EU membership will be an asset for the Common Foreign and Security Policy.

Can Buharalı offers a Turkish view of his country's contribution to European security. The author recalls that Turkey has been an important security provider not only as a full member of the Atlantic alliance but also as a participant in several peace-keeping missions deployed in crisis spots around the world. Nevertheless, Buharalı contends that in the post-Cold War era, several developments (most notably Cyprus' EU membership) have caused the erosion of Turkey's position in the European security architecture. The chapter recommends that the EU elaborate a way to integrate Turkey within its security structures even in advance of its full European accession.

In the next chapter Özgür Ünal Eriş explains why the fight against illegal immigration has received greater salience in the Union in recent years. This policy development has impinged upon the evolution of the *acquis communautaire* and, by extension, had an impact on the EU–Turkish accession negotiations. Eriş briefly presents the country's relevant institutional framework, the main deficiencies in terms of conformity with European standards and the progress that has been registered since Turkey was proclaimed a candidate for EU membership. The chapter suggests that Turkey confronts a difficult dilemma; it must implement costly changes to its asylum and illegal-immigration policies, while it does not know whether it will be eventually admitted into the EU.

The contribution of Panayotis J. Tsakonas explores the capacity of the Union to positively transform the Greek–Turkish conflict. The author ventures a combination of rational-institutionalist and constructivist theoretical approaches to claim that the ability of the EU to change the interests and the identity scripts of Greece and Turkey is dependent upon the fulfilment of two conditions. The first concerns the Union's legitimacy and credibility in the eyes of the two conflict parties as well as the strength of the norms it exerts upon them. The second condition refers to the depth of internalisation that results from the Europeanisation process (i.e., whether it is targeting solely the elites or society as well).

Kostas Ifantis elaborates on Greece's security policy towards Turkey and analyses historically the view Athens has had of EU–Turkish relations. The author explains how Greek policy has evolved over time from a firm stance against any step towards the further institutionalisation of the Union's (and previously the EEC's) relations with Turkey, to a position in favour of Turkey's EU candidacy. Ifantis concludes that the success of the present Greek strategy of engaging and anchoring Turkey in the EU will hinge upon the preservation of the prospect for full membership, Ankara's response to the Greek openings and the progress made towards the resolution of the Cyprus question, the domestic developments in the candidate country and its determination to implement the required reforms.

The chapter by Eugenia Vathakou employs Luhmann's modern systems theory to study the Greek–Turkish peace processes of the 1996–1999 period. The author demonstrates that the evolution of bilateral relations depends on the complexity and contingency of their environment and the connectability of the themes of conflict or cooperation. The chapter suggests that the process of Turkey's accession to the EU has increased the complexity of the environment of the Greek–Turkish conflict, creating structures such as themes, roles and institutions, which can guide the operations of different social systems in the direction of peace. Vathakou points to the fact that the same process also has the potential to cause chains of multiple connections among existing social systems on each side of the conflict to emerge.

Dimitris Keridis discusses in his contribution the content of European identity as the latter was constructed and transformed in recent historical times. Keridis stresses that Turkey's exclusion from Europe is not due to geographical and religious factors. It is instead related to its non-participation in WW II, which was for Europe a key defining moment. Turkey disassociated itself from the European regional subsystem, and Kemalism (i.e., its constitutive ideology) was not delegitimised and defeated as happened with other interwar authoritarian ideologies. If European identity is recent, evolving and civic, as the author suggests, then Turkey can reform its state ideology and bring it into conformity with modern European realities.

In the next chapter, Ranier Fsadni offers a cultural anthropological view of the question of Turkey's EU admission. The author presents the main cultural arguments that have been articulated for and against Turkish membership in Europe and discovers that, quite surprisingly, they share the same four assumptions: religion always dominates culture in Muslim countries, radical differences exist between Islam and the West, cultures are separate entities demarcated by clear boundaries and civilisations can clash or make alliances. Fsadni elaborates on the false premises of these assumptions and stresses that, while Europe's identity and future is at stake in the debate on Turkey's membership, the terms in which this debate is conducted highlight the increasing Americanisation of European politics.

Ali Ihsan Aydin claims that Europeans seem to have rediscovered in Turkey a mirror of the cultural and religious heritage of Europe. An existential reflection on the content of European identity has been launched, in which European Christian churches are actively participating. Although the latter do not consider that Turkey's European integration should be obstructed because of Turkey's religion or culture, the churches are not enthusiastic about this prospect either. Considering that European integration has from its inception been a reconciliation project, Aydin recommends that the EU seize the opportunity offered by the Turkish candidacy to achieve a historic reconciliation between Muslims and Christians.

The chapter of Mustafa Akyol adopts a critical stance on Kemalism. Akyol challenges the mainstream view that Turkish Islam is exceptional because of Kemal's secularism. The author argues that Islamic modernisation had commenced long before and that it was indeed the Ottoman legacy that gave rise to both Atatürk and modern Turkey. Akyol also reveals the illiberal content of Kemalism, which is in sharp contrast with the forms of secularism that were put forward in western democracies. The chapter concludes that the modernisation of the Islamic world will come about through the spread of democracy, freedom and economic opportunity rather than through secularist tyrannies or western military interventions that may fuel radicalism.

Finally, Pantelis Sklias deals in his chapter with the political economy of Turkey's accession to the EU. The author compares Turkey's candidacy with those of the Central and Eastern European countries (CEECs) that were admitted to the Union in the fifth round of its enlargement and highlights four major differences: Turkey's more advanced trade integration ahead of its European accession, its lower human capital in terms of education, skills and culture, its greater demographic dynamism and its larger pool of prospective immigrants to Europe. Sklias concludes that although Turkey's European integration will probably be a lengthy and difficult process, its political-economic transformation will be in the EU's interest.

Altogether, the book undertakes a comprehensive and multidimensional approach to the question of Turkey's admission into European structures, an event that will ultimately have ramifications not only for the future of enlargement but also, more importantly, for the medium-term prospect of the European integration process itself.

References

Alpay, S. (2008). Making sense of Turkish politics. *International Spectator*, *43*(3), 5–12.

ESI. (2008). *Turkey's dark side: Party closures, conspiracies and the future of democracy*. ESI Briefing. Berlin, 2 April.

European Commission. (2005). *Negotiating framework*. Luxemburg, 3 October. Available at http://ec.europa.eu/enlargement/pdf/st20002_05_TR_framedoc_en.pdf

European Commission. (2007). *Turkey 2007 progress report*. Brussels. COM 663 final, SEC 1436, 6 November.

Font, N. (2008). The domestic politics of the EU in the constitutional treaty referendums. *Perspectives on European Politics and Society*, *9*(3), 301–315.

İçener, E. (2007). Privileged partnership: An alternative final destination for Turkey's integration with the European Union? *Perspectives on European Politics and Society*, *8*(4), 415–438.

Müftüler-Baç, M. (2008). Turkey's accession to the European Union: The impact of the EU's internal dynamics. *International Studies Perspectives*, *9*(2), 201–219.

Nugent, N. (2007). The EU's response to Turkey's membership application: Not just a weighing of costs and benefits. *Journal of European Integration*, *29*(4), 481–502.

Qvortrup, M. (2006). The three referendums on the European Constitution treaty in 2005. *The Political Quarterly*, *77*(1), 89–97.

Sedelmeier, U., & Young, A. R. (2006). Editorial: Crisis, what crisis? Continuity and normality in the European Union in 2005. *Journal of Common Market Studies*, *44*(annual review), 1–5.

Sjursen, H. (2002). Why expand? The question of legitimacy and justification in the EU's enlargement policy. *Journal of Common Market Studies*, *40*(3), 491–513.

Sjursen, H., & Smith, K. E. (2005). Justifying EU foreign policy: The logics underpinning EU enlargement. In T. Christiansen & B. Tonra (Eds.), *Rethinking European Union foreign policy* (pp. 126–141). Manchester: Manchester University Press.

Whitman, R. G. (2007). Europe's next steps. *International Affairs*, *83*(1), 227–230.

Enlargement Governance and the Union's Integration Capacity

Constantine Arvanitopoulos and Nikolaos Tzifakis

1 Introduction

EU enlargement is widely appreciated as Europe's most powerful foreign policy instrument and most effective conflict prevention mechanism (Miralles & Johansson, 2002). Yet enlargement was not originally viewed as a means of EU external policy-making. Historically, the EEC (the predecessor of the EU) entered into accession negotiations with candidate states long before it even considered the possibility of developing policies and instruments towards a common foreign policy. Indeed, enlargement began to be viewed as an external-relations instrument only after the EU commenced shaping a community foreign policy, rather than the other way around. Enlargement stands out from and transcends all EU pillars instead of being located in one of them (e.g., the Common Foreign Policy and Security Policy pillar).

In terms of credibility, while the capacity of the Union to manage ethnic conflicts and safeguard international security has frequently been challenged, its ability to 'widen' itself with the acceptance of new member states has never been questioned. As a result, the association of EU conditionality clauses with the prospect of membership has lent unparalleled leverage to the relevant community policies. This leverage has not been a feature of European policies towards non-candidate states.

This chapter contends that employing enlargement by and large as a foreign policy tool towards Turkey and the western Balkan countries has injected the deficiencies of the EU's external-relations policy into the enlargement process. The most important deficiency in the EU's international policies has been conceptualised by Christopher Hill (1993) as an 'expectations–capabilities gap'. This gap refers to the distinction between what Europe is expected to do and what it can indeed accomplish. Hill's analytical scheme highlights the EU's aspiration to play a world role, on the one hand, and its institutional, political and military deficiency in sustaining the relevant policies, on the other. The expectations–capabilities gap in the enlargement process has emerged in the debate that has resurfaced during the last 3 years concerning the EU's capacity to integrate more member states. It describes the distinction between the EU's practice of offering candidate (and 'potential candidate') status to several south-eastern European countries, on the one

C. Arvanitopoulos (Ed.), *Turkey's Accession to the European Union*

hand, and its readiness to proceed with the implementation and assume the implications of such decisions, on the other.

The chapter is divided into three parts. The first section discusses how enlargement has increasingly worked as a form of governance of third countries. In this way, the EU has come to rely more and more on enlargement for the accomplishment of foreign policy objectives. The second part elaborates on the debate around the EU's absorption capacity, which has cast doubts on the very completion of the current enlargement process. The chapter concludes that the Union should attempt to directly tackle the expectations–capabilities gap in its foreign policy, instead of by-passing it through enlargement.

2 Enlargement Governance

As one analyst asserts, enlargement puts the EU in a position to shape large parts of applicant states' policies in a way that seems to set aside traditional principles of non-interference in other states' domestic affairs (Sjursen, 1998). For Friis and Murphy (1999, p. 226), enlargement represents a form of governance in the sense that the EU creates a negotiated order whereby the applicant countries are governed by a constant process of negotiations. Jan Zielonka (2004, p. 23) presents enlargement as a means of asserting the EU's 'imperial' control over less stable European regions. Altogether, enlargement governance is an 'asymmetrical process' that puts the candidates in the position of adopting rules that have been determined by the EU (Dimitrova, 2002, p. 175).

Enlargement governance is made possible largely by the attaching of conditionality clauses to EU policies towards the applicant countries. Schimmelfennig, Engert and Knobel (2003, p. 496) explain that EU conditionality generally works through a strategy of 'reinforcement by reward'. The EU offers (or withholds) financial and technical assistance and institutional ties to applicant countries in response to progress in their compliance with the accession requirements. However, in the course of the negotiations, the EU does not take into account the cost-benefit calculus of the candidate states, in the sense that it avoids causing extra costs or offering extra assistance (Schimmelfennig et al., 2003, pp. 496–497). Enlargement governance works efficiently to the extent that the applicant countries perceive the benefits of membership as outweighing the costs of compliance with accession requirements (Moravcsik & Vachudova, 2003, p. 49). In one analyst's words, the prospect of EU membership has so far represented the 'golden carrot' that has provided the incentive for many aspirants to undertake far-reaching reforms (Larrabee, 2007).

EU conditionality does not have a uniform impact on every issue. For instance, with respect to the *acquis communautaire,* Hughes, Sasse and Gordon (2004, p. 525) argued that the leverage of EU conditionality depends on how 'thick' this *acquis* is in a particular policy issue. The thinner the *acquis*, the larger is the ambiguity surrounding the policy recommendations. Furthermore, EU conditionality has not been undifferentiated through each round of enlargement and towards every candidate state.

The Treaty of Rome stated that every European state could apply for membership (Article 237) and no political or economic conditions were raised during the first round of EEC enlargement (apart of course from the adoption of the *acquis*). As for the second and third rounds (i.e., with Greece, Spain and Portugal), these enlargements were conditional merely on the restoration in the candidate states of representative democracy and respect for human rights (Sjursen & Smith, 2005, pp. 130–131). The so-called Copenhagen criteria[1] were indeed articulated in 1993 in respect precisely to the associated countries from Central and Eastern Europe. Yet the political and economic criteria for membership are flexible and vague enough to permit the Union to politically interpret the extent to which an applicant meets them (Grabbe, 2002; Maniokas, 1999, p. 12). As a result, Brücker, Schröder and Weise (2003) claimed – through the employment of the framework of a 'war of attrition' bargaining game – that the distribution of benefits deriving from enlargement, between the existing members of the Union, on the one hand, and the applicant country, on the other, eventually determines how favourable the accession terms will be (e.g., an insistence on weaker or more thorough reforms).

Above all, the leverage of EU conditionality is not constant throughout the entire accession process. Haughton (2007) argues that the EU's power to transform the applicant states is at its maximum the moment that a decision is about to be taken on the opening of accession negotiations. This is so because candidates know that once they have reached that stage, a credible possibility of membership is being offered. The fluctuation during the accession process of the leverage of EU conditionality has also been researched by other analysts. Based on empirical evidence, Steunenberg and Dimitrova (2007) note that the effectiveness of conditionality decreases sharply once the accession date is set. To a great extent, this is explained by the fact that the candidate states know that they have accomplished their objective of membership. Along the same line of argument, Barnes and Randerson (2006, p. 356) point to the possibility that new member states might be tempted to roll back commitments, once their EU accession process is successfully completed.

Nevertheless, if EU enlargement boiled down in the end to little more than a rational calculation and a bargaining game, one would expect that neither the effectiveness of EU conditionality, nor the long-term compliance of new member states should be taken for granted. As a result, enlargement governance uses conditionality as part of a larger process of 'Europeanisation'. The latter combines rational institutionalism through policies of political and economic conditionality with sociological institutionalism through norm diffusion and social learning (Emerson, 2004, p. 2). Enlargement entails the long preparatory work of 'gradual

---

[1] These are 'stability of institutions guaranteeing democracy, the rule of law, human rights and respect for and protection of minorities, the existence of a functioning market economy as well as the capacity to cope with competitive pressure and market forces within the Union'. The Copenhagen Conclusions additionally stated that 'membership presupposes the candidate's ability to take on the obligations of membership including adherence to the aims of political, economic and monetary union' (European Council, 1993, 13).

and formal horizontal institutionalisation of organisational rules and norms' (Schimmelfennig & Sedelmeier, 2002, p. 503). Emilian Kavalski describes this process, using the term 'socialization' to denote how 'institutions, practices and norms are transmitted between international actors'. The accession process is perceived as consisting not only in a compliance component (through the instrument of conditionality) but, additionally, in a learning component concerning how to comply (Kavalski, 2003, p. 77). EU aspirants are expected at the end to enter an enlarged 'European identity' that is constructed around common values and norms facilitating compromise and consensus-building and leading to the emergence of shared interests (Adler & Crawford, 2002, pp. 4–8).

The Union has been tempted, therefore, to generate expectations of membership in third countries in order to capitalise not only on the readiness of third countries to comply with accession requirements, but also on the potential of Europeanisation to bring about change. However, enlargement governance is not an infinite process. It is destined to eventually affect EU governance itself as it results in changes to the composition and the nature of the Union's structures. Enlargement additionally represents a process of reconstructing the Union's own identity (Tzifakis, 2007, pp. 58–59). This is why the Union has recently reflected on its capacity to meet the candidates' expectations and accept them as new member states. The next section elaborates on the debate regarding the EU's absorption capacity.

3 The Union's Integration Capacity

According to Olli Rehn, Commissioner for Enlargement, absorption capacity is about whether the EU can take in new members while continuing to function effectively (EurActiv.com, 22 May 2006). The term implies that it is not sufficient that a candidate member state meet every political and economic requirement for EU integration. It is equally important that the EU itself affirm its capacity to receive the state in question as a new member. The term was originally articulated during the discussion concerning the criteria for EU membership that took place during the Copenhagen Summit of 1993. The Presidency Conclusions state that

> [t]he Union's capacity to absorb new members, while maintaining the momentum of European integration, is also an important consideration in the general interest of both the Union and the candidate countries. (European Council, 1993, p. 13)

France was at the time sceptical about the repercussions of enlargement on EU governance, while Greece, Spain and Portugal feared the loss of access to EC structural funds. As for the Benelux countries, they worried about the impact of enlargement on their own influence within the Union (Friis & Murphy, 1999, p. 221). Yet the EU's absorption capacity was not really treated as a criterion in the fifth round of enlargement. Indeed, it is widely acknowledged that the Amsterdam and Nice Treaties failed adequately to prepare EU institutions for the accession of 12 new member states (Baldwin et al., 2001; Friis & Murphy, 1999, p. 223;

Heinemann, 2002). As for the European Constitutional Treaty, although it envisaged more substantial reforms of EU institutions, its ratification was not made a precondition for the accession of the 12 new member states either. Thus the lack of progress in improving the effectiveness of European institutions did not eventually inhibit the EU's 'big-bang' enlargement.

The European Commission denied the validity of the argument that it had not in the past considered the repercussions of each enlargement. The Commission claimed that in all rounds of enlargement, its opinions on the applications for membership included assessments of the impact of accession on the Union (European Commission, 2006, p. 19). Yet the question about its capacity to absorb new members has not consistently been raised before. 'Absorption capacity' has entered only recently into European rhetoric around enlargement, triggered, in fact, by the reservations surrounding the Turkish candidacy for EU membership. As Frank Vibert (2006) remarks, the term has been doubly useful because it generalises the issues posed by enlargement beyond that of Turkish membership alone, and it deflects attention from political arguments about whether Turkey belongs or not to Europe.

The French and Dutch 'No' votes on the ratification of the European Constitutional Treaty complicated further EU enlargement and added another dimension to the discussion of the EU's capacity to integrate more members. Katinka Barysch (2006, p. 79) argues that the national referenda on the Constitutional Treaty (and those on accession held in the new member states) have set an important precedent in the sense that the days of integration and enlargement 'by stealth' are over. In the future, Barysch (2006) continues, 'the EU will not be able to significantly change the way it works, move into new policy areas or take in more countries without asking the people in a popular vote'. Suffice it to recall here that while Austria unequivocally stressed as early as December 2004 that it would organise a referendum ahead of Turkey's EU accession (Associated Press, 17 December 2004), France enacted a constitutional amendment in March 2005 to the effect that any future EU accession, beyond that of Bulgaria and Romania, be submitted to a vote by its citizens.

The failure of the ratification of the European Constitution additionally damaged what Charles Grant (2007, p. 16) calls the 'implicit bargain' between 'deepeners' and 'wideners' inside the Union. The parallel advancement of integration and enlargement processes has helped both of the aforementioned camps to make mutual concessions during the last 20 years. The deepeners secured the implementation of several EU reform treaties, while the wideners got approval for subsequent rounds of enlargement. Hence the pause in the march towards European integration, owing to the non-adoption of the European Constitutional Treaty, implied that the deepeners had lost an important incentive to concede further enlargement. In this respect, absorption capacity became the point of convergence between two heterogeneous groups; namely, those who opposed further EU enlargement and those who wanted EU reforms to proceed despite the rejection by France and the Netherlands of the European Constitution. On the other hand, the Commission and a group of states led by the UK urged that the EU cannot go back on its promises to the region, and warned of the negative repercussions from such a perspective for the stability of the Turkey and the Western Balkans (Deutsche Presse-Agentur, 25 May 2006). In any case, the EU decided to put on hold the process of enlargement as long as the constitutional crisis was not resolved. As was repeatedly suggested, there would be no more rounds of EU enlargement on the basis of the Nice Treaty after the entry of Bulgaria and Romania.

The debate on the EU's absorption capacity was institutionally launched in November 2005 with the publication of the Commission's *2005 Enlargement Strategy*. The document states that

> [t]he Union has to ensure it can maintain its capacity to act and decide according to a fair balance within its institutions; respect budgetary limits; and implement common policies that function well and achieve their objectives. (European Commission, 2005, p. 3)

In February 2006, the European Parliament followed suit with the adoption of a resolution requesting the Commission to submit a report by 31 December 2006 setting out the principles underpinning the concept of 'absorption capacity'. The resolution claimed that comprehension of this concept required 'defining the nature of the European Union, including its geographical borders' (European Parliament, 2006, p. 4). In other words, the question of the Union's absorption capacity was not perceived as a problem merely of institutional adjustment, it also incorporated a geographic dimension concerning Europe's borders (if not also a cultural one on its identity).[2] What is more, the European Parliament (2006) called on the Commission and the Council to submit proposals for a close multilateral relationship between the EU and all European countries currently without a membership perspective.

Upon the insistence of France, Denmark and the Netherlands (Deutsche Presse-Agentur, 25 May 2006), the Brussels European Council of 16 June 2006 discussed the expediency of introducing 'absorption capacity' into the list of EU membership criteria. Josep Borrell Fontelles, President of the European Parliament, claimed that 'it is impossible to keep adding new floors to the building without making sure the foundations are solid' (EUPolitix.com, 16 June 2006). Jacques Chirac, France's President, endorsed this viewpoint: 'we should continue with enlargement, but in a process that is controlled and better understood.' He further added that absorption capacity had not only a financial but also a political dimension, implying that the European nations should be given the opportunity to say if they accept or not (EurActiv.com, 16 June 2006). On the other hand, Prime Minister Goran Persson of Sweden said that it was not up to incoming countries to take responsibility for absorption (The New Anatolian, 17 June 2006). Along the same lines, Dimitrij Rupel, the Foreign Minister of Slovenia, noted that absorption capacity was an internal problem of the EU and could not be a criterion for the accession of a new country (Slovenian Business Week, 19 June 2006). The European Council (2006a, para. 53) eventually decided to debate the question again at the summit of December 2006 and, like the European Parliament, requested that the Commission prepare a report on the EU's absorption capacity by the year's end.

[2]For an argument in favour of the elaboration of a 'Union-al' identity, see Fakiolas (2007).

The introduction of absorption capacity into European discourse on enlargement has been sharply criticised by several analysts. Emerson et al. (2006, p. 9) suggested that, in contrast to the political and economic accession criteria, absorption capacity was not officially defined. As it stood, the term could be taken to refer to the capacity for enlargement in many areas, such as the common market, society, EU institutions and budget and the Union's strategic security (2006). As a result, the concept had a vague and loosely defined content and this in turn allowed populist politicians to manipulate it (Senem, 2007, p. 3). Moreover, the EU has been criticised for treating absorption capacity as a static concept. The Union seems to assume that contemporary assessments of its capacity to widen itself will be valid in the future. The EU's absorption capacity is taken as constant. However, several analysts argue that exactly the opposite is the case. According to Esen (2007), once the recent round of enlargement is consolidated and considered successful, the scepticism of the European people might be reversed. To the extent that we don't really know the context in which the next round of enlargement will take place (with the notable exception of Croatia, no other country is expected to be admitted any time soon), the entire discussion of the Union's capacity to receive new member states within its ranks is viewed as premature and meaningless (Emerson et al., 2006, p. 11). Finally, as Ülgen (2007) points out, the uncertainty that has been cast on the eventual accession of current applicant countries has rendered it more difficult for the latter to implement unpopular reforms. In other words, the debate on the Union's absorption capacity has inflicted damage on EU conditionality and undermined the compliance efforts of the candidates.

In November 2006, the European Commission issued a special report on the Union's absorption capacity, as requested. First of all, on the level of semantics, the Commission suggested the replacement of the term 'absorption capacity' with the term 'integration capacity'. Whereas several countries aspire to be integrated into the European Union, none of them envisages being absorbed. The term 'absorption' is obviously more negatively charged from the perspective of the candidate states. Second, the Commission's report dealt with the issue of Europe's borders raised earlier by the European Parliament. Although the Commission detached the question of the EU's integration capacity from any geographical consideration, it declined to express its view on where the boundaries of Europe should be drawn.[3] The report instead argued that

> [t]he shared experience of ideas, values, and historical interaction cannot be condensed into a simple timeless formula and is subject to review by each succeeding generation. (European Commission, 2006, p. 18)

Hence, while the Commission acknowledged that the Union need not necessarily accept all applications, it simultaneously proposed an inclusive definition of the EU in relation, first and foremost, to its values (European Commission, 2006). Above

---

[3] This is not to claim that the Union has not attempted to draw its external boundaries through its policies. For a relevant discussion, see Tzifakis (2007).

all, the Commission's communication pronounced on the conditions that would enable the Union to integrate new member states. First of all, the EU should ensure that it can maintain its capacity 'to function, in the interest of its present and future citizens'. This implies that the EU should make sure that its institutions work effectively, its policies meet their goals and its budget is commensurate with its objectives and with its financial resources (European Commission, 2006, p. 20). The Commission clearly conditioned further enlargement on progress in the EU's own institutional development. As the document stressed, 'A new institutional settlement should have been reached by the time the next new member is likely to be ready to join the Union' (European Commission, 2006, p. 18).

Second, the Commission asserted that conditionality should be strictly applied in respect of the implementation of rigorous reforms by the applicant countries. Finally, the Commission's report suggested that the advantages and the challenges of enlargement should be better communicated by the Union to its citizens (European Commission, 2006, pp. 23–24).

The report's approach was affirmed and endorsed in subsequent Council Conclusions (European Council, 2006b, para. 4–9), European Parliament resolutions (e.g., European Parliament, 2008), and Commission communications (European Commission, 2007). In addition, the Brussels European Council of 15 December 2006 requested that the Commission prepare impact studies on key policy areas in its regular assessments of every country's application for membership (European Council, 2006b, para. 9).

The signing of the Treaty of Lisbon temporarily generated the hope that the EU would come out of its constitutional crisis and that enlargement would resume once the Union's institutions were eventually reformed. Nevertheless, the Irish 'No' vote on the ratification of the Treaty soon demonstrated that the Union's period of introversion was not yet over. Both French President Nicolas Sarkozy and German Chancellor Angela Merkel made it clear that no round of EU enlargement would take place if the Lisbon Treaty did not enter into force (John, 2008). On the other hand, the European Commission and a group of countries such as Austria, Poland and Slovenia maintained that the negative result in the Irish referendum on the Treaty of Lisbon should not impinge upon enlargement (especially on Croatia's case) (Deutsche Presse-Agentur, 19 June 2008; John, 2008).

Even if we discount entirely the discussion concerning the EU's material and institutional capacity to widen itself, we cannot also ignore the widespread 'enlargement fatigue' and absence of enthusiasm for more new entrants into the Union. According to the Eurobarometer (2007, pp. 30–33), only 49% of EU-27 citizens are in favour of further enlargement of the Union, while 39% are opposed. As for the EU-15, support for enlargement is even weaker, amounting to 43% of the population. Indeed, there is a widely shared perception that enlargement causes the outsourcing of economic growth to new member states (Stefanova, 2006, p. 252). For many Europeans, 'enlargement fatigue' denotes 'immigration fatigue' or 'unemployment fatigue'. However, as Emerson et al. (2006, pp. 5–6) note, there is a reality–perception gap in the attitudes of European citizens towards the fifth round of enlargement, in the sense that there is a large discrepancy between the costs as widely perceived and the actual costs of enlargement. European leaders have, indeed, all these years underestimated the need to explain to their people the economic, geopolitical and other benefits of EU expansion. As a result, populist politicians and certain interest groups have been given the opportunity to portray enlargement in a negative light and associate it with, for example, the legitimation of vast waves of immigration (Vachudova, 2005, p. 68). The latter phenomenon has, in turn, been embedded in the discourses that construct a 'security continuum' encompassing some of Europe's most serious socio-economic problems, that is to say, unemployment, terrorism and organised crime (Huysmans, 2000, p. 760). Public opposition to enlargement, therefore, presumably represents a policy of containment against the threats facing contemporary European societies.

4 Conclusions

The chapter claimed that the EU has increasingly utilised enlargement as an instrument for the attainment of foreign policy objectives. Enlargement governance has emerged as a very powerful means of influencing much more than the immediate policies of third countries. The process of Europeanisation is intended to have an impact on their long-term attitudes as well. Nevertheless, EU enlargement has become the victim of its own success. The transformative power of enlargement has tempted the EU to generate expectations of membership in third countries that the Union was not genuinely intending, ready, or able to pursue (Fakiolas & Tzifakis, 2008; Tzifakis, 2006, pp. 237–241). There is an expectations–capabilities gap in EU enlargement policy that is widely apparent in the discussion that has taken place during the last three years concerning the Union's absorption capacity.

Irrespective of whether it attempts to represent objective reality or merely public sentiment, reflection on the Union's capacity to integrate more members highlights the limits of enlargement. This assertion is not a call for the demarcation of Europe's frontiers. In any case, no such frontiers can leave outside those countries whose candidate (and potential candidate) status has at the minimum signified an acknowledgement by the EU of their European identity. The chapter instead argues that enlargement can no longer be used as a foreign policy tool. The EU should develop alternative means to lend credibility to its policies of conditionality. Enlargement is, after all, not a far-reaching external relations instrument. This is because it represents a transitional phase in bilateral relations eventually leading to the 'domestication' of problems (Sjursen, 1998). To put it differently, the EU's influence cannot be restricted only to candidate members with which external relations are terminal (i.e., till their accession). The EU should honour all of its actual commitments and attempt to directly tackle the expectations–capabilities gap in its foreign policy instead of by-passing it through enlargement.

References

Adler, E., & Crawford, B. (2002). Constructing a Mediterranean region: A cultural approach. In *The convergence of civilizations? Constructing a Mediterranean region*. Lisbon: Instituto de Estudos Estratégicos e Internacionais, 6–9 June.

Baldwin, R. E., et al. (2001). *Nice try: Should the Treaty of Nice be ratified?* London: Centre for Economic Policy Research, Monitoring European Integration Report 11.

Barnes, I., & Randerson, C. (2006). EU enlargement and the effectiveness of conditionality: Keeping to the deal? *Managerial Law, 48*(4), 351–365.

Barysch, K. (2006). Is enlargement doomed? Towards a more 'flexible and fuzzy' Europe. *Public Policy Research, 13*(2), 78–85.

Brücker, H., Schröder, P. J. H., & Weise, C. (2003). Doorkeepers and gatecrashers: EU enlargement and negotiation strategies. *European Integration, 26*(1), 3–23.

Dimitrova, A. (2002). Enlargement, institution-building and the EU's administrative capacity requirement. *West European Politics, 25*(4), 171–190.

Emerson, M. (2004). *European neighbourhood policy: Strategy or placebo?* Brussels: Center for European Policy Studies, CEPS Working Document 215.

Emerson, M., et al. (2006). *Just what is this 'absorption capacity' of the European Union*. Brussels: Center for European Policy Studies, CEPS Policy Brief 113.

Esen, A. T. (2007). Absorption capacity of the EU and Turkish accession: Definitions and comments. *TEPAV Policy Brief*, 9 May.

Eurobarometer. (2007). Public opinion in the European Union: First results. *Standard Eurobarometer*, 67, June, 9 November.

European Commission. (2005). *2005 Enlargement strategy paper*. Brussels, COM(2005) 561 final.

European Commission. (2006). *Enlargement strategy and main challenges 2006–2007: Including annexed special report on the EU's capacity to integrate new members*. Brussels, COM(2006) 649 final, 8 November.

European Commission. (2007). *Enlargement strategy and main challenges 2007–2008*. Brussels, COM(2007) 663 final, 6 November.

European Council. (1993). *European Council in Copenhagen. Conclusions of the Presidency: 21–22 June 1993*, SN 180/1/93 REV 1.

European Council. (2006a). *Brussels European Council: Presidency conclusions (15–16 June 2006)*. 10633/1/06, REV 1, 17 July.

European Council. (2006b). *Brussels European Council: Presidency conclusions (14–15 December 2006)*, 16879/06.

European Parliament. (2006). *Report on the Commission's 2005 enlargement strategy paper (2005/2206(INI))*, Committee on Foreign Affairs, Final A6-0025/2006, 3 February.

European Parliament. (2008). *European Parliament resolution of 10 July 2008 on the Commission's 2007 enlargement strategy paper (2007/2271(INI))*. Committee on Foreign Affairs, P6_TA-PROV(2008)0363, A6-0266/2008.

Fakiolas, E. (2007). The European Union's problem of cohesion. *New Zealand International Review, 32*(2), 19–23.

Fakiolas, E. T., & Tzifakis, N. (2008). Transformation or accession? Reflecting on the EU's strategy towards the Western Balkans. *European Foreign Affairs Review, 13*(3), 377–398.

Friis, L., & Murphy, A. (1999). The European Union and Central and Eastern Europe: Governance and boundaries. *Journal of Common Market Studies, 37*(2), 211–232.

Grabbe, H. (2002). European Union conditionality and the *acquis communautaire*. *International Political Science Review, 23*(3), 249–268.

Grant, C. (2007). The strategic implications of the EU malaise: Enlargement, variable geometry and a stronger neighbourhood policy. In M. Emerson (Ed.), *Readings in European security* (Vol. 4, pp. 15–27). Brussels, London and Geneva: Centre for European Policy Studies, International Institute for Security Studies and Geneva Centre for the Democratic Control of Armed Forces.

Haughton, T. (2007). When does the EU make a difference? Conditionality and the accession process in Central and Eastern Europe. *Political Studies Review, 5*(2), 233–246.
Heinemann, F. (2002). The political economy of EU enlargement and the Treaty of Nice. *European Journal of Political Economy, 19*(1), 17–31.
Hill, C. (1993). The capability–expectations gap, or conceptualizing Europe's international role. *Journal of Common Market Studies, 31*(3), 305–328.
Hughes, J., Sasse, G., & Gordon, C. (2004). Conditionality and compliance in the EU's eastward enlargement: Regional policy and the reform of sub-national government. *Journal of Common Market Studies, 42*(3), 523–551.
Huysmans, J. (2000). The European Union and the securitization of migration. *Journal of Common Market Studies, 38*(5), 751–777.
John, M. (2008). Germany backs French on EU enlargement doubt. *The Guardian*, 20 June.
Kavalski, E. R. (2003). The international socialization of the Balkans. *The Review of International Affairs, 2*(4), 71–88.
Larrabee, F. S. (2007). L'Elargissement et ses opposants. *Politique Etrangère, 2*, 353–365.
Maniokas, K. (1999). Methodology of the EU enlargement: A critical appraisal. *Lithuanian Political Science Yearbook.*
Miralles, D., & Johansson, E. (2002). *The EU enlargement and the Mediterranean.* Barcelona: Observatory of European Foreign Policy.
Moravcsik, A., & Vachudova, M. A. (2003). National interests, state power, and EU enlargement. *East European Politics and Societies, 17*(1), 42–57.
Schimmelfennig, F., Engert, S., & Knobel, H. (2003). Costs, commitment and compliance: The impact of EU democratic conditionality on Latvia, Slovakia and Turkey. *Journal of Common Market Studies, 41*(3), 495–518.
Schimmelfennig, F., & Sedelmeier, U. (2002). Theorizing EU enlargement: Research focus, hypotheses, and the state of research. *Journal of European Public Policy, 9*(4), 500–528.
Senem, A. D. (2007). 'Absorbing' Turkey?: The integration capacity debate in the EU. *TESEV Foreign Policy Bulletin, 4*, 3–5.
Sjursen, H. (1998). *Enlargement and the common foreign and security policy: Transforming the EU's external policy?* University of Oslo, ARENA – Centre for European Studies, Working Paper 18.
Sjursen, H., & Smith, K. E. (2005). Justifying EU foreign policy: The logics underpinning EU enlargement. In: T. Christiansen & B. Tonra (Eds.), *Rethinking European Union Foreign Policy* (pp. 126–141). Manchester: Manchester University Press.
Stefanova, B. (2006). The 'No' vote in the French and Dutch referenda on the EU constitution: A spillover of consequences for the wider Europe. *PS: Political Science & Politics, 39*(2), 251–255.
Steunenberg, B., & Dimitrova, A. (2007). Compliance in the EU enlargement process: Institutional reform and the limits of conditionality. In J. M. Josselin & A. Marciano (Eds.), *Democracy, freedom and coercion: A law and economics approach* (pp. 221–250). Cheltenham: Edward Elgar.
Tzifakis, N. (2006). The intentions–declarations gap in the EU policies towards the Western Balkans and the Southern Mediterranean. *Journal of Political and Military Sociology, 34*(2), 237–246.
Tzifakis, N. (2007). EU's region-building and boundary-drawing policies: The European approach to the Southern Mediterranean and the Western Balkans. *Journal of Southern Europe and the Balkans, 9*(1), 47–64.
Ülgen, S. (2007). Le 'critère d'absorption', un tête-à-queue pour l'elargissement. *Le Figaro*, 15 October.
Vachudova, M. A. (2005). Promoting political change and economic revitalization in the Western Balkans: The role of the European Union. *Slovak Foreign Policy Affairs, 6*(2), 67–73.
Vibert, F. (2006). 'Absorption capacity': The wrong European debate. *OpenDemocracy*, 21 June, http://www.opendemocracy.net/democracy-europe_constitution/wrong_debate_3666.jsp.
Zielonka, J. (2004). Europe moves eastward: Challenges of EU enlargement. *Journal of Democracy, 15*(1), 22–35.

The EU–Turkey Negotiations: Between the Siege of Vienna and the Reconquest of Constantinople

Julio Crespo MacLennan

The official opening of negotiations for the entry of Turkey into the European Union was a moment of great importance in the history of European integration. It provided yet more evidence of the success of the European Union as an organisation and showed that its political system and model of society can be transplanted even beyond the traditional geographic and cultural boundaries of mainstream Europe. Yet these will undoubtedly be the most difficult negotiations for entry in the history of European integration, since Turkey is a large country with a political system that is still far from meeting European standards and a relatively backward economy. Above all, it is considered not wholly European. To put it bluntly, the country is too big, too poor and too different, as has frequently been pointed out. Many Europeans feel that the eventual entry of Turkey will be a new siege of Vienna – recalling the episode when the Ottoman Empire threatened to overrun the Christian world – and that on this occasion Europe will succumb to the foreign invasion. On the other hand, for Turkey, the prospect of accession into the EU means a great step forward in the country's modernisation and the culmination of a process of Westernisation that began in 1923 with the establishment of a Turkish Republic. Yet the price that the EU will demand might be too high and perhaps even humiliating for an ancient and proud imperial nation, and some Turks have voiced their concern that the process of negotiations with the EU might mean the European reconquest of Constantinople, which the Ottomans captured in 1453. Cultural prejudices and historical fears are playing a much more important role than was originally expected in these negotiations, to the extent that they could lead to a catastrophic failure.

In this chapter we will analyse the impact of negotiations between the EU and Turkey on the political development of the two parties and also the possible outcomes that may result from the present deadlock in negotiations.

1 What the European Union Means for Turkey

The EU is synonymous with economic development, political stability and modernisation in all aspects of society. This is the main reason why there has been a long list of candidates for entry ever since the creation of the European Economic

C. Arvanitopoulos (Ed.), *Turkey's Accession to the European Union*

Community in 1957. It has been so attractive that candidates for entry have not been exclusively European: Morocco, for example, applied for entry, arguing that not being part of the European continent should not be considered an obstacle to its membership. While there never was any possibility of Morocco joining a European organisation, Turkey's candidacy is certainly legitimate as it has very good grounds for considering itself a European country.

Turkey's goal of membership in the EU is coherent with the political nature of its state as a secular republic that is part of the Western world. It also constitutes the culmination of a policy of Westernisation originally imposed by the founder of the Turkish Republic, Mustafa Kemal Atatürk. Atatürk was a devoted Europeanist who used all his influence as head of state from 1923 to ensure that Turkey would be firmly anchored in Europe, and that the West would be Turkey's future not only from the point of view of political and economic development but also from the cultural point of view.[1]

As a member of NATO since 1952, the country has played an important role in Western defence. The Turkish government aimed at getting the country involved in European organisations from the early stages of the process of European integration. Turkey became a member of the Council of Europe in 1949, it applied for the opening of negotiations with the European Economic Community in 1959 and became an associate member in 1963. After decades of negotiations, Turkey officially applied for entry into the European Community in 1987 and it obtained a customs union agreement in 1996. When accession negotiations officially began in 2005, Turkey was no stranger to European institutions and Western organisations. It could boast a much older relationship with Western organisations than many of the present EU members, and its accession, if and whenever that may happen, will be the culmination of what could rightly be called the long march towards Europe.

Turkish reasons for aiming at membership in the EU go beyond the economic and political benefits that this powerful organisation can provide. Membership is associated with the country's modernisation and the pursuit of its most ambitious aims. Oxford historian Timothy Garton Ash (2005) wrote that the continent was divided between the West that has Europe and no longer really believes in it and the East that believes in Europe because it symbolises the fulfilment of all its aspirations. Turkey is clearly in the latter category, as were Greece, Spain and Portugal in the 1960s and 70s and the countries in the former communist bloc in the 1980s.

Europe has had a mythic dimension for many of the continent's modernisers. 'If Spain is the problem, Europe is the solution', stated José Ortega y Gasset, reflecting on his country's problems (quoted in MacLennan, 2000, p. 12).[2] This quote, with which the famous Spanish philosopher summarised Spain's idea of Europe in the 1920s, can clearly be applied to what Turkey expects from the EU at present. In fact, Turkey has strengthened its diplomatic and cultural ties with Spain over the last decade partly because the Turkish elite has seen Spain as the

---

[1] For the role of Atatürk and Kemalism in contemporary Turkey, see Lewis (2001), Mango (2006).

[2] For Europeanism in Spain see MacLennan (2000).

ideal model of a European Mediterranean country to follow and because the Spanish government has been one of the most enthusiastic supporters of Turkish entry into the EU.

There are interesting similarities between Spain and Turkey. Both are large Mediterranean countries situated at strategically important corners of the continent. Both are former imperial nations with strong cultural links and interests beyond Europe. They also share a politically unstable past and a tradition of military interventions that have constituted an obstacle to integration into mainstream Europe. Yet, despite these undeniable similarities, there is one important difference between the two: Spain is an old European nation which could not join the European Community at an early stage due to unfortunate political circumstances, whereas Turkey is a nation whose European identity is questioned not only from abroad but also within the country. This is why there was political unanimity on the issue of Spain's membership in the European Community and there has been virtually no Euroscepticism ever since the country joined the EC, whereas in Turkey political elites are deeply divided over this issue. Although there is a clear Europeanist majority within the population, there are influential nationalist and Islamist groups that argue that both for reasons of national self-interest as well as for religious and cultural reasons, Turkey's future is not in the European Union. Failure to make progress in negotiations with the EU will strengthen these anti-European groups and their influence on Turkish society.

2 What Turkey Means for the European Union

The EU's attitude towards Turkey has experienced a remarkable evolution over the last 20 years. Various factors have contributed to a change in the official position, which led to the European Council at Helsinki in 1999 declaring itself in favour of Turkey's candidacy. Geopolitical factors have played a very important role; Turkey has important assets that can contribute to strengthening the EU as an economic superpower and enhance its global role.

Turkey's candidacy undeniably constitutes a great advantage for Europe from the energy point of view. The country is well endowed with natural resources, particularly gas, which could help to diminish the dependence on Russia. In the long run its young population of over seventy million could be a great compensation for Europe's ageing population and solve its serious demographic problem. The fact that the overwhelming majority of its population is Muslim would contribute to strengthening the EU's credentials as a secular state capable of welcoming and assimilating non-Christian societies. This would also contribute to strengthening liberal democracy in the Middle East where Turkey is very influential, as this country would become a bastion of liberal democracy and Western values in a traditionally turbulent and politically unstable area. Finally, enlargement with the inclusion of a country that includes Constantinople, the capital of the Roman and Byzantium empires as well as important remains of ancient Greece, would also make great sense from the cultural heritage point of view.

Yet the apparent advantages are also the main obstacles in the short run. Although Turkey undeniably has great advantages in the long run, in the short run it may be too poor and too large for the EU's economy to assimilate. Turkey's rural population, constituting a third of its total, would imply a great investment in structural funds that is difficult to imagine. With respect to the fact that this is a largely Muslim country, religion should not be an issue when negotiating between secular states but it inevitably plays an influential role when we consider the impact of religion on politics and society. The Western world is different from the Islamic world, their societies have developed different values that are not easily compatible and religion is largely responsible for this.

The clash between Christian and Muslim societies becomes an issue of great importance when considering the power that should be granted to Turkey as an eventual member of the EU. With its present growth rate, Turkey's population in the next 20 years will be as high as 90 million, which would make it the most populous state in the EU. As a result, it should have more seats in the European Parliament than Germany or France, currently the two largest states, and consequently more voting power. That the most powerful state within European institutions would be a Muslim country is difficult to accept, not only due to the still-powerful prejudices against Muslims within Christian nations, but also because it is feared that ideas defended by Muslims might clash with Western values, and in this way Western values might eventually be undermined as a result of Turkish entry. Turkey has a long and firmly entrenched tradition as a secular state but, on the other hand, it is undeniable that Islamic fundamentalism plays an influential role, particularly in rural areas and within the poorest sector of the population. Another matter of great concern is the degree to which a governing party that calls itself Islamist can seriously commit itself to Western secular values. It is true that Turkey's governing party, the Islamist conservative AKP led by Recep Tayyip Erdoğan, has proved to be an enthusiastic pro-European party, but not long ago this party was discussing the possibility of making adultery punishable by law, which clearly indicates that its ideology is not fully compatible with European secular values. In short, there is still a strong perception among Europeans of Turkey as a historic enemy and its entry into the EU as a new siege of Vienna.

Finally, another crucial element of Turkey's eventual entry that will deeply affect the EU is the concept of Europe that would need to be adopted. What kind of Europe? Two concepts of Europe have traditionally been at stake in the process of European integration: a Europe of nations in which national governments will retain great independence; and a federal Europe in which nations transfer sovereignty to supranational institutions. A federal Europe requires not only great commonality in political and economic development but also strong cultural ties. Enlargement has always been bad news for advocates of federalism because it has always prevented a deepening of institutional links. This is the reason why advocates of the concept of a Europe of nations have always been the most enthusiastic supporters of enlargement, well aware that the more the EU grows, the looser the institutional links will be and, therefore, the more difficult it will be to defend a federalist vision. Enlargement into Eastern Europe has constituted a severe blow for federalism and the eventual entry of Turkey would give federalism its *coup de grâce*.

Another issue that has to be faced if the EU eventually accepts Turkey is the question of where Europe ends: What is the eastern border of Europe? The EU has avoided pronouncing on the issue of the continent's eastern border for the obvious reason that there is no clear boundary from the geographic point of view.[3] Drawing a line from St Petersburg to Istanbul and saying that the territory east of this line is not Europe is too arbitrary. Leaving Turkey and Russia out of European history is not an easy option, particularly from the Europeanist point of view. On the other hand, the lack of a definition of the eastern boundary implies that enlargement can continue indefinitely and that Turkey will be one of many countries in that immense geographic area known as Euro-Asia to join the EU.

European Councils have been deliberately ambiguous about defining clearly where Europe ends, and the consequences of this ambiguity are easily predictable. If negotiations have been opened with a country like Turkey, whose frontiers clearly go beyond what has traditionally been defined as Europe, those countries that are clearly within those boundaries will demand that they have more right to join the EU, and it is predictable that some countries in the Balkan area like Croatia will achieve it in the foreseeable future. With the initiation of Turkey's negotiations, a Pandora's box has been opened for countries from the so-called Euro-Asian zone to apply for membership in the EU. If Turkey joins the EU, there are no good reasons for denying entry to countries on Turkey's frontier, like the Caucasian republics of Georgia, Armenia or Azerbaijan, nor can the republics of the former Soviet Union like Ukraine, Belarus or Moldavia be kept out. Even Russia should have the right to join the EU if it hypothetically wished to do so. Over the next decades, therefore, it is likely that the EU will find itself overwhelmed with the great number of countries applying for membership and negotiating with countries that wish to enjoy the benefits of belonging to the European world but whose populations have very little to do with European heritage. Is it possible and desirable to accept all these countries? This issue will have to be addressed before Turkey's eventual entry is decided.

In the negotiations with Turkey, therefore, there is something more at stake than the entry of this particular country. Turkey will influence the concept of Europe that determines the future of the EU as well as the question of where Europe ends. These are two essential questions that have caused major disputes and will have a deep influence on the continent's future.

3 Turbulent Negotiations with an Uncertain Future

Negotiations for entry into the EU have always been long and complex. With the exception of Austria, Sweden and Finland, which, due to their economic and political development, enjoyed a short and smooth process of negotiation, all other countries

---

[3] The EU treaties, from the Treaty of Rome to the European Constitution, include no reference to the eastern border of Europe or to the definition of Europe.

aiming to join this organisation or its predecessor, the European Community, have had to endure humiliating rebuffs from Brussels institutions and self-interested demands from arrogant member states. But in the case of Turkey, negotiations are bound to be more complex and fraught with risk than those with any other country and their final outcome more uncertain than ever.

From the beginning of negotiations it was obvious that the EU would demand from Turkey no more than it has demanded from any other candidate for membership, but certainly no less. The problem with Turkey is that accepting the same demands as the rest of the candidates will be a bigger effort than it was for any other. Not only does it have to undergo deep economic, political and social reforms, it must also solve several historic problems and radically improve its external image.

The most difficult problem that Turkey has to solve is the conflict with Cyprus, which is the indirect consequence of a rivalry with Greece that is several centuries old. Since the Turkish invasion of Cyprus in 1974 and the subsequent division of the island, this issue not only has been a constant source of international tensions, but it also has become the main obstacle to progress in the negotiations.

Turkey made a symbolic gesture that won international acclaim when the Turkish Cypriots agreed to endorse the United Nations plan presented in 2004 for the reunification of the country. The plan was rejected by the Greek Cypriots to the dismay of both the UN and the EU. Despite the failure of the island's reunification, Cyprus joined the EU in 2004, to Turkish indignation, and ever since it has become an insurmountable obstacle in the negotiations. Several member states demanded that Turkey recognise Cyprus before the start of accession talks, and although the Turkish government with characteristic pride managed to avoid this demand, it was soon to become the main obstacle to progress in the negotiations. In November 2006, European Commission President José Manuel Durao Barroso sent Ankara an ultimatum: that it open its ports and airports to Cyprus in order to implement a customs union, in accordance with EU regulations. Failure to respond to this ultimatum has been the main cause for the decision of EU foreign ministers to suspend eight out of thirty-five chapters of the *acquis* in Turkey's negotiations to join the EU. An unexpected event that raised hope for an eventual solution to the Cyprus conflict was the dismantling by Greek Cypriots on 9 March 2007 of the so-called green line dividing Nicosia, the last dividing wall in Europe. But it remains to be seen whether a satisfactory solution can be negotiated in the near future.

Another historic problem that has become a great obstacle to progress in negotiations has been the Armenian issue. The Armenians have maintained over the past decades that the event that took place in Anatolia, in which several thousand members of their community died, was a state-sponsored mass killing or genocide. Hundreds of thousands of Armenians perished between 1915 and 1917 in Anatolia as a result of a confrontation between members of this community and the Turkish government, but Ankara maintains that the deaths were the result of civil war, disease and famine. This issue has become a great source of tension between Turkey and Europe due to the presence of an influential Armenian diaspora, which is particularly numerous in France and Germany. The passing of a bill in the French National Assembly making it illegal to deny the Armenian genocide was another serious blow to Ankara and further evidence of the lack of understanding between Turkey and several European governments.

What makes the Armenian issue particularly problematic is not just its implications from the human rights point of view. After all, what happened in Armenia during the First World War is just one more example in the history of barbaric European acts and many governments have failed to come to terms with their past. It is the fact that the event is linked to issues of freedom of expression and civil rights in Turkey, a basic aspect of democracy without which Turkey will never be accepted into the EU.

The Turkish penal code includes a notorious article, Article 301, by which it is a crime to publicly insult Turkish identity. This article has been used to prosecute intellectuals for expressing views that were not considered orthodox. In August 2006, this article was used to bring charges against Orhan Pamuk, Turkey's most famous novelist, because he had declared in Switzerland that there had been an Armenian genocide despite the failure of the government to admit it. The trial against Orhan Pamuk, for what is considered in any democracy a simple case of freedom of expression, greatly inflamed European public opinion against Turkey. It put all those in favour of Turkish entry in a very difficult position. As Denis MacShane, the UK's former Minister for Europe, declared: 'If the authorities persist with this attack on a great European writer then many of us who are strong supporters of Turkey will be forced to change our minds' (Quoted by Chislett, 2005).

The Turkish government was well aware that prosecuting Orhan Pamuk would cause an international scandal that would greatly affect the country's chances of joining the EU in the future. For this reason the proceedings against Pamuk were dropped. A few months later Orhan Pamuk was awarded the Nobel Prize for Literature. This award was considered by some nationalists as a new insult to Turkey. Less-well-known intellectuals were more directly affected by their use of freedom of expression over the Armenian issue. Armenian journalist Hrant Dink was condemned to 6 months in prison for an article in which he defended the need for the re-establishment of relations with Armenia, and in January 2007 he was murdered. After his murder, Orhan Pamuk, who had received threats from the person accused of murdering Dink, decided to leave the country because he feared for his life. Although the government cannot be blamed for fanatics who take these measures against intellectuals, the fact that the internationally acclaimed novelist cannot live in his own country is bad news for the cause of freedom of expression in Turkey.

Another complicated issue is the increasing tension between the Islamist party in government, the AKP, and the secularist opposition. As has happened so often in contemporary Turkish history, the success of the Islamist party provoked vehement reactions from the Kemalists and even rumours of a coup d'etat. The appointment of Yasar Buyukanit as head of the Military Staff in 2007 raised fears of a possible intervention by the army in politics to put an end to the Islamist advance. However much it has been argued that the intervention of the army in Turkish politics has always had a modernising effect, this is unacceptable in any democracy and the EU Commissioner for Enlargement, Olli Rehn, warned that any attempted army coup would provoke an immediate end to negotiations with Turkey (Rehn, 2007).

Although such warnings from Europe have had a stabilising effect on Turkish politics, the secularist opposition continues to argue that the Islamists in power have a secret agenda. The relationship between government and opposition is failing to meet the standards of a normal European democracy.

All these issues where a conflict has arisen or where Turkey has failed to comply with European institutional demands have been welcomed by opponents of Turkish membership and have increased pressure on the Commission to announce not only a suspension of negotiations but an eventual abandonment. The fact that a country's entry into the EU needs to be unanimously approved by the 27 member states shows how vulnerable the Turkish cause is. It was only after much pressure from several states, including the United States, that Austria agreed to vote in favour of opening negotiations with Turkey. France and Germany have a clear majority opposed to Turkish entry and it seems that this opinion will have a great influence at the government level. If the CDU had been in power, Germany would not have voted in favour of opening negotiations with Turkey. The present Chancellor, Angela Merkel, has made it clear that her preference is to establish a privileged relationship with Turkey. France has experienced a similar evolution. Despite the fact that former President Valéry Giscard d'Estaing stated that Turkey's entry would destroy the European Union, President Chirac, with characteristic ambivalence, declared himself in favour of the eventual entry of Turkey. Nevertheless, France's centre-right seems to be clearly in favour of a privileged relationship, as is the current President, Nicolas Sarkozy, whose plan for the so-called Mediterranean Union was originally conceived with the aim of giving Turkey a special role in the Mediterranean that could compensate for the denial of full membership in the EU.

There is certainly a strong case for the establishment of a privileged relation with Turkey: because of the country's geographic position and cultural and religious identity, it cannot claim to be purely European. But what do we mean by privileged relationship? The country has had a privileged relationship since 1996 when a customs union was established, but this is far from satisfactory. The privileged relationship has to be defined in more depth in order to be taken seriously.

What would be the consequences of a definitive break in negotiations between Turkey and the EU? However tortuous the negotiations may be, both parties must consider the price to be paid if the EU halts negotiations or if the Turkish government decides to walk away from them. Ruling out Turkish membership would certainly spare the EU many economic problems in the short run but would also rule out important benefits in the long run. It would contribute to undermining the EU's credibility in the Islamic world. Finally, failure to contribute to Turkey's political and economic transformation would greatly affect the EU's reputation as a democratising force through its neighbourhood policy.

For Turkey the impact of a breakdown in negotiations could be very dramatic. The incentive of EU membership has not only contributed to the country's modernisation and economic development over the past years but it has also contributed to making it more compatible with Western democracies. Kemalist secularists in the army, the judiciary and the civil service and the Islamist AKP in government have worked well towards the common goal of membership in the European Union, but if this goal disappears this difficult balance of power would be destroyed and very likely tilt in favour of the nationalists and Islamists who feel cheated by the West. It could also have a dramatic effect on the country's secularism. The results would be disastrous and it would suffer both political instability and economic turmoil. The lack of a firm alliance with the EU would lead Turkey to look for allies elsewhere. The most likely partners could be Russia or the Organisation of Islamic States. Some senior figures from the Kremlin have argued that both countries are outcasts from the European mainstream and should therefore stick together. The AKP has also been active in the Organisation of Islamic States and there could be a possibility that Turkey would seek a deepening of relations with the Islamic world, which would also lead to a progressive re-Islamisation of Turkish society.

When negotiations between Turkey and the EU were officially opened, opinion polls indicated that the majority of the European population opposed this country's membership. Anti-Turkish feeling was particularly high in France, Germany and Austria. It is for this reason that the President of the European Union, Durao Barroso, warned in 2004 that the success of Turkey's candidacy would require an improvement in Turkey's image within European public opinion. Unfortunately, four years after the beginning of negotiations there has been no improvement of Turkey's image among Europeans. Although opinion polls should not influence progress made in negotiations, it is particularly dangerous for the EU to ignore public opinion. In fact, anti-Turkish opinions and opposition to enlargement greatly influenced many of those who voted 'No' in the referendums on the European Constitution in France and the Netherlands. The experience of the European Constitution showed that a lack of harmony between EU governing elites and the population can have disastrous results and lead to failure. Surveys of the attitude of the Turkish population towards the EU show that there has been a considerable decline in Turkish Europeanism. Support for Turkish membership in the EU dropped in 2005 to 63%, and there is an increasing number who believe that a privileged relationship might be the best option (Eurobarometer, 2005). Particularly worrying is the fact that a 2006 Eurobarometer survey showed that only 35% of Turks trust the EU (Eurobarometer, 2006).

Not only have prejudices and cultural stereotypes played an important role in negotiations, but Europeans have not improved their opinion of the Turks and, worst of all, Turks seem to be increasingly disappointed with the EU. To prevent further alienation between the two parties would require, on the one hand, more serious compromises from the Turkish government to improve its external image and, on the other, a bigger effort by EU institutions to explain to European citizens the political and economic advantages of a Turkish rapprochement with the EU. Only then can negotiations make progress with better prospects for success.

The negotiations for Turkish entry into the EU have so far been, as expected, the most problematic in the history of European integration. Theoretically the opening of negotiations constitutes the start of an irreversible process in which the candidate starts to be seen as an EU member. This has not been the case with Turkey, as this chapter has shown. Yet, however problematic Turkey's candidacy might be from the political, economic and cultural point of view, an eventual definitive break in negotiations would be disastrous for both sides. For the EU it would mean forsaking a great asset that could considerably strengthen its position as a global power. It would also undermine its formidable soft power, which has made it a very efficient external factor promoting democracy and economic development among its neighbours. For Turkey it would mean putting an end to a process of modernisation and Westernisation, which could have catastrophic results for the country as well as for the Western world. For this reason it is necessary to overcome prejudices and continue the negotiations, which are bound to take a very long time but which should culminate in a mutually beneficial agreement.

References

Chislett, W. (2005). Turkish delight: The EU begins accession negotiations. *Real Instituto Elcano*, 4 October, http://www.realinstitutoelcano.org/wps/portal/rielcano_eng/Content?WCM_GLOBAL_CONTEXT=/Elcano_in/Zonas_in/ARI+122-2005/.

Eurobarometer. (2005). *Public opinion in the European Union*. National Report, Executive Summary, Turkey 63, Spring, http://ec.europa.eu/public_opinion/archives/eb/eb63/eb63_exec_tr.pdf.

Eurobarometer. (2006). *Public opinion in the European Union*. National Report, Executive Summary, Turkey 65, Spring. http://ec.europa.eu/public_opinion/archives/eb/eb65/eb65_tr_exec.pdf/.

Garton Ash, T. (2005). *Free world*. London: Penguin.

Lewis, B. (2001). *The emergence of modern Turkey*. Oxford: Oxford University Press.

MacLennan, J. (2000). *Spain and the process of European integration, 1957–85*. Basingstoke: Palgrave.

Mango, A. (2006). *The Turks today*. New York: Overlook.

Rehn, O. (2007). A military coup has been avoided, but early election looms. Turkey's problems are postponed not solved. *The Economist*, 27 April–3, May.

Turkey and Europe: The Importance of Predictability

Diba Nigar Göksel

Predictability is a notion that runs through many dimensions of Turkey–EU relations. Being anchored in the integration process gives Turkey a predictable course to follow, which is very important for business and society at large. Part of the problem in the 1990s was frequently changing governments, each with its own policy agenda and little interest in investing in a far-reaching goal.

On the other hand, for Turkey to stay the course, the outcome needs to be more or less predictable, so that if Turkey attains the standards required for membership the path will not be blocked for reasons that cannot be changed – such as religion or size. The inability to count on membership would not only demoralise the society and political circles but also change the calculation of the political expedience of taking on the challenges of harmonisation with the *acquis*.

Turkey has been wracked with polarising infighting particularly since spring 2006. The turmoil is multi-faceted and has been manifest recently in the political crisis over the election of the president in summer 2007 and the court case brought against the ruling AKP in March 2008 that could result in the banning of the party and/or 70 of its members. Hate crimes and assassinations that seem to be politically motivated (many of which have recently been linked to an ultra-right group) and rising nationalism have shaken the country.

The shift in power from the traditional elites to a new segment of society is one dimension of the bitter confrontation, which has political, economic and socio-cultural elements. Underlying these elements, however, is also a lack of trust that those with privilege will not exploit their power, that the law will not be breached and that rights will not be trampled upon. In other words, the AKP has not been able to convince the critical mass it needs to in order for there to be social harmony that it operates in a different way than did previous holders of power. The unpredictability has also been reflected in foreign policy – which may have been inevitable given the shifting of global fault lines in recent years. This could have been managed, however, in a way that projected more clarity and vision.

As a single-party government with weak competition from other parties, it is in the AKP's interests to take the extra step in order to consolidate meritocracy, the rule of law, pluralism and increased freedoms across the board – creating a clear break with the heritage of Turkish politics. The society has matured, and has come to expect this, while the politicians have not matured enough to deliver it. In this

C. Arvanitopoulos (Ed.), *Turkey's Accession to the European Union*

period of disconnect, the EU process is critical to provide a roadmap for politics and confidence to domestic and international players.

1 The Promise of Joining the Club

Looking at the track record of the EU's soft power over candidate countries, it is clear that the promise of Europeanisation fosters stability and improvements in living standards.

In Central Europe, eight post-communist states, each in quite diverse circumstances, transformed themselves into full-fledged EU members in the last decade. The rapid transformation of Spain, Ireland and Greece after they become EU candidates is also a remarkable story. Certainly there were factors other than EU integration that played a role in these success stories; however, on the whole the EU factor appears to have been the catalyst.

One decade ago, leading European statesmen such as former French President Giscard D'Estaing were saying that Bulgaria should never be part of the EU, that it was part of a different civilisation: Orthodox and post-Ottoman. The country was also economically devastated. It was when the government associated itself with the EU that steps in the political and economic sphere – which had been recommended for years – were finally put into action. These bold shifts were carried out in the context of the prospect of EU membership. The Prime Minister promised the Parliament in 1997 that in 10 years Bulgaria would be a member of the EU. This prospect provided the framework for the progress made thereafter. Governments changed, but since this goal remained, public policy was stable and predictable. Investors saw Bulgaria not for what it was, but for what it would be, an EU member. A virtuous cycle caught on (ESI, 2007b). Today, Bulgaria is a full-fledged member.

In complex societies, with many problems and tensions, the prospect of accession to the EU creates a common goal – an incentive – and a clear action plan for structural reforms. It makes governments predictable; the process of change is anchored. And it creates a self-fulfilling circle of positive expectations. The transformation becomes irreversible as domestic stakeholders are empowered on the basis of accountable and effective work.

2 Turkey's Virtuous Cycle

To see that the same dynamics caught on in Turkey, it is enough to compare the 1990s – Turkey's lost decade – with the five years after candidacy was granted in 1999. In the 1990s, although everyone knew what should be done, governments were populist and policies shifted with each change in government. The short-term concerns of parties drove the decision-making process. Until EU candidacy was granted to Turkey, no political actor had the incentive to change this cycle.

The formula of political expediency shifted in Turkey with the beginning of the EU process in 2000. Two consecutive governments of very different political orientations and composition followed through with profound reforms in legislation and policies. Both the 1999 coalition government – of the Motherland Party of Turkey (Anavatan Partisi, ANAP), the Democratic Left Party (Demokratik Sol Parti, DSP) and the Nationalist Action Party (Milliyetçi Hareket Partisi, MHP) – in power between 1999 and 2002, and the single-party government formed by the AKP, pursued the EU recommendations with constitutional amendments and reform packages. The EU accession negotiations with Turkey began in October 2005.

To name a few of these reforms: civilian control over the military was strengthened and the political role of the military was reduced significantly, freedom of expression for and the cultural rights of Kurds were broadened, laws governing the rights of women were brought up to EU standards and reform of the very centralised and ineffective public administration system finally began. For decades, calls for reform on these very issues from advocacy groups and intellectuals had been ignored.

A social consensus was built around EU aspirations – the conservatives, the arch-secularists, the security establishment, the business community and the society at large united around this vision. The EU process also empowered the modernisers in society and politics, depriving anti-Western agendas of their appeal. The EU track satisfied the demands of seemingly incompatible social segments simultaneously – it promised meritocracy rather than cronyism, freedom rather than patronisation and rational and effective policy rather than disjointed, weak institutions.

Predictability was achieved and investors who hadn't previously been interested felt confidence in Turkey's future. The role of the IMF programme for macroeconomic stability is of course central; however, without political stability it would not have had the same results.

A stark example of how the EU integration process directly and indirectly impacted policymaking in Turkey is the process and content of the new Penal Code that was enacted in 2004. After repeated calls from the EU about the need to reform the Penal Code, the AKP launched a participatory process – reaching consensus with the opposition Republican People's Party (Cumhuriyet Halk Partisi, CHP) on the composition of the commission formed to revise the draft, sharing developments with the press on a daily basis and listening to the perspectives of feminists. Almost all the players in this multi-faceted process admitted that the EU had played a role, directly or indirectly, in the timing, scope and motivation for the reform of the Penal Code and that the process reflected a progressive approach to citizen–state relations (ESI, 2007a). This virtuous cycle seemed to fizzle out in 2005, however.

3 Downturn: Loosing the Momentum for EU Accession

There is a deeply rooted tendency in Turkey to see the world as plotting against Turkey, and a susceptibility to the belief that it is surrounded by adversaries. After 2005, it seemed to many in Turkey that Turkey's membership was too unlikely to be worth the investment of political capital and 'national pride': The (relatively) 'Turkey-friendly' European leaders of France and Germany were replaced by sceptics, the debate in Europe about Turkey centred on Islam and an existential divide, the claim that Turkey had committed genocide against Armenian Christians 90 years ago was made repeatedly and demands that Turkey officially recognise the Republic of Cyprus resonated loudly. The conviction that Europe was behind Kurdish separatists was coupled with uproar at the US's unwillingness to crack down on the PKK (Partiya Karkerên Kurdistan, Kurdistan Workers' Party) bases in northern Iraq. Increasingly, the 'sincerity' of the US and EU was brought into question; the mood was manifest also in the conspiracy theories promoted in best-selling books and popular movies that depicted the attempts of Western countries to wrest land and power from Turkey. Faced with this climate, opposition parties, rather than calling for calm, incited heightened emotionalism by framing these events as Turkey's 'loss of honour' and calling for more hawkish policies against the EU and US.

Prior to the Brussels Summit of December 2004, discussion in Europe about Turkey boiled down to whether an alternative (privileged partnership) to full membership should be offered. The media coverage in Turkey of the negative statements emanating from leading Europeans played on Turkish pride and insecurities. Rather than treating the goal of EU accession as a national cause, it was largely seen as a process that would increase support for the AKP. Rather than claiming that they could pursue the EU goal more effectively than the AKP, the opposition parties undermined the goal itself. And the intellectual elite did not use its ability to frame the events more constructively.

In fact, the disheartening discourse emanated mostly from Austria and France and from Christian Democrats in Europe. Reasons put forth for Turkey's un-Europeanness were largely about culture and identity. Then Interior Minister Nicolas Sarkozy said that 'if Turkey were European, we would know it'. It was recalled that Valéry Giscard d'Estaing, the former President of France, had said in 2002 that Turkey was not European for cultural reasons.

In 2005 only 20% of French public opinion supported Turkey joining the EU, and in February 2005 the French constitution was amended such that a referendum would be held after the conclusion of negotiations for any future enlargement. Sarkozy, the vocal opponent of Turkey's membership, became President in May 2007.

The Christian Democrat Angela Merkel, a hardliner about Turkey compared to former Chancellor Schröder, became Chancellor of Germany in September 2005.

At the EU Foreign Ministers meeting in November 2005, Austria delayed the opening of accession negotiations with Turkey for a day by insisting that negotiations should be for something other than full membership. Austrian public support for Turkish accession stood at only 5% according to the 2006 Eurobarometer survey (ESI, 2008a).

Seen from Turkey, the new face of Europe was that of a tough if finally inconvincible audience.

The rejection of the European constitution in France and the Netherlands, in May 2005 and June 2005 respectively, and particularly the fact that the political debate in both countries had revolved around Turkey's potential membership, was a further reason for demoralisation.

Meanwhile, domestic developments fuelled nationalism and led Turkish public opinion to be particularly receptive to the belief that the EU was humiliating Turkey through issues like resolutions recognising the Armenian genocide and the perceived hypocrisy regarding Cyprus.

The return of PKK terror and the nationalist backlash played an important role in the transformed social psyche. Acts of intolerance against religious minorities seemed like an extension of the reactionism. Disturbing assassinations such as the killing of a priest in Trabzon in February 2006, of a judge of the Council of State in May 2006 and of a well-known Armenian-Turkish journalist in January 2007 indicated how dramatic the consequences of this new state of affairs could be.[1]

During this period, the country's opposition parties played the nationalist card, feeding into conspiracy theories that Turkey's troubles were the result of Western ill will. Anti-American sentiments have also been fuelled by the perception that the US hypocritically turned a blind eye to the PKK presence in northern Iraq – the US was seen to have double standards when it came to terror. A significant majority of Turks feels that the EU does not appreciate the threat of separatist terror that Turkey faces. The European emphasis on the need to expand rights for ethnic minorities, at a time when ethnicity is being used as a mean to divide, has been framed as Europe's way to weaken Turkey and has awakened memories of Sèvres – the treaty that the Ottomans were forced to sign – which divided up Anatolian lands among various European countries and Turkey's neighbours.

The pursuit by the well-financed Armenian diaspora of genocide resolutions in different legislative bodies around the world also fed into the sentiment of being singled out by the global community. In October 2007, the Foreign Affairs Committee of the US House of Representatives approved a resolution recognising the Armenian massacre in 1915 in Anatolia as genocide. Though the resolution was never brought to the House floor, it ignited fierce bitterness in Turkish public opinion.

In a nationwide survey conducted jointly by the ARI Movement and Terror Free Tomorrow in early 2007, 20% of Turks expressed a favourable opinion of the US; among these, four-fifths stated that their opinion would deteriorate if the resolution formally recognising an Armenian genocide (which was, at the time, being considered in Congress) were to pass (Ballen, 2007). A similar dynamic exists in Turkish opinion about the legislatures of European countries passing genocide resolutions.

When in October 2006 the French parliament adopted a bill making it a crime to deny that Armenians suffered 'genocide' at the hands of the Turks, there was widespread anger in Turkey and harsh reactions from the Turkish foreign ministry. This incident fed into the sense that 'the West' was hypocritical and had double standards when it comes to Turkey. Turkey's chief negotiator in EU membership talks, Ali Babacan, said: 'This is violating one of the core principles of the European Union, which is freedom of expression' (*International Herald Tribune*, 12 October 2006). Though the bill did not become law because the French Senate and President did not approve it, it left a bad taste in Turkey's mouth.

Because Turkish Cypriots voted in favour of the Annan Plan for the resolution of the Cyprus deadlock in 2004, the perception that Turkey was 'punished' by the EU for not

[1] By 2008 it was alleged that many of these incidents were linked to an ultra-right gang named Ergenekon.

recognising the Cyprus Republic (i.e., implementing the Ankara Protocol on Cyprus) heightened popular conviction of Europe's hypocrisy on Turkey-related issues.

Arguments that Turkey was not being dealt with according to the principles of fairness and equal treatment have been formulated intellectually (Senem, 2006) and resonated widely in public discourse. Unfortunately the policy implications of this approach boiled down to resigning to fate, which was convenient for those who had a different vision for Turkey to begin with. The AKP and Prime Minister Erdoğan went out of their way to prove their nationalist credentials, with tougher talk on issues such as minority rights and a stalling of progress on EU-related reforms.

What is puzzling is that EU enthusiasts in Turkey did not put up a struggle, and the AKP, instead of using its high ratings and the Prime Minister's talent for persuasion to lead the public debate, bought into it. It was Turkey-friendly Europeans who tried to remind the Turks that enlargement fatigue was not new in Europe.

In 1977, Francois Mitterand warned that 'Neither Greece nor Spain are in a position to join the Community. Accession is neither in their interest nor is it in our interest'. Soon after, however, Greece, Spain and Portugal joined the Union.

Opinion polls gauging whether EU citizens favoured the accession of the then candidates identified similar levels of opposition towards countries that today have joined as now exist towards Turkey. For example, until 2002 there was little difference between Austrian views towards Turkey and towards other EU candidates (ESI, 2008a).

Despite the existence of people who have always believed that Turkey should never join, the process has proceeded, albeit with a fair degree of brinkmanship. Just because there are vocal Europeans that are against Turkey's membership does not necessarily mean the process will be obstructed.

That being said, concern about the unpopularity of Turkey in Europe is justified and Turkey does indeed need to launch a more proactive and effective campaign in Europe.

Nilgun Cerrahoglu terms the convenient ambiguity as 'a gentlemen's agreement' in which the Turkish government 'pretends' to be working towards EU membership in order to avoid facing the consequences of not doing so, and the EU 'pretends' the process in on track – again, in order to prevent the consequences of a clear derailment.[2] Meanwhile, alternatives are proposed.

4 Maximising Turkey's Potential through Alternate Policies

Faced with this domestic environment and disillusioned by the EU and the US, the government may have made a calculation that too much emphasis on EU integration at the expense of maximising other potential relations was not wise. A more 'self-sufficient' and neighbour-focused policy rhetoric came about.[3]

Some analysts maintain that the motivation of AKP loyalists for EU integration was also shaken by the decision of the European Court of Human Rights, in

[2] Nilgun Cerrahoglu on Kanalturk, TV programme hosted by Mine Kirikkanat, 27 April 2008.

[3] Various arguments to this end are made in Göksel (2007).

November 2005, rejecting the appeal of Leyla Sahin, who argued that her inability to study in university wearing a headscarf was discrimination that violated the right to education (BBC News, 10 November 2005).

Others see the tilting of foreign policy eastwards as a pragmatic shift in light of unease within the Turkish populace about making too many ‘concessions’ to the EU and US, and in light of ‘external challenges’, including post-Cold War and post-9/11 economic and strategic realities (Giragosian, 2007).

Though some in the government no doubt conceived this shift with pragmatic intentions, ‘less West and more East’ is also in line with the visions of the ideologically or emotionally motivated currents in the ranks of the AKP, the conservative nationalist circles in society as well as certain state institutions.

In fact, whether the shift amounted to a conscious ‘calculation’ or whether it was more erratic and reactionary can be debated. Conflicting voices from within the circle of decision-makers could be heard from 2005 onwards. Should Turkey lead the Middle East from its current disarray into a global powerhouse? Should Turkey focus on Eurasia, using its Turkic card or the Muslim card? Should Turkey pragmatically foster relations with countries like Russia and Iran, be a key energy player and expect Europeans to wait at its own doorstep? A mixture of pride, ambition and confusion resonated in the debate on Turkey’s direction in 2006.

The name widely perceived to be behind the cultivation of renewed foreign policy parameters was Professor Ahmet Davutoğlu, adviser to the Prime Minister. His book *Strategic Depth* offers a new conceptualisation of Turkey’s place in the post-Cold War setting. *Branding* Turkey proactively rather than drifting in the currents of globalisation appears to be the goal.

Davutoğlu writes that Europe is keeping Turkey as its economic *hinterland* while geoculturally excluding Turkey. He argues that one of the most important strategic requirements of Turkey in the near future is to develop alternative policies towards its neighbouring regions so that it has a wide space to manoeuvre, with political alternatives, and is not isolated when in 20 years Eastern Europe is totally integrated into the EU and Turkey is left out (Davutoğlu 2002).

Interestingly, the maximisation of Turkey’s unique historic, geographical and cultural/religious assets was an area in which the AKP and the statist bureaucracy – be it foreign policy, security or other – have increasingly converged. Though the Foreign Ministry bureaucracy at times has been left out of the policy implementation and there have been incidents where different official bodies seemed to be on a different page, the growing perception, for example, that the interests of the US and Turkey diverge has been shared across the board.

The recognition of the need to collaborate with Russia, based on both countries having legitimate spheres of influence, was one pillar of this approach – and one that did not necessarily sit well with the US or other NATO partners. On the other hand, the lack of a united approach in the EU towards Russia and the pursuit of national interests among EU member states seemed to justify Turkey’s decision to diverge from traditional blocs of power. Moreover, given the difficulties and mistrust the US faced in the region, Turkey did not encounter a high cost for frequent inconsistency between its message and its actions.

Whether the 'spheres of influence' of Turkey will accept themselves as such, whether Turkey has the credentials and human resources to substantiate the bulk of the new responsibilities entailed by its ambitious rebranding, are open questions. With ambiguity as to the strategy and capacity to substantiate claims to regional power, the claim can backfire.

Moreover, there are arguably junctures where actors need to choose between parties at odds with each other or where bilateral relations cannot be viewed in isolation from global dynamics. The AKP has yet to demonstrate that it will be able to do so. Playing different hands with different partners may result in loosing the confidence of all.

Partially because the parameters of this new approach were not communicated clearly to domestic or international stakeholders, concerns were voiced that the AKP aimed to change the course of Turkey, severing ties the country had traditionally treasured. There was not an informed debate in the country and this left a vacuum in terms of both domestic leadership and clarity with respect to counterparts.

The AKP government, given its strong following, should be able to sway public opinion in line with a foreign policy it perceives to be in Turkey's strategic interests. Thus it needs to take on the responsibility of articulating a comprehensive vision and project a clear, integrated approach that will generate predictability and confidence among not only international partners but also the domestic populace.

Otherwise, emotionally disposed Turks will be ever more vulnerable to speculation that leverages fears based on historical traumas, insecurities and notions of pride and honour.

Such perspectives also have far-reaching domestic implications, as it is often assumed that it is the minorities in the country that will be used as tools in the plot to dismember Turkey. The question of what it means to be a Turk is intertwined with foreign policy dynamics.

The much-needed loosening of taboos has unleashed as much negative as positive discourse. In the clash of religious conservative circles and liberals of an anti-state disposition with those of nationalist and statist approaches, voices that have the legitimacy necessary to bridge the divide and foster tolerance have been absent.

5 Domestic Troubles: Systemic, Cultural and Conjectural

The slowdown of reforms that would transform Turkey into a more democratic and stable country, coupled with the rising ratings of the conservative AKP, fuelled some segments' concern about Turkey's direction.

5.1 Deficiencies of Pluralism and the Rule of Law

Turkey has a relatively weak system of checks and balances. Especially when a single-party government is in power, the executive has a strong hold over the legislature and even the judiciary. This stems both from the legislative framework and the assumption that the winner takes all; and is also embedded in the lack of confidence in the rule of law. The oversight over the executive is weak. The Party Law ensures loyalty to the party leader rather than the constituency (Freedom House, 2008). And the judiciary can come under the sway of the executive – especially through political appointments or pressure from a strong government. The reverse is also true, in that the state – including but not limited to the security apparatus – has had unchecked power through various mechanisms. The fine-tuning of limitations on the power of the elected and appointed classes has remained unresolved.

In the political scene of Turkey until recently, the judiciary and the presidency played the role of a check on government power by nature of their intrinsic split from the AKP. Acting at times at the limit of 'opposition for the sake of opposition' both President Ahmet Necdet Sezer, until he stepped down in August 2007, and the high courts have blocked AKP moves that they found to be questionable.

The realisation that the 'former Islamists' would be in the position to approve the appointment of enough high judges of their own choice to tilt the balances in the high courts was terrifying for those who believe that this will result in a pro-Islamist judiciary. The fears were fuelled by those who risked loosing privileges by the ascendance of the AKP. Thus the thorny process that finally brought Abdullah Gül to Presidency in August 2007 after his election was blocked by the highly controversial decision of the Constitution Court that a two-thirds quorum was required in the Parliament for the election to be valid.

Efforts to homogenise the population have been prevalent in Turkey since its establishment. Pressure to conform, restriction of the rights of ethnic groups and religious minorities and acts of intolerance have been means through which this drive has surfaced over the years.

The problem goes much further back than the AKP's entrance into the political scene. AKP supporters will argue that the establishment's prescriptions about how to live and think, by definition excluded the conservative religious segments of society. Indeed, a tolerance for differences was not widely internalised by the time the AKP appeared and the conviction started to spread that a new totalitarian approach based on the right way to live would be imposed. It is against this backdrop that concerns heightened that the conservative political movement that the AKP represents was making progress in increasing the prominence of religion in people's lives.

5.2 *Could the AKP Have Maintained the Consensus or Was Such a Far-Reaching Clash Inevitable?*

The AKP made strides towards empowering a new generation of like-minded people in the media and business circles of their own camp – establishing symbiotic relationships. This was indeed a pattern previous governments in the decade of the 1990s had also pursued; however, in this case the camp also had ideological underpinnings.

When the AKP started to give priority to the rights and prominence of its traditional base, these acts were framed as a threat to the existing order and even to the regime. Discrimination in bureaucratic appointments in favour of men whose wives wear the headscarf, Islamist statements and publications of AKP municipalities, the initiative to open the way for women wearing the headscarf to study at universities, and the apparent success of the AKP in winning the hearts and minds of the Kurdish population through emphasising religious bonds were put forth as signs that a Pandora's box was being opened.

In fact, a number of the reactions were out of proportion and ill conceived – undermining the legitimacy of the opposition. For example, the uproar against the AKP for amending the Constitution in January 2008 to open the way for women to wear headscarves in university was hardly justified. In fact, 'banning students to enter university grounds wearing headscarves is a relatively new phenomenon. Until 1998, though with short-lived periods of restriction, girls could attend university with their headscarves… What now constitutes the "ban" is largely based on rulings of the Constitutional Court that interpret the wearing of a headscarf in university to be a violation of secularism and thus unconstitutional' (ESI, 2008b). The MHP voted with the AKP for this amendment, which is supported by a strong majority of the country. The efforts to portray the AKP as a dire threat based on this move are not credible.

The AKP may not have tried hard enough to reassure the people who are not within their constituency that they do not wish to carry out a vendetta against those who held social and political prominence in the decades prior. On the other hand, it is not wise for those opposed to the AKP to paint a large segment of society as a threat, whose empowerment needs to be blocked by all means, democratic or not. This can only strengthen conceptualisation along the same lines on the other side, which it has done. By now, neither side can back down for fear of looking weak.

Had the AKP kept to a EU-integration-driven reform agenda and demonstrated the will to stand up for the rights of those not a part of its traditional constituency, it might have preserved the wider support base it needed to be immune from the drastic efforts exercised by the establishment to curb its power, such as the closure case against the AKP accepted by the Constitutional Court on 31 March 2008.

On issues such as freedom of expression, the rights of religious minorities or fighting corruption, the AKP proved not to be a 'revolutionary' reformer. The AKP appeared unpredictable and unprincipled – perhaps due to the tight space for manoeuvre it was left with as it played its hand in Turkey's political maze. Trying to please the conservatives, nationalists, liberals, status quo defenders and special interest groups at once, the AKP appeared contradictory. At times appeasing the establishment and selling out the ideals it had come to represent for different segments of the country, it was perhaps inevitable that the AKP would not be able to deliver on all the promises it had made. Confidence in the AKP has been shaken among various segments of society in the past couple of years. When the nationalist vote seemed to slip, the AKP made a gesture to win it back; when the religious base was frustrated, a statement to cater to their ideals would follow. The AKP could not project courageous and consistent leadership possessing a transparent vision through these seemingly disjointed moves.

It is also true that the confrontational opposition to the AKP, emanating from not only opposition parties but also segments of the state apparatus and civic society, did stir up instability and to an extent served the goal of shaking public and international confidence in a Turkey governed by the AKP. Stoking the fire by spreading the conviction that a Turkey ruled by the AKP would constantly suffer crises may have contributed to the turmoil itself.

5.3 Who Competes with the AKP on Solutions?

Part of the problem is the reality of the lop-sided political spectrum in Turkey. It is puzzling that, in a country with significant disparities and development problems, a social democrat vision is not advocated.

On Women's Day, on 8 March 2008, Prime Minister Erdoğan promoted the need for each woman to have at least three children. This, while his party scorns the notion of widespread institutional childcare as a choice for women. The structural grounds for this policy are hardly present: Turkey already has enough trouble absorbing the one million young people that enter the workforce each year and women are hardly empowered to make rational choices, for the following reasons: a very low level of women's participation in the workforce, the absence of institutionalised childcare and the cultural pressures for traditional gender roles.

In certain provinces of south-east Anatolia, over 50% of women are illiterate despite primary education having been mandatory for more than 80 years, the average family size is seven plus, unemployment is rampant, most live on subsistence agriculture or seasonal work, domestic violence is widespread and shelters for women are non-existent, while state institutions are perceived to be patronising. Girls not registered at birth and/or married only in a religious ceremony are outside of the law, as their marriage is not recognised and their existence not known. Most urbanites in this region lived in mountains as villagers until they were displaced due to the conflict in the region with PKK in the 1990s.

The state has limited capacity for delivering the services and opportunities necessary for individuals to break out of this vicious cycle. The environment is conducive for entrenched traditions to outlive their natural course. Extended families and clan-like informal feudal structures establish the values, ensure their implementation and match favoured people with the few job opportunities. Honour killings and councils of elders are just two of the means through which the official judicial process is circumvented. Official plans have thus far not been able to trigger economic development and for decades politicians have opted to appease regional power figures rather than empower individuals to break out of this stubborn system of quasi-feudalism.

Making the delivery of services a priority and levelling the chasm of opportunity should naturally be the priority of the left of the political spectrum. As the base of their votes (the educated and relatively well-to-do) demonstrates, the main opposition party, the centre-left CHP, is not seen to be searching for solutions for the less privileged.

In environments of poverty and displacement, the AKP offers its own party organs (such as local AKP representatives) as a solution for people's problems, reaching out a helping hand. In the short term, of course, this works to the benefit of the party's support. However, it is not being complemented with long-term investment to strengthen state institutions and render them able to deliver people's needs in an ideologically neutral fashion. To the extent that state institutions are strengthened, it is often linked to the appointment of like-minded bureaucrats. Turkey cannot afford not to practice full meritocracy in public administration at this juncture.

One should not be surprised by the swell of conservatism in an environment where morality is intertwined with efforts to even out the vast social discrepancies in opportunity.

It is clear that a stronger welfare state is needed – there are too many citizens trapped with no means to actualise their potential. Informal communities based on a set of values, such as religious sects, have fertile ground to recruit followers whom they 'guide' by defining the traditions and rewards of modernity that should be embraced, the right lifestyle, the right way to think, coupled with job opportunities and a sense of meaning.

In districts of Istanbul as different as Umraniye and Kadikoy, a majority of the residents were born outside of the city, most having migrated from rural settings. Facing a dramatically different environment, having to adapt to a new lifestyle and lacking the traditional social networks, all the elements of rapid urbanisation and moder-nisation are inevitably experienced.

The bright side is this: the transformation Turkey is experiencing today is like that which many European societies experienced only a few decades ago. The rising rate of education and access to opportunity especially among the young generation is heartening and signals positive trends.

However, institutional solutions to the new challenges are needed. The generations of educated young people, growing up in cities, need ways to reconcile family life with economic activity. While prosperous districts like Kadikoy are able to meet these needs, the results are not so heartening in districts where the market is not strong enough and public institutions need to compensate during the transformation.

Without strong social services provided by politically and ideologically neutral state institutions, large segments of society will continue to lack the ability to make choices for themselves. Dependence on extended families and on communities to which one has to prove one's ideological credentials to be accepted, does not offer a level playing field where the power of persuasion is the basis for political competition.

The political actors on the scene today each have a set of prescriptions (for the right way to live and think and believe). Rather than competing on the basis of catering to people's needs, the competition has taken on an ideological nature. Exploiting nationalism or offering conservative worldviews as a way to cater to emotional vulnerabilities are the grounds on which the political competition is pursued. The AKP has managed to garner support through more efficient and accessible services, particularly through functioning municipalities as well as the ideologically associated Islamist movement (Milli Görüş) and various religious sects that act with them on an occasional basis.

Those concerned that the AKP is also promoting a conservative lifestyle should get into the arena with solutions to the challenges that Turkish citizens face rather than expending their energies on formulas to bring down the AKP.

6 The EU: An Anchor for Turkey in Limbo

Especially in the absence of such merit-based domestic political competition, the EU plays the role of a sensible opposition in Turkey – pointing out the weaknesses of the democratic system and benchmarking higher standards of governance.

The pursuit of the institutional and structural reforms the EU integration path requires appears to be the strongest guarantee of the rule of law and pluralism in Turkey today.

During the closure case of the AKP, leading actors of the EU used firm rhetoric in favour of democracy in Turkey, which many in the country perceived to be in support of the AKP. In turn, the AKP brought the issue of EU reforms back on the agenda in its rhetoric. Among AKP voters, the favourability of the EU increased. However in the same period the amendment to Article 301 of the Penal Code, one of many articles used to curb freedom of expression, was hardly satisfactory as many of the changes made were largely cosmetic. The case against the AKP did not result in its closure. Whether genuine commitment to European values will be pursued from this point onwards is an open question.

The AKP re-established its strong public support in the July 2007 elections; the President in office will clearly not block the party's reasonable steps; and European Commission President Jose Manuel Barroso reiterated in April 2008 that Turkey's progress will determine the results of the accession process. It is timely that the AKP push forward with pending reforms. The recent turmoil should spur a renewed understanding that a pro-reform social coalition is critical for both the AKP's success and Turkey's progress. Passing a new constitution to replace the authoritarian spirit of the 1982 Constitution will go a long way to getting Turkey out of the limbo it currently appears to be stuck in.

References

Ballen, K. (2007). Wrong resolution on Turkish killings. *Baltimore Sun*, 15 March, http://www.terrorfreetomorrow.org/upimagestft/6%20BSun%20March%2015%202007(1).pdf/.

Davutoglu, A. (2002). *Stratejik Derinlik – Türkiye'nin Ulusrarasi Konumu [Strategic Depth – Turkey's International Position]*. Istanbul: Küre Yayinlari.

ESI. (2007a). *Sex and power: Islam, feminism and the maturing of Turkish democracy*. Berlin/Istanbul: European Stability Initiative, 2 June, http://www.esiweb.org/index.php?lang = en&id = 156&document_ID = 90/.

ESI. (2007b). *From laggard to EU member*. Berlin/Istanbul: European Stability Initiative, October, http://www.esiweb.org/.

ESI. (2008a). *A referendum on the unknown turk: Anatomy of an Austrian Debate*. Berlin/Istanbul: European Stability Initiative, 30 January, http://www.esiweb.org/index.php?lang = en&id = 156&documentID = 101/.

ESI. (2008b). *Turkey's dark side – party closures, conspiracies and the future of democracy*. Berlin/Istanbul: European Stability Initiative, 2 April, http://www.esiweb.org/index.php?lang = en&id = 156&document_ID = 104/.

Featherstone, K., & Kazamias, G. (Eds.) (2001). *Europeanization and the southern periphery*. London: Frank Cass Publishers.

Freedom House. (2008). *Turkey in transit-democratization in Turkey, 2006–2007*. Budapest.

Giragosian, R. (2007). Redefining Turkey's strategic orientation. *Turkish Policy Quarterly, 6*(4), 33–40, http://www.turkishpolicy.com/.

Göksel, D. N. (Ed.) (2007). Special issue: The international architecture of global governance and Turkey. *Turkish Policy Quarterly, 6*(4), http://www.turkishpolicy.com/.

Minority Rights Group International (2007). *A quest for equality: Minorities in Turkey*. London, 11 December, http://www.minorityrights.org/?lid = 4572/.

Terror Free Tomorrow & the ARI Movement. (2005). *The perception among Turkish public of the United States and of Americans*. July, http://www.ari.org.tr/.

Senem, A. D. (2006). *Seeking Kant in the EU's relations with Turkey*. Istanbul: Turkish Economic and Social Studies Foundation (TESEV) 2(3).

Tertium Datur: Turkey's Application for EU Membership

Thomas Silberhorn

1 The Application as Seen in the Light of Each Side's Identity Problem

In previous negotiations on EU enlargement, the readiness of the member states to accept the candidates was never in doubt. Turkey's application, however, faces long-standing, deeply divided opinion, especially in France and Austria, where binding referendums are to be held. But in Germany, too, there exists a broad and stable popular majority against Turkey's possible accession.[1]

The question as to Turkey's accession capability and the Union's capacity for enlargement affects both sides as they strive to realise their identity. In Turkey, there is a rift between the Kemalists, found notably in the military and judicial establishment, who had been at one time the protagonists of a pro-European Turkey, but who now believe that accession would jeopardise the country's secular system, and conservative Islamic factions, who today want closer relations with the EU principally to gain political ground at home. The Union's enlargement to include the Central and East European states has rekindled the debate on the finality of integration. The vision of some for an ever-closer union[2] contrasts with a vision of a loose economic community, whose main proponents are to be found in Great Britain and the Czech Republic – who, not surprisingly, are among the strongest supporters of Turkey's accession to the EU.

Thus EU accession negotiations with Turkey are accompanied by factional disputes on both sides. These open quarrels cannot be explained away by the fact that, for the first time, accession negotiations that have already begun have been

[1] In the Eurobarometer surveys commissioned by the European Commission, only 21% (2005) and 16% (2006) of respondents in Germany were in favour of Turkish EU membership. See Eurobarometer (2005, 2006).

[2] See the Preamble to the Treaty on European Union (1992).

C. Arvanitopoulos (Ed.), *Turkey's Accession to the European Union*

declared open-ended (European Council, 2004). Indeed, in contrast to all previous applications for accession, there is a real possibility, if not a probability, that some member states will refuse to admit Turkey. What is more, the pendulum in Turkey itself could swing against EU membership.[3]

2 Turkey Caught between Secularism and Islamisation

Undoubtedly, the prospect of EU membership is generating the impetus for reform in Turkey. However, the reform efforts are proceeding on shaky foundations, as the progress reports of the European Commission have shown.[4] The growing intensity of the dispute between secular Kemalist and conservative Islamic factions, culminating in the proceedings before the Turkish Constitutional Court aiming to ban the AKP, accentuates the schism in the country and poses serious questions about its internal stability.

The role of the armed forces and the question of religious freedom are examples of the contentious areas at issue. As Turkey moves towards EU membership, it will be forced to make decisions that could undermine its stability. The primacy of political control over the military establishment is an indispensable precondition for accession. On the other hand, unlimited parliamentary oversight would mean that the military high command would forfeit its role as the guarantor of the Kemalist system; this prospect is perceived as involving the risk of the country's Islamisation.[5] Equally crucial for EU membership is recognition of religious freedom, which, in practice, is far from the reality in Turkey despite the fact that, as a party to the European Convention on Human Rights, it is already under obligation to respect that freedom (Oehring, 2008). Without disregarding the discrimination against and marginalisation of Christian and Jewish minorities (Oehring, 2008, p. 31; Sommer, 2008, pp. 19, 21). it is clear that the main objective of the government through the Office for Religious Affairs is to control the Islamic majority. It seems that religious freedom, too, conjures up the unwanted risk of Islamisation in the eyes of the secularists.

This dilemma of proceeding towards EU membership whilst preserving the nation's secularism can be overcome only by Turkey itself. In this context the maintenance of domestic stability is essential if the EU's efforts to support the reform process in Turkey are to prove meaningful.

[3] In the Eurobarometer surveys, approval for EU membership among all Turkish respondents ranged between 55% in autumn 1955 and 44% in spring 2006. See Eurobarometer (2007).

[4] The most recent being the European Commission (2007).

[5] Concerning the role of the armed forces, see Sezer (2007).

3 The EU's Quandary: Being Supportive or Accommodating?

The closest possible cooperation between the EU and Turkey is, without question, in the strategic interests of both sides. Moreover, there is a long-standing tradition for this: Turkey's membership in NATO and the Council of Europe, and through the Ankara Agreement.[6] However, the description of Turkey's prospects in Article 28 of that agreement amounted to no more than an undertaking by the EEC to examine the mere possibility of accession. Furthermore, that commitment related only to the former European Economic Community and was subject to the condition that the results of the agreement had been sufficiently positive.

It was not until 1997 that the European Council confirmed Turkey's eligibility for full membership (European Council, 1997, p. 2). It then confirmed, in 1999, that Turkey was 'destined to join the Union' (European Council, 1999, p. 4). Within the scope of the accession partnership and the accession strategy document signed in 2001, a programme for bringing Turkey closer to the EU was adopted, which led to the opening of accession negotiations, though still as an 'open-ended process' (European Commission, 2005, p. 1).

Despite receiving wide-ranging support from the EU, Turkey has not yet fulfilled its obligations. By refusing to ratify the supplementary protocol of 29 July 2004 to the Ankara Agreement and open its harbours and airports to Cypriot ships and aircraft, it is preventing the extension of free trade to Cyprus, a member of the EU, and in this way trying to avoid *de facto* recognition of the Republic of Cyprus. Hence Turkey has failed to fulfil one of the preconditions for accession negotiations. Negotiations with the aim of membership nonetheless commenced on 3 October 2005.[7]

In effect, this enabled Turkey to use recognition of the Republic of Cyprus as a pawn in the negotiations on its own membership. It came as no surprise, therefore, that when Turkey failed to meet the deadline in 2006 (European Council, 2005, p. 2) for ratifying the supplementary protocol to the Ankara Agreement, the EU's response was to suspend eight negotiation chapters and continue with the rest (European Council, 2006, p. 9). This may have been regarded by Turkey as confirmation of its consistent approach and the Union's toleration of Turkey's continuing disregard for its obligations towards the Republic of Cyprus and the EU as a whole.

This compromise approach was also reflected in the accession of Bulgaria and Romania on 1 January 2007 without their first having been required to meet the criteria for membership. This considerably eased the pressure on these countries to

[6] The Agreement establishing an Association between the EEC and Turkey (64/733/EEC, Official Journal No. P 217, 29 Dec. 1964, 3687) was signed on 12 September 1963 and entered into force on 1 January 1964.

[7] The Federal Republic of Germany was represented by the Red-Green Federal Government, which was still in office because the 16th Bundestag, although already elected, had not yet been constituted.

carry out the necessary reforms and has, to this day, hampered their integration into the EU. It is obvious that such special concessions undermine agreed standards and justify the concern that political discounting is tantamount to debasing the criteria for membership.

This is the main reason why, notwithstanding its acceptance of open-ended negotiations, the Christian Social Union has included in its new Basic Programme a clause rejecting full membership in the EU for Turkey (CSU-Landesleitung, 2007, p. 154). Its objectives and its opposition to any qualification of the objective criteria for accession are described in the following sections.

4 The Spatial Dimension of a Common Identity in the EU

Turkey's application for accession confronts the EU – and also Turkey, of course – with the question of how it sees itself. A common identity shared by the Union's citizens is essential if the aim of a political union – supported by two-thirds of Germans (Schoen, 2008, p. 68) – is to be achieved. A feeling of belonging together can, however, be developed only on a foundation of shared historical and cultural experiences. The influence of these experiences inevitably has geographical limits, because they are always shared only within a specific area. The development of a common identity therefore has a spatial dimension. Thus, in addition to its geographical limits, the EU reaches its limits where there is a lack of common ground in historical and cultural terms.

Turkey and the EU do not to a sufficient degree form an area with a common history and culture based on shared experiences. On the contrary, there are serious differences in their understanding of the fundamental principles of law and values held by the European community. Although Turkey is based on democratic structures and the rule of law, and has committed itself to respecting fundamental and human rights, in reality the implementation of the constitution is not consistent with these fundamental European values. This is demonstrated by the status of the military and the situation of religious communities in Turkey, as well as by the widespread practice of honour crimes and forced marriages.

It is true that EU citizens have far more in common with the political and economic elite in western Turkey than with the people living near Turkey's borders with Iran, Iraq and Syria. Nonetheless, Turkey's history and culture have undeniably been defined by a different understanding of the principles of democracy and the rule of law and of fundamental and human rights – part of the political criteria established by the European Council in Copenhagen for accession to the European Union (European Council, 1993, p. 13) – than that of the EU member states.

The view that Turkey is not part of Europe in cultural terms is the primary explanation for the German population's opposition to Turkish accession to the EU (Schoen, 2008, p. 78). In practice, Christian faith is irrelevant in this context (Schoen, 2008, p. 78). This is, in any case, not a question of religious affiliation: it is about the understanding of religious freedom, which holds a different cultural status in the EU than it does in Turkey, due to the EU's heritage of Judeo-Christian values, humanism and the Enlightenment.

The fact that it has not been possible to satisfactorily resolve in Turkey the fundamental issues relating to values – so important to the EU's understanding of itself as a political union – after almost 100 years of Kemalism, nearly 60 years as a member of the Council of Europe, and more than 40 years of association with the EU, suggests that a common identity cannot be expected to develop in the span of a few years in the course of accession negotiations. The timeline of cooperation between Turkey and the European Union instead implies that alternatives to full Turkish membership in the EU should be developed. Otherwise, there is a danger that, if Turkey became a member, the EU's power to integrate would be overstretched, its internal homogeneity would be lost and the aim of a political union would be endangered.

5 The Need for a Third Way

There is also a danger that any Turkish accession could fail as a result of the likely consequences for the EU. Due to growing socio-economic disparities (see Quaisser & Wood, 2004, p. 23), the Common Agricultural Policy and the Structural Funds could be opened to Turkey only at considerable additional cost over a long period of time, and not without substantial reforms (see Quaisser & Wood, 2004, p. 45). From a security-policy perspective, it is far from certain that Turkish integration into the EU would produce an increase in stability; in fact, the difficult geopolitical environment and the long borders with Syria, Iraq and Iran could even have the opposite effect, if one considers the Turkish army's operation against PKK positions in northern Iraq in 2007/2008.

It is in any case entirely possible that the EU's accession negotiations with Turkey, if conducted according to the principle of 'all or nothing', could come to nothing. The damage in terms of foreign policy would be almost incalculable. In place of an 'in or out' dichotomy, a third way must therefore be offered. This involves diversifying the forms of cooperation and integration between the EU and its neighbouring countries.

There may initially be no incentive for Turkey to consider options other than full membership in the EU, so long as accession is the aim of the negotiations. But in the face of an impending failure of these negotiations, Turkey will not be able to ignore the possibility of a third way, because it is in the country's own best interests to have as close ties to Europe as possible, and there are no serious alternatives to this for Turkey.

Irrespective of the situation with Turkey, the EU is faced with the task of developing a third way between EU membership and the European Neighbourhood Policy. A glance at the differences between the states bordering the EU to the south and east makes it clear that differentiated models, ranging from closer cooperation to partial integration into EU structures, are essential in order to take account of each individual neighbouring state that is unable or unwilling to become a member of the EU.

6 The Nature of a Third Way

Diversifying the forms of cooperation and integration between the EU and its neighbouring countries would expand the possibilities open to both sides. While neighbouring countries would have the option of tailoring their relations with the EU flexibly in line with their own interests, the EU would be able to differentiate according to the willingness and ability of its neighbouring countries to deepen relations.

The models under discussion in Turkey's case range from forms of intergovernmental cooperation – such as a privileged partnership (zu Guttenberg, 2004), Extended Associate Membership (Quaisser & Wood, 2004, p. 50) or a European Economic Area Plus (Brok, 2005, pp. 15, 17) – to forms of graduated membership (Karakas, 2007, p. 4; Wissmann, 2006, p. 64) involving partial integration at a supranational level. What all of these models have in common is the aim of linking Turkey as closely as possible to the EU's structures if full Turkish membership should not be feasible.

Only a brief outline can be given here of the almost unlimited range of issues that a third way could potentially involve. A more advanced form of the customs union that has been in place since 1996 is the minimum, while the maximum is anything which would overstretch the EU's capacity for integration, such as unrestricted freedom of movement or full Turkish inclusion in the Common Agricultural Policy and structural policies. Within these limits, closer cooperation is conceivable within the framework of the Common Foreign and Security Policy, the European Security and Defence Policy or the fields of justice and home affairs; equally conceivable is an extension of the customs union to become a comprehensive free trade zone or even partial Turkish integration into the single market.

From an institutional perspective, the possibilities range from the establishment of joint bodies (zu Guttenberg, 2004, p. 16) to Turkish involvement in the Council, whether solely with rights of participation and consultation or with co-decision rights in specific areas (Karakas, 2007, p. 16; Wissmann, 2006, p. 68). However, the granting of limited co-decision rights can be considered only if Turkey is given the option of partial integration; a right of veto must in any case be ruled out.

The specific nature of a third way will depend to a crucial extent on Turkey's political and economic development and its willingness to surrender sovereignty. The EU's task is to set conditions on which the level of cooperation or integration depends. For example, it must already be ensured during the ongoing accession negotiations that only those negotiation chapters are open which are relevant to the form of closer cooperation or partial integration that both sides have agreed on as their aim.

7 Looking Ahead

Diversifying the forms of cooperation and integration between the EU and its neighbouring countries would not only reflect the shared interest of both sides in striving together to achieve the best possible form of closer relations. It would also take into account the challenge of connecting the existing islands of regional integration, a challenge which globalisation is increasing. It is forging links that is essential, not forming blocs.

Turkey is a geostrategic interface between Europe and its eastern neighbours. Full integration into the EU will not enable it to fulfil this function, however; this can only be achieved if Turkey combines the forming of closer ties with the EU with the expansion of its political, economic and cultural relations with the Caucasus and the Middle East. The more successful Turkey is in this respect, the greater the benefits of closer relations with Turkey would be for the European Union.

References

Brok, E. (2005). Eine neue Erweiterungsstrategie für die EU – Perspektiven nach dem Verhandlungsbeginn mit der Türkei. *Die Politische Meinung, 433*, 15–18.

CSU-Landesleitung. (2007). Chancen für alle! In Freiheit und Verantwortung gemeinsam Zukunft gestalten. Grundsatzprogramm der Christlich-Sozialen Union in Bayern, http://www.csu.de/partei/unsere_partei/grundsatzprogramm/index.htm/.

Eurobarometer. (2005). TNS Opinion and social: National report Germany, executive summary. *Eurobarometer 64*, Autumn.

Eurobarometer. (2006). National report Germany, executive summary. *Eurobarometer 66,* Autumn.

Eurobarometer. (2007). TNS Opinion and social: National report Turkey, executive summary. *Eurobarometer 67,* Spring.

European Commission. (2005). *Negotiating framework*. Luxemburg, 3 October, http://ec.europa.eu/enlargement/pdf/st20002_05_TR_framedoc_en.pdf.

European Commission. (2007). *Turkey 2007 progress report*. SEC (2007) 1436, Brussels, 6 November.

European Council. (1993). *Copenhagen European Council, presidency conclusions, (21–22 June 1993)*, SN 180/1/93.

European Council. (1997). *Luxembourg European Council: Presidency conclusions, (12–13 December 1997)*, SN 400/97.

European Council. (1999). *Helsinki European Council: Presidency conclusions, (10–11 December 1999),* SN 300/99.

European Council. (2004). *Brussels European Council: Presidency conclusions, (16–17 December 2004),* 16238/1/04 REV 1.

European Council. (2005). *Turkey, declaration by the European Community and its member states, (21 September 2005)*, 12541/05 (Presse 243).

European Council. (2006). Press release, 2770th Council meeting general affairs and external relations (General Affairs). 11 December 2006, 16289/06 (Presse 352).

zu Guttenberg, K. T. (2004). *Die Beziehungen zwischen der Türkei und der EU – eine 'Privilegierte Partnerschaft'*. München: Hanns-Seidel-Stiftung e.V. (Ed). Aktuelle Analysen, 33.

Karakas, C. (2007). EU – Türkei: Abgestufte Integration als Alternativmodell zur Vollmitgliedschaft?. *Südosteuropa Mitteilungen, 47*, 4–19.

Oehring, O. (2008). Religionsfreiheit in der Türkei. In CDU/CSU-Gruppe im Europäischen Parlament (Ed.), *Europa und die Türkei*. Schriften zur Europäischen Integration, 1/08, 31–34.

Quaisser, W., & Wood, St. (2004). EU member Turkey? Preconditions, consequences and integration alternatives. *Forschungsverbund Ost-und Südosteuropa* (Ed.). Arbeitspapier, 25.

Schoen, H. (2008). Die Deutschen und die Türkeifrage: Eine Analyse der Einstellungen zum Antrag der Türkei auf Mitgliedschaft in der Europäischen Union. *Politische Vierteljahresschrift, 49*, 68–91.

Sezer, E. (2007). Das türkische Militär und der EU-Beitritt der Türkei. *Aus Politik und Zeitgeschichte, 43*, 27–32.

Sommer, R. (2008). Menschenrechte und Grundfreiheiten in der Türkei. In CDU/CSU-Gruppe im Europäischen Parlament (Ed.), *Europa und die Türkei*. Schriften zur Europäischen Integration, 1/08, 19–23.

Treaty on European Union (1992). *EC Official Journal*, C191, 29 July, http://eur-lex.europa.eu/en/treaties/dat/11992M/tif/JOC_1992_191__1_EN_0001.pdf.

Wissmann, M. (2006). Das Modell der gestuften Mitgliedschaft. *Internationale Politik,* 5(6), 64–68.

Europeanisation and Its Discontents: Turkey, 1959–2007

Hakan Yılmaz

1 Introduction

In the last few years, there has been in Turkey an intense questioning of the country's relationship with the European Union. The EU is blamed for a lack of understanding and respect in its relations with Turkey. According to the Eurosceptic narrative, the moment Turkey lost its strategic value for Europe in the aftermath of the Cold War, Europe began to revive its historical demands on Turkey, which had been most clearly manifested in the articles of the 1920 Treaty of Sèvres. Hence, the narrative has it, pressure has been put on Turkey to accept the Armenian genocide, to yield to Kurdish demands for autonomy and independence, to recognize Greek authority over Cyprus, and to make all the reforms demanded by the EU, without being offered any timetable for membership.

The extent to which the elite-level Eurosceptic discourse has been internalised by the general public can be observed in the findings of a nation-wide opinion survey, which was conducted in October and November 2003 as part of a research project led by the author (Yılmaz, 2004; 2005b).[1] We found that the feelings of being excluded by the EU were very strong among the people. In all, 60% of our respondents agreed with the view that the EU treated Turkey according to double standards, that it imposed on Turkey conditions that it had not demanded from the other candidate states and that it did not view Turkey as a European state. On the question of whether EU demands in the area of human rights and minority rights were similar to the terms of the Sèvres Treaty, the respondents were roughly divided into three equal groups: approximately one third said that they shared this view; another third said that they disagreed with it; and the remaining one third said that they did not know enough about those historical events to reach a judgment. Yet a third element of the elite-level Eurosceptic discourse was that Turkey's EU

[1] The research took place among a national, random, multi-layered sample of 2,123 people, aged 18 and above. The respondents were selected from 17 provinces and the three big metropolitan areas (Istanbul, Ankara, Izmir). In total, 68% of the interviews were conducted in the urban areas and 32% in the rural areas, reflecting the rural–urban division of the Turkish population. This research project, and the related opinion poll, was the first attempt to obtain an empirical measure of the degree of the reaction to Eurosceptic themes and issues among the general public.

C. Arvanitopoulos (Ed.), *Turkey's Accession to the European Union*

membership would result in the rise of ethnic separatism and the eventual loss of its national unity and territorial integrity. Our survey revealed that 45% of the general public agreed (as opposed to 20% who disagreed) that ethnic separatist movements would definitely increase if Turkey joined the EU. However, 50% of the respondents disagreed (as opposed to 35% who agreed) that EU membership would result in a disintegration of Turkey along ethnic lines.

In this chapter we are going to examine the evolution of the major Eurosceptic themes and movements in Turkey, from the early years of the EEC–Turkey relations in the late 1950s until the Turkish general elections in 2007. In the first three sections, a historical overview of EU–Turkey relations will be given, beginning with the era between the EEC–Turkey association agreements of 1963 and the military intervention of 1980; continuing until the membership application of 1987; and finishing with the rise of Euroscepticism in Turkey during the radicalised and polarised political atmosphere of the 1990s. The following two sections will be devoted to an assessment of the outcomes of the elections of November 2002 and July 2007, which resulted in the ex-Islamists and new 'Conservative Democrats' coming to power, the turn of Islamic conservatism towards Europe and Europeanisation and democratisation under a 'Conservative-Democratic' leadership.

2 The Early Years of EU–Turkey Relations: From the Association Agreement of 1963 to the Military Intervention of 1980

The contractual relations between Turkey and the EU began close to a half-century ago, in 1959, when, on 31 July of that year, the Turkish centre-right government of the Democratic Party (Demokrat Parti, DP) applied for membership in the European Economic Community (EEC). This application reflected, on the one hand, the overall Western and European orientation of Turkish foreign policy since the end of the Second World War. Indeed, Turkey had already been a member of such critical Western and European organizations as the Council of Europe, the OECD and NATO. Thus, its desire to become a member of the EEC was entirely normal. Moreover, another equally strong motive behind the Turkish application was without a doubt the fact that Greece, Turkey's regional rival, had already applied just two weeks previously. Because the economies of both countries were underdeveloped, the EEC decided not to offer them full membership status. A relationship termed as 'association' was formulated in the association agreements that were signed, first with Greece in November 1962 (the Athens Agreement), and then with Turkey in September 1963 (the Ankara Agreement). The Ankara agreement envisaged a three-stage transition period (a preparatory stage, a transitional stage and a final stage) first to a customs union and then to full accession to the EEC. Article 28 of the agreement stated that 'as soon as the operation of this Agreement has advanced far enough to justify envisaging full acceptance by Turkey of the obligations arising out of the Treaty establishing the Community, the Contracting Parties shall examine the possibility of the accession of Turkey to the Community'.

During the 1960s and 1970s, Turkey was characterised by ideological radicalisation and political polarisation. The radical right was represented in the political arena by two political parties: the MHP embodying Turkish ethnonationalism, and the National Salvation Party (Milli Selamet Partisi, MSP) representing Islamism. Both the radical left and the radical right were vehemently opposed to Turkey's entry into the EEC. In the parlance of the radical left, the EEC was an appendage of American imperialism, from which they were trying to save Turkey. In the eyes of the Islamists linked with the MSP, the EEC was nothing but a 'Christian club', sponsored and maintained by the Vatican, in which a Muslim Turkey would have absolutely no place. Turkish nationalists in the MHP, on the other hand, while adopting the rhetoric of both the radical left and the Islamists, put the emphasis on the claim that joining the European community would give the European states a historic opportunity to meddle in Turkey's internal affairs. They feared that the EEC's purpose was to divide the country and take its various parts under control by weakening state institutions and provoking the minorities and 'over-westernised' Turks to rebel against the state. After the mid-1970s, when three other southern European countries – Greece, Portugal and Spain – which had just come out of US-supported dictatorships, were determinedly progressing towards democratic Europe, Turkey was taken hostage by radical parties, groups and ideas. This early period of EEC–Turkey relations came to an abrupt end with the military takeover in Turkey in September 1980.

3 EU–Turkey Relations from the Military Intervention of 1980 to the Membership Application of 1987[2]

The military regime in Turkey lasted for two years, during which time the political system, from top to bottom, was speedily and nearly completely redesigned. Depoliticisation was the driving idea behind this development, which would be achieved by dramatically curbing freedom of speech and political participation. The military regime formally ended when new elections took place in November 1983 and a newly elected civilian government, under Turgut Özal and his party (ANAP), took office in December of that year. It took more than a year for the EEC to suspend its relations with Turkey in protest of the military intervention of 12 September 1980. The suspension, which came into force in January 1982, was lifted in September 1986, when the EEC–Turkey Association Council met for the first time after a long hiatus. The decision of the EEC to normalise its relations with Turkey was no doubt motivated by Turkey's return to civilian rule and the efforts at liberalisation, particularly in the economic sector. The Özal government had already set its

[2] For excellent reviews of the early years of EU–Turkey relations, see the contributions in Evin and Denton (1990).

mind on making Turkey a member of the EEC. On 17 April 1987, the Özal government handed in Turkey's formal application for membership in the EEC. It took nearly two years for the European Commission to draft its opinion on the Turkish application. It was published on 18 December 1989. The Commission reiterated Turkey's eligibility for membership in principle, but claimed that neither Turkey nor the EEC were ready to start membership talks. Turkey, according to the Commission, was not ready to take on the obligations of membership, given its existing level of economic and political underdevelopment. The EEC, on the other hand, had to put its own house in order first and complete the transition to a single market before contemplating any further enlargement. The Commission then went on to underscore the need for a comprehensive cooperation programme aimed at facilitating the integration of Turkey into the EEC, and added that the customs union should be completed in 1995 as envisaged.

Although the membership application in 1987 did not bring any tangible results, it did put Turkey back on the EEC's agenda. Moreover, it once again brought Europe to the centre of political decision-making and public debate in Turkey. It is a fact that EEC–Turkey relations, particularly in the commercial and economic area, continued to expand in the years that followed the membership application. Because Turkey underwent the Özalist reforms of economic and, to a lesser extent, political liberalisation during the 1980s, in the beginning of the 1990s, the country had reached the point of undertaking the obligations of a customs union with the EC. In the eyes of the Turkish government of the day, under Turkey's first woman Prime Minister, Tansu Çiller, the customs union would have been the first step towards full membership. However, for many European leaders, Turkey had to be firmly linked to the EEC, but it had to be left beyond the borders of the Community. Hence, for them, the customs union with Turkey represented the end-point of EEC–Turkey relations.

4 The 1990s in Turkey: Political Radicalisation, Ideological Polarisation and the Rise of Euroscepticism[3]

On 6 March 1995, while Turkey was governed by the 'grand coalition' of Tansu Çiller's centre-right True Path Party (Doğru Yol Partisi, DYP) and Deniz Baykal's centre-left CHP, the EU–Turkey Association Council took a decision regarding the inauguration of a customs union between the EU and Turkey, following the pattern set out in the Ankara Agreement of 1963 and the Additional Protocol of 1970.[4] The Council's decision received the European Parliament's assent on 13 December 1995, enabling it to enter into force on 1 January 1996. Following the Association

[3] For first-rate examinations of the rise of identity movements in the 1990s, see Göle (1997) for the Islamic movements; Mutlu (1996) for Kurdish movements; Vorhoff (1998) for the mobilisation of the Alevi identity; and Bora (2003) for the transformations of Turkish ethnonationalism.

[4] See the official website of the EU at http://europa.eu.int/comm/dg1a/turkey/overview.htm.

Council's customs union decision, in July 1995, the Turkish government launched a series of democratising and liberalising reforms, which were the first-ever package of amendments to the 1980 military-era Constitution. It is apparent that the tactical goal of the Turkish government for initiating the reforms was to persuade the European Parliament to give its consent to the Association Council's customs union decision. The government's strategic goal, on the other hand, was to bring Turkey closer to full membership in the EU, by fulfilling the necessary political conditions as they were formulated in June 1993 during the meeting of the European Council in Copenhagen.

The 1990s were a time of economic, political as well as cultural crises. Perhaps the most important facet of politics in the 1990s was the politicisation of identities. It was the first time that there appeared on the public political scene movements organised around Kurdish, Sunni Muslim and Alevi identities. This was quickly followed by political and civic movements, which attempted to mobilise their followers by appeals to gender, region, life-style, sexual choice, age and other subjective and mostly symbolic issues, feelings and attachments.

The armed Kurdish secessionist movement led by the PKK, which reached its peak in the second half of the 1990s, was no doubt the most important cause of the political crisis of the 1990s. Apart from the high cost in human lives, perhaps the most detrimental consequence of PKK terrorism was the creation, within the state apparatus and the security forces, of various paralegal or utterly illegal organisations. These organisations, which were referred as 'the gangs' in Turkish popular parlance, brought together state officials and mafia members who operated largely outside of the control of the democratic authorities and followed their own personal agendas. These self-appointed protectors of the state ruined, to some extent, the credibility of the state in the eyes of a large part of the masses and were a severe blow to efforts to build a state based on the rule of law. A second and equally destructive impact of PKK terrorism was that it gave rise, among the Turkish masses, to nationalist extremism of unprecedented proportions. This nationalist extremism at the same time fuelled anti-Western and anti-European sentiments among the Turkish people, who believed that Western governments were supporting, tacitly or openly, the PKK.

Another source of the crises of the 1990s was the rise of political Islam. This tendency was represented in the political arena by the parties of the National Outlook (Milli Görüş) movement (the Welfare Party [Refah Partisi, RP], the Virtue Party [Fazilet Partisi] and the Felicity Party [Saadet Partisi]), all founded and led by Necmettin Erbakan. The continual strengthening of political Islam was partly due to the increasing inability of the secular parties to deal with the pressing problems of the country. The intense Islamisation of Turkish educational and intellectual life, which followed the military coup of the 1980s – launched in an attempt to immunise the country against the power and under the threat of communist ideology – was another cause. The massive internal migration of the 1980s should also be seriously considered as the third factor in the rising power of Islamist politics. This migration, it has been claimed, resulted in the formation of impoverished communities on the urban peripheries, made up of people of rural origin who were very receptive to religious indoctrination and mobilisation.

The third source of the political crisis of the 1990s was an unexpected and non-political event, namely, the Marmara earthquake of August 1999. The utter inability of the government and more generally of state institutions to deal with the problems created by the earthquake discredited not only the political parties that were then in power but the political establishment in general. The resulting mood of protest became especially obvious during the general elections of November 2002, when all the major parties of the 1990s were almost annihilated electorally.

The 1990s was also the decade of the decline of pro-institution and centrist parties and the rise of radical politics. As usually happens in moments of crisis, radical solutions began to be articulated and applied to serious problems. Hence the 1990s witnessed the severe and sometimes violent radicalisation and polarisation of political choices, cultural identities and even economic policies. While the combined electoral power of the centrist parties of the left and the right fell from 83% to 57% from 1991 to 1999, that of the radical parties, largely of the right, rose from 17% to 42% during the same period. Perhaps a more dramatic expression of the rise of radical politics can be seen if we contrast the electoral performance of the centre-right parties with that of the radical-right parties. The total vote of the centre-right parties, which had been 51% in 1991, fell steeply to 26% in 1999. At the same time, radical-right parties, of the nationalist and Islamist varieties, doubled their combined electoral support from 17% to 34%. Although there was no marked increase in the support for the radical-left parties (their total vote increased from 0.2% 1995 to 1.3% in 1999), the electoral base of the Kurdish nationalist parties continued to grow, from 4.2% in 1995 to 5.6% in 1999.

5 The Elections of November 2002 and July 2007 and the Turn of Islamic Conservatism towards Europe[5]

The outcome of the 3 November 2002 general elections in Turkey was an 'expected surprise' for observers of Turkish politics. It was expected, because the general ranking of the parties in relation to one another had been predicted by many people. It was, on the other hand, a surprise, because no one had predicted precisely the strong performance of the AKP or the very low percentages achieved by the parties of former Prime Minister Bülent Ecevit (the DSP) and former Foreign Minister İsmail Cem (the New Turkey Party [Yeni Türkiye Partisi, YTP]). Moreover, contrary to the estimate of many analysts, the secularist–social democratic CHP did not succeed in making a strong showing, despite its last-minute recruitment of Kemal Derviş, the widely respected former Economy Minister, into its ranks.

[5] For thorough analyses of the causes and consequences of the November 2002 elections, see Çarkoğlu (2002) and Öniş and Keyman (2003). For the AKP's role in the consolidation of Turkish democracy see İnsel (2003). Çarkoğlu (2008) offers an expert look at the determinants of party support in the July 2007 elections.

The AKP was the undisputable victor of the elections, with 34% of the votes and 66% (363 out of 550) of the parliamentary seats. The CHP, the second party, won 20% of the votes and 34% of the seats (178 out of 550). No other party managed to break through the national threshold of 10%. As a result, slightly more than 45% of the voters, nearly half of the electorate, remained unrepresented in the new Parliament. In all, 70% of the voters voted for the right-wing parties and 30% for the left-wing parties. The right-wing votes were divided among the 'conservative-democratic' right of the AKP (34%), the radical (Turkish ethnonationalist or Islamist) right of the Nationalist Action Party, the Felicity Party and others (22%), and the centre-right of the True Path Party, ANAP and others (15%). The left-wing votes, on the other hand, were divided among the centre-left of the CHP, the DSP and others (22%) and the radical left of the pro-Kurdish Democratic People's Party (DEHAP) and others (7%). Finally, 77% of the electorate chose parties that had declared themselves as 'Eurosupporters', whereas 23% of the electorate preferred the 'Eurosceptic' parties of the left and the right.

In what follows, we will examine the social composition of the AKP and CHP voters and their attitudes towards the EU, based on the findings of a public opinion survey that was conducted in May 2002 (Yılmaz, 2005a). The first remark to be made regarding the profile of AKP supporters is that 60% of them thought that their primary identity was 'Muslim', whereas the national average was only 35%. In a similar vein, 40% of AKP supporters identified themselves primarily in national terms (as 'Turks' or 'citizens of the Republic of Turkey'), while the national average was 60%. It is clear therefore that AKP supporters perceived themselves as being 'more Muslim' and 'less Turkish' than the average Turkish citizen. Secondly, AKP supporters turned out to be less educated than the average respondent, and much less educated than CHP supporters. Of those who voted for the AKP, 54% had only 5 years of elementary school education, while the national average was 42%. Of AKP supporters, 33% had gone to middle or high school, while the national average was 40%. Finally only about 8% of AKP supporters were university graduates, whereas the national average was 12%. All in all, the AKP has a constituency of which 60% identified itself as being primarily Muslim and which was less educated than the average Turkish citizen.

A brief look at AKP voters' attitudes towards Europe and Turkey's membership in the EU reveals that they cannot be labelled Eurorejectionists, but they manifested significantly more Eurosceptic tendencies when compared with the national average and with the voters of the opposition party, the CHP. In a hypothetical referendum on Turkey's membership in the EU, 56% of AKP supporters would vote 'yes'. This was significantly below the national average of 64% and far below the CHP figure of 82%. Similarly, when they were asked whether their lives would change for the better in case of EU membership, the 'yes' rate among AKP supporters was only 34%, though this was slightly above their 'no' rate of 30%. The percentage of 'yes' votes was far below the national average of 42% and the CHP average of 53%. When it comes to the harm expected from EU membership, 78% of AKP supporters said that the most important disadvantage of EU membership for Turkey would be a possible corruption of national and religious values. This emphatic sensitivity of AKP supporters on the issue of the negative impact of Europeanisation on Turkish national and religious values, reaching a total of 78%, far exceeded the national average of 64% and the CHP average of only 46%.

A clear majority of the general respondents turned out not to believe that the EU was sincere about accepting Turkey as a full member. This overall Eurosceptic tendency was much more pronounced among the supporters of the AKP. Thus, around 60% of the respondents said that Europeans did not understand Turkey and its citizens. Furthermore, a similar percentage of the responents claimed that the EU was not sincere about accepting Turkey as a full member, and that the Union had imposed conditions on Turkey that it had not imposed on the other candidate states. Among AKP supporters, the ratio of those who shared a similar scepticism towards Europe and the EU rose to about 70%. In a similar vein, close to 50% of all the respondents believed that the EU would not accept Turkey as a full member, even if Turkey fulfilled all the preconditions required for membership. Agreement with this question was found to be around 60% among the potential voters of the AKP. Finally, concerning the final question, whether Turks perceived the EU as a 'Christian club' or not, the overwhelming majority of AKP supporters, close to 75%, said 'Yes'. This was significantly higher than the national average of 54% and much higher than the CHP average of 46%. It seems that, because they primarily identified themselves as 'Muslim', using a religious criterion, AKP supporters perceived Europe in religious terms also and defined it as being Christian before everything else.

In striking opposition to its constituency's Eurosceptic attitudes, the leadership of the AKP, from the day the elections were won, committed itself to the cause of bringing Turkey into the EU. Hence, the AKP turned out to be a party with the most Eurosceptic and isolationist constituency and the most Eurosupportive and integrationist leadership. Given this dramatic discrepancy between the tendencies of the party's base and its leadership, it would not be a big surprise if clashes and tensions occurred between this generally conservative, inward-looking and isolationist constituency and the self-declared liberal, outward-looking, integrationist leadership of the AKP. In the years since it came to power, the AKP leadership, to its credit, was admittedly more inclined to bring its own constituency into the sphere of European values rather than yielding to the easier, populist method of playing on the nationalist and Islamist sentiments of its supporters in order to cover up mistakes and mismanagement.

In the general elections that took place in July 2007, nearly five years after it came to power in November 2002, the AKP increased its share of votes by 13 percentage points over the previous election, from 34% to 47%. This was the second time in Turkish democratic history that a party has increased its support from one election to another while in government (the first such party was the centre-right Democratic Party of the 1950s). Moreover, this was the largest share of votes that a party had received in general elections since the electoral victory of the centre-right Justice Party (AP) in 1969. All in all, the AKP won a historic victory in July

2007. Almost all the other major parties (the Turkish nationalist MHP, the Kemalist CHP and the Kurdish nationalist DTP) got most of their votes from certain regions of the country: the CHP from the coastal zones of the Marmara and the Aegean regions, the MHP from the inner Anatolian regions and the DTP from the Kurdish-populated southeast Anatolian regions. Only the AKP received votes from every corner of the country, including people of Kurdish origin.

The high percentage of votes, and the more or less even distribution of its electoral support across the country, can be taken as indicators for the success of the AKP's decision to make the drastic move to occupy the centre-right mainstream of the Turkish political spectrum. However, this statement has to be qualified. The AKP did not simply occupy an empty centre-right; it also set out to redefine the centre-right mainstream of Turkish politics along three new axes: Islamic conservatism in politics, neo-liberalism in economics and a pro-EU orientation in foreign relations. What we are observing can be interpreted as the birth pangs of a 'Muslim democracy' in Turkey, which are not very different from the problems encountered during the formative years of Christian Democrat parties and ideologies in countries like Italy and Germany in the 1950s and 1960s, and later on in Spain (Popular Party) and Greece (New Democracy Party) in the 1970s and 1980s. The AKP deserves the benefit of time, and a lot of European help, so that it can successfully complete its historic transition from a party promoting anti-Western Islamism to one promoting pro-Western Muslim democracy.

Why did so many people go and vote for the AKP, despite the allegations, voiced by no less than the chief of the general staff, that the party might endanger the secular character of the Turkish regime? The oft-cited reasons for its success usually revolve around the general macroeconomic improvement during the years of the AKP government, which revealed itself, for the common people, as a drastic fall in the inflation and unemployment rates and a slight improvement in income distribution. On the more political side of the picture, one can pinpoint three other reasons that might help us understand how the AKP could gain the favour of so many voters. One reason could be that the AKP was the only party that based its electoral campaign on a list of 'do's', positive promises and a general tendency towards optimism, as opposed to the other parties that stressed their 'don'ts', making negative promises and talking pessim-istically. The electorate never had the opportunity to learn what the opposition parties were planning to do if they formed the government. All they heard was what the other parties would not do or would not let other people do. A second probable reason behind the choice of the AKP could be that the AKP appeared to be the only party that talked about multiple issues, while each of the other parties stressed a single issue only: secularism by the CHP, Turkish nationalism by the MHP, Kurdish nationalism by the DTP. A third probable reason behind the electorate's choice of the AKP was the AKP's generally flexible and pragmatic stance as opposed to the ideological, inflexible and extremist discourse of the other parties. In the eyes of the average voter, the hard-line discourse of the opposition parties might have rung the alarm bells that, were they to come to power, the country would drift towards some sort of crisis.

6 Europeanisation and Democratisation under Islamic Conservative Leadership: Future Prospects

What can be said about the ex-Islamists' strategic choice for the EU and how different it is from their earlier tactical rapprochement towards the EU? Admittedly, the pro-EU attitudes of the AKP elites were initially a tactical choice, a matter of finding European protection against the oppressive policies of the Turkish secularist establishment. However, this tactical choice seems to have evolved into a strategic one. This strategic choice is closely connected with the defeat of Turkish political Islam – which has been traditionally represented in the political arena by Necmettin Erbakan and by the so-called National Doctrine parties he led – as a result of the shock waves of the 'post-modern' military intervention of 28 February 1997. Since then, anti-Kemalist revanchism, the top-down transformation of society along Islamic lines and using democracy as no more than an instrument for coming to power, this quintessentially political project has proved to be futile. Erdoğan, who was a radical Islamist in the pre-28 February period, once said that democracy was but a train and that one should get off of the train at the right station. Once his party took power, the same Erdoğan started to say that he and his party rejected any project of 'social engineering', that is, the use of political power to change society according to the precepts of a certain ideology, including the Islamist one. He also started to deny vehemently that his party was Islamist or even that it was a religiously based party. In quest of a more appropriate appellation that would better reflect the party's new orientation away from political Islam and towards the centre, the party ideologists came up with the term 'conservative democrat'.

The strategic choice seems to involve the following dimensions. The first dimension has to do with ideological decoupling from political Islam, as well as institutional decoupling, while the second aims at Europeanising the Turkish public sphere to accommodate public displays of Islamic identity, particularly by passing legislation that would allow Muslim women wearing a headscarf to have a legitimate presence in the universities and government institutions. Here the issue is the compatibility of Muslim identity and European modernity. In this respect, the Kemalist-nationalist understanding of modernity is too restrictive, too exclusive for the desired integration of Islamic identity and modernity. Hence, a new, more liberal, more inclusionary version of modernity – one could say a more 'post-modern' definition of modernity, such as the one that is upheld by the EU – would offer much better grounds for that integration to take place. The Kemalist understanding of modernity is, paradoxically, too modernist, too much attached to an earlier, French revolutionary, nineteenth-century definition of modernity to allow the manifestations and performances of Islamic identity in the public sphere. On the other hand, the current European understanding of modernity is, again paradoxically, much less 'modernist' than Turkey's. Therefore a Europeanised public sphere in Turkey would more easily tolerate the free display of Muslim identity. Two forces will resist this project, however. The first of these is Euroscepticism and nationalist isolationism in Turkey: nationalist isolationists will not leave the battleground without, at least, a fierce final battle. Nationalists will be particularly willing to mobilise public opinion against the government, whenever the latter attempts to touch upon such nationally sensitive issues as secularism and the Kurdish and Cyprus questions. The second force is likely to be Turkoscepticism towards and rejectionism of Turkey in Europe. European rejectionists of Turkey, such as the French President Nicolas Sarkozy, sticking to the theses of cultural and civilisational incompatibility between Turkey and Europe, will make it harder for Turkey to be integrated into the EU, alienating many Muslim supporters of the AKP, while at the same time playing into the hands of Turkish nationalist isolationists.

The success of the conservative-democratic project for Europeanising Turkey depends essentially on an external and uncontrollable factor, namely, EU policy towards Turkey. Squeezed between Turkish Euroscepticism and European Turkoscepticism, the AKP project may very well fail. If it fails, then Islamism, as a political ideology, will surely return. Kurdish secessionism would most probably follow suit, as Kurds would lose hope of expanding their community rights in a democratic Turkey. As a result, Turkish politics would again revert to a battlefield, much the same as in the 1990s, of Islamism, Kurdish nationalism and Turkish isolationism. If Turkey's integration within the EU makes a leap forward with the smooth progression of the accession negotiations that were opened in the fall of 2005, then the expected short-term consequence of this would be felt, on the political front, in the form of the consolidation of a more democratic and liberal atmosphere. In such an atmosphere, it would be easier for the AKP to build a wide-ranging consensus for the purpose of integrating Muslim identity into the liberalised Turkish public sphere. That would satisfy the party's more religious constituency and provide the party leadership with enough ideological ammunition to fight against, and detach themselves from, their Islamist critics. In this way the AKP could pass a critical threshold in its journey towards the secular centre of Turkish politics, and this would surely make a significant contribution to the stabilisation and consolidation of the democratic regime in Turkey.

References

Bora, T. (2003). Nationalist discourses in Turkey. *The South Atlantic Quarterly, 102*(2–3), 433–451.

Çarkoğlu, A. (2002). Elections in Turkey: Whither politics as we know it? *TUSIAD-US*. Available at http://www.tusiad-us.org, 10 October.

Çarkoğlu, A. (2008). *Ideology or economic pragmatism: Determinants of party choice in Turkey for the July 2007 elections*. University of Aberdeen, Centre for the Study of Public Policy, Working Paper No. 439.

Evin, A. O., & Denton, G. (Eds.). (1990). *Turkey and the European community*. Opladen, Germany: Leske and Budrich, Schriften des Deutschen Orient-Instituts.

Göle, N. (1997). The quest for the Islamic self within the context of modernity. In S. Bozdoğan & R. Kasaba (Eds.), *Rethinking modernity and national identity in Turkey* (pp. 81–94). Seattle: University of Washington Press.

İnsel, A. (2003). The AKP and normalizing democracy in Turkey. *The South Atlantic Quarterly, 102*(2–3), 293–308.
Mutlu, S. (1996). Ethnic Kurds in Turkey: A demographic study. *International Journal of Middle East Studies, 28*(4), 517–541.
Öniş, Z., & Keyman, E. F. (2003). Turkey at the polls, a new path emerges. *Journal of Democracy, 14*(2), 95–107.
Vorhoff, K. (1998). Let's reclaim our history and culture! Imagining Alevi community in contemporary Turkey. *Die Welt des Islams, 38*(2), 220–252.
Yılmaz, H. (2004). *Euroskepticism in Turkey: Manifestations at the elite and popular levels.* Research project co-supported by a grant from the Open Society Institute Assistance Fund (Grant No. 20010556) and Boğaziçi University Research Fund (Project No. 03M105), July.
Yılmaz, H. (2005a). Swinging between Eurosupportiveness and Euroskepticism: Turkish public's general attitudes towards the European union. In H. Yılmaz (Ed.), *Placing Turkey on the map of Europe* (pp. 152–181). Istanbul: Boğaziçi University Press.
Yılmaz, H. (2005b). Indicators of euroskepticism in the Turkish public opinion by the end of 2003: Basic findings of a survey. In H. Yılmaz (Ed.), *Placing Turkey on the map of Europe* (pp. 182–185). Istanbul: Boğaziçi University Press.

The European Union, Islam and Turkey: Delineating Europe's Soft Power

Aristotle Tziampiris

Why have we been wavering for the last two hundred years?
Where does Turkey belong? In the East? In the West?[1]

1 A Unique Source of EU Soft Power: The Lure of Accession and Turkey

The European Union is often portrayed as an international actor excelling in the projection of soft power:

> The ability to establish preferences tends to be associated with intangible power resources such as culture, ideology and institutions. This dimension can be thought of as soft power (Nye, 1990, p. 32). This soft power – getting others to want the outcomes that you want – co-opts people rather than coerces them. (Nye, 2004, p. 5)[2]

The Union, as opposed to states, enjoys a unique source of such power that is integrally related to the desire of entire countries to become full members (Nye, 2004, pp. 77–78). Membership is viewed as an exceptionally attractive prospect and not only because it might contribute to the EU's economic and political vitality (Leonard, 2005, pp. 81–82). Accession is justifiably

> [l]inked to the consolidation of democracy, the preservation of peace and security, and full participation in common European institutions … EU membership will be unavoidably linked to the process of modernization and Europeanization in the new members. (Tsoukalis, 2003, p. 170)

In effect, soft power reinforces the Union's overall power by facilitating improvements in the social, political and economic standards of future members.

This process is inevitably restricted in scope and applies only to states that are perceived and accepted as belonging to Europe.[3] Furthermore, it involves a certain

[1] Niyazi Berkes (a Turkish scholar), cited in Kotsovilis (2006, p. 63).

[2] In many ways Nye's (1990) study on soft power is academically more rigorous than his subsequent somewhat popularising effort.

[3] The idea of Europe has been dynamic and not static throughout the centuries. For a discussion, see Pocock (2002).

C. Arvanitopoulos (Ed.), *Turkey's Accession to the European Union*

degree of asymmetry and conditionality, with Brussels having the upper hand in areas of importance and dispute. References to accession negotiations are misleading, since '95 per cent [of the *acquis*] is untouchable' (Schrijvers, 2007, pp. 32–33).[4] Given satisfactory progress on the *acquis* and the concomitant fulfilment of the Copenhagen criteria,[5] a state is deemed ready to finally accede.

In this manner, the EU model links soft power and accession prospects, thus fuelling a process of Europeanisation that demands the implementation of highly technical legislation. The result is a uniquely dynamic process that has been repeated in the Union's various enlargements. However, the candidacy of Turkey is posing a fundamental challenge to this model.

A Eurobarometer study demonstrated that among the peoples of the EU-25, a clear majority of 52% considered that Turkey's accession would be in the primary interest of Turkey, only 20% viewed it as a mutually beneficial outcome, a mere 7% saw it in the interest of the Union and a paltry 3% believed that it would be in the interest of their own country (Eurobarometer, 2006, p. 69).

Crucially, 48% of EU-25 citizens did not want Turkey to accede to the Union *even if* she fulfilled all her pre-accession obligations (Eurobarometer, 2006, p. 70).[6] In certain states the numbers opposed to such an outcome regardless of Turkey's performance were overwhelming: 81% in Austria,[7] 54% in France, 69% in Germany, 69% in Luxembourg, 68% in Cyprus and 67% in Greece (Eurobarometer, 2006, p. 71).

This fact is of the utmost importance since it is the 'European citizens [who] will make the final decision regarding Turkish membership' (Tacar, 2007, p. 127), and it should be remembered that France has amended its Constitution to require a referendum on future members, while the government of Austria has made clear its political intention for a similar course of action on Turkey.

If the people of Europe are the final arbiters of Turkey's accession, and many are unwilling to accept such an outcome regardless of Copenhagen criteria–related progress, then it is possible that certain identitarian criteria (based upon religious, historical, cultural and identity-related considerations) are at work. According to some sophisticated (if tentative) research,

> [s]upport for Turkish membership is not only low, it is also declining … Public support for Turkish membership can be understood along three different dimensions: instrumental, identitarian and post-national (or civic) … Supporters for Turkish accession are mostly counted among the ranks of those having a post-national vision of the EU. Conversely, those against Turkish accession are more likely to be so departing from identity-related arguments … The utilitarian dimension is the least important of the three. (Ruiz-Jimenez & Torreblanca, 2007, p. 23)[8]

---

[4] She is relying upon Grabbe (2004, p. 2).

[5] For the Copenhagen criteria, see European Council (1993).

[6] Turkey's accession is welcomed by 39% provided it has fulfilled all of it obligations.

[7] For an important discussion on Austrian attitudes towards Turkey's EU accession, see ESI (2008).

[8] 'Utilitarians conceive the EU pragmatically, as a problem-solving entity to which they lend their support depending on a cost-benefit analysis'. An identitarian approach focuses on issues such as 'identity, history, culture and traditions'. The post-national approach is primarily based upon considerations of 'universal principles and values, such as democracy, human rights and the rule of law' (Ruiz-Jimenez and Torreblanca, 2007, pp. 2–3).

In other words, although not formally grounded in the Treaties or part of the Copenhagen criteria, an identitarian outlook may prove decisive.

This essay will present the basic factors that shape the identitarian opposition to Turkey's EU membership. We will thus focus on various perceptions and claims, based on a specific reading of the historical, social, cultural and demographic interactions of Islam with Europe. The validity and potential consequences of such claims will be evaluated. By extension, we will also attempt to assess whether Europe's enlargement-based soft-power capabilities might be limited (or even negated) by suspicion, hostility or dismissal of Islam in a post-9/11 world.

2 The Identitarian Fear of Islam and Turkey in Europe

The historical interaction between Europe and Islam since the eighth century AD has been far from peaceful and harmonious. Christian Europe was at times seriously imperilled, first by Arabs and subsequently by Ottoman Muslim forces. 'For almost a thousand years, from the first Moorish landing in Spain to the second Turkish siege of Vienna, Europe was under constant threat from Islam' (Lewis, 1993, p. 13).

Western historiography focuses on a number of episodes and turning points. The initial Arab invasions were relatively sudden but proved far ranging. Between the seventh and eleventh centuries, large parts of the Iberian peninsula,[9] Sardinia, Sicily, Malta, Crete, Cyprus and Rhodes fell under Muslim occupation, while parts of France and key cities such as Rome, Constantinople, Thessaloniki, Bordeaux, Lyons, Marseilles, Pisa and Genoa were attacked and some even sacked.[10] Most of Western Europe would probably have been conquered had it not been for the Battle of Poitiers in 732.[11] Otherwise, as Jenkins (2007, p. 108) commented, who quoted Edward Gibbon, 'Perhaps the interpretation of the Koran would now be taught in the schools of Oxford and her pulpits might demonstrate to a circumcised people the sanctity and truth of the revelation of Mahomet.'[12]

The subsequent Crusades contributed additional episodes of enmity and war over a period of centuries.[13] Even after the demise of the Arab threat, a new Muslim power came to the forefront: the Ottoman Turks.[14] They succeeded in overrunning

[9] The Christian Reconquista of the Iberian Peninsula was only completed in 1492.

[10] For a full account of what is perceived to be Muslim military aggression, see Stenhouse (2007).

[11] For some interesting comments on how the Battle of Poitiers was seen in Western and Arab historiography, see Lewis (1993, p. 11). For a revisionist history of Europe's first encounter with the Arab conquering forces that includes an excellent account of the Battle of Poitiers, see Lewis (2008). He essentially bemoans the defeat of the Arabs given the subsequent 'creation of an economically retarded, balkanised and fratricidal Europe that, by defining itself in opposition to Islam, made virtues out of hereditary aristocracy, persecutory religious intolerance, cultural particularism, and perpetual war' (Lewis, 2008, pp. xxiii, 174).

[12] Jean-Baptiste Duroselle argues that 'it was the Arab conquest that brought the word "Europe" back into use and, moreover, for the first time gave it a political meaning' (Duroselle, 2004, p. 136).

[13] For an excellent new account of the Crusades, see Tyerman (2006). It is tellingly titled *God's War*.

[14] For a succinct history of the Ottoman Empire, see Goodwin (1999).

the Christian Byzantine Empire (Constantinople fell in 1453)[15] and subsequently conquered most of south-eastern Europe (and kept it under control until the nineteenth and twentieth century). Described by an 'Elizabethan historian … "as the present terror of the world" … they threatened the heart of Europe for almost two centuries' (Esposito, 1999, p. 40). The defeat of the Ottoman navy at Lepanto in 1571[16] proved a turning point, as was their failure during the second siege of Vienna in 1683. Ottoman decline accelerated after the Karlowitz Treaty in 1699, a process that was paralleled by the West's global political, economic, military and scientific ascendancy.[17] The early twentieth century witnessed not only the dissolution of the Ottoman Empire (1919) but also most Muslim states becoming colonies of Western European countries.

What emerges is a historical record that includes memories and perceptions of occupation, war, fear, suspicion and enmity[18] (although, admittedly, this is only a partial record; peaceful coexistence and mutually beneficial trade relations were also present at times). In effect,

> [d]espite common theological roots and centuries-long interaction, Islam's relationship to the West has often been marked by mutual ignorance, stereotyping, contempt and conflict. Ancient rivalries and modern conflicts have so accentuated differences, as to completely obscure the shared theological roots and vision of the Judeo-Christian-Islamic tradition. Both sides have focused solely on and reinforced differences, and have popularized rather than united these three great interrelated monotheistic traditions. (Esposito, 1999, p. 23)

Partly as a result of this situation, it has been argued that

> The … Western depiction of Muslims and Islam has not changed for the past fourteen hundred years, or even the past forty … What has remained constant has been a nervousness and distrust of those associated with these terms, a persistent sense that to be Muslim is to be a distrusted Other. (Gottschalk & Greenberg, 2008, pp. 10–11)

In Europe today, Muslims (and by extension Turks) are clearly perceived by many as being the 'Other'. A worrisome link seems often to be made between Muslims and potential terrorists. It should be kept in mind that the 1999 Helsinki European Council that bestowed upon Turkey the status of a candidate state (Jorgensen, 2007, p. 17) took place prior to the events of 9/11 and the subsequent 'war on terror'. Since then, Islamic terrorist activities have also taken place in Europe, the most deadly manifestations being the bombings in Madrid on 11 March 2004 and London on 7 July 2005. Despite the fact that Sunni terrorists represent an extremely tiny minority of the world's (and also Europe's) Muslim population,

---

[15] Runciman (1990) remains the classic account of the siege and fall of Constantinople.

[16] For an excellent historical account of the Lepanto naval battle, properly set in its historical context, see Capponi (2006).

[17] The classic account of Europe's ascendancy is Jones (1987). The process began around 1500.

[18] Commenting on only one such instance that involved the Ottoman conquest of Cyprus in 1571 and the subsequent flaying alive of Venetian commander Marco Antonio Bragadin – his skin was stuffed with straw – despite assurances of safety, Niccolò Capponi (2006, p. 236) stresses that these 'actions would for a long time be cited as an example of Ottoman – indeed Muslim – duplicity, and even today Bragadin's straw-stuffed hide casts a shadow over East-West relations'.

these events have created a climate of anxiety and suspicion. A typical example of such apprehension stresses that

> Britain houses around two million Muslim citizens out of a population of some sixty million. How many more Muslim youths, people wondered, might similarly be planning mass murder against their fellow Britons? (Philips, 2006, pp. 8–9)

At the same time, others are raising concerns about the inability of Muslims to assimilate and accept European cultural norms, arguing that 'Islam in Europe has not followed a process of Westernization' (Ye'or, 2006, p. 10). Muslims are thus characteristically presented as hailing from non-European, poor, and religiously conservative backgrounds, relying heavily upon welfare, hostile to homosexuality, unsympathetic to women's rights (men often beat their wives) and inadequately educated (Bawer, 2006).

Population trends make this situation even more alarming for those who endorse such a viewpoint. For them, it is ultimately the demographic problem that constitutes 'the most severe' crisis in Europe (Laqueur, 2007, p. 15). To reach such an anxious conclusion, the rapid rise of the number of Muslims in various states is first highlighted (see Table 1)[19]:

These increases are then contrasted with the projected decline in population for a series of European states (see Table 2):

Furthermore, the projected decline in population by 2050 is 34% for Bulgaria, 25–27% for Latvia and Lithuania, 20% for Croatia, 18% for Hungary and 17% for the Czech Republic (Laqueur, 2007, p. 15).

In other words, what is found by many as alarming is that the projected significant overall decline in European populations will be simultaneously coupled with the rise in the number of Muslims on the Continent. In their trepidation over such possible trends, some have gone even further, predicting that the dominance of Islam in Europe will lead to the effective creation of a 'Eurabia' (Ye'or, 2006). Subsequently, Mark Steyn stressed that 'much of what we loosely call the Western world will not survive this century, and much of it will effectively disappear within our lifetimes' (quoted in Jenkins, 2007, p. 4).

Table 1 Population of Muslims in 2006 (in millions)

France	5.3 (doubled since 1980)
Germany	3.6 (6,800 in 1961)
Britain	1.6
Netherlands	1.0 (tripled since 1980)
Denmark	0.3 (25,000 in 1982)
Italy	0.9 (120,000 in 1982)
Spain	1.0 (120,000 in 1982)

Source: Laqueur (2007, p. 37)

[19] For a comprehensive table of the increase in the population of Muslim in Western Europe between the years 1900 and 2000, see Jenkins (2007, p. 117; Chap. 5, Table 1).

Table 2 Projected decline in population

Country	Present population (in millions)	2050 (projection)	2100 (projection)
France	60	55	43
United Kingdom	60	53	45
Germany	82	61	32
Italy	57	37	15
Spain	39	28	12

Source: Laqueur (2007, pp. 24–25)

Perhaps all the strands of contemporary European suspicion of Islam (historical, cultural and demographic) come together and are presented in an extreme manner in the arguments of Oriana Fallaci. According to Talbot (2006), who quotes Fallaci, she

> [w]rites that Muslim immigration is turning Europe into 'a colony of Islam,' an abject place that she calls 'Eurabia' which will soon 'end up with minarets in place of the bell-towers, with the burka in place of the mini-skirt.' Fallaci argues that Islam has always had designs on Europe, invoking the siege of Constantinople in the seventh century, and the brutal incursions of the Ottoman Empire in the fourteenth and fifteenth centuries. She contends that contemporary immigration from Muslim countries to Europe amounts to the same things – invasion – only this time 'with children and boats' instead of 'troops and cannons'.[20]

Turkey's candidacy and potential accession prospects have exacerbated the aforementioned fears for identitarians. This is partly because Turkey is considered (at best) a 'torn state'[21]:

> Turkish leaders regularly described their country as a 'bridge' between cultures ... A bridge, however, is an artificial creation reflecting two solid entities but is part of neither. When Turkey's leaders term their country a bridge, they euphemistically confirm that it is torn. (Huntington, 1996, p. 149)

The prospect of a torn state, whose population is projected to reach 100 million by 2050 according to Laqueur (2007, p. 26), acceding to the European Union compounds the concerns of those adopting an identitarian outlook towards such a development. Focusing on Europe's history of antagonism with Islam, they view the addition of a populous Muslim country to the Union with apprehension because it raises the spectre of a European demographic imbalance in favour of Islam. Furthermore, they consider Muslims a potential source of jihadist terrorism and conclude that they are fundamentally unable (or unwilling) to assimilate into mainstream European society. As a result, they steadfastly oppose Turkey's membership even if the Copenhagen criteria are fulfilled. Whether these concerns are justified, as well as their potential consequences for the Union's soft power, will be discussed next.

---

[20] Fallaci even more controversially compares the situation in contemporary Europe with 'the pact in Munich, when England and France did not understand a thing. With the Muslims we have done the same thing. Islamicism is the new Nazi-Fascism' (quoted in Talbot, 2006).

[21] According to Samuel Huntington (1996, p. 138), 'a torn country ... has a single predominant culture which places it in one civilization but its leaders want to shift it to another civilization'.

3 Assessing the Consequences of European 'Islamophobia'[22]

The grim situation concerning the status and implications of Islam in Europe that was presented above requires additional scrutiny, not least because the projected democratic deluge of Europe by Muslims constitutes, upon closer inspection, a rather problematic proposition. In 34 European states (excluding Turkey) taken together, the number of Muslims as part of the entire population is a mere 4.6% (Jenkins, 2007, Table 1). Thus the various alarmist voices are concentrating on only 28.2 million Muslims out of Europe's total population of 521 million. In other words, the Continent is far from being overrun by Islam. France has the largest percentage of Muslims but it is still short of 10% (8.3% to be precise) (Jenkins, 2007, Table 1).

On a more substantial level, references to Muslims suggest that Islam is somehow monolithic and often imply close connections with extremism. This is far removed from reality; Islam exhibits antagonisms and variations (Sunni, Shia, Wahhabi etc.) not unlike Christianity (Catholic, Protestant, Orthodox etc.). Muslims in Europe simply do not share exactly the same theology or politics nor do they have identical backgrounds. In effect, referring to Europe's Muslim population is an oversimplification unless one is willing to accept a very loose (and subsequently less meaningful) standard of categorisation (Jenkins, 2007, pp. 18–19).

Problems with education, employment and cultural assimilation clearly exist, and are probably more pronounced in states such as France. But it cannot be simply assumed that these problems are linked to religion or will lead to religiously inspired terrorism. The number of Muslim terrorists is insignificant and it is unacceptable to apply such a label (even potentially) to all adherents of the faith of Muhammad. Furthermore, the possibility should not be discounted that, over time, European secularism and social policies may affect Islam in ways similar to the way that they affected Christianity in the Continent.[23]

European 'Islamophobia' is exaggerated but not necessarily completely irrational or based merely on fantasies. Nevertheless, the question remains whether these 'Islamophobic' concerns might begin to coincide more with reality in the case that Turkey accedes to the European Union. In the event of such an occurrence, the percentage of Muslims in European states as a whole would jump to almost 16% (Jenkins, 2007, p. 256), a not insignificant number. Some brief observations on the nature of Islam in Turkey are thus required.

Perhaps the most significant observation is that Islam in Turkey has persistently and consistently exhibited signs of moderation; it is thus not a coincidence that the existence of terrorist Islamic groups has been minimal and marginal (Netherlands Scientific Council for Government Policy, 2004, pp. 132–137). Crucial factors in creating

[22] Those who use the term 'Islamophobia' should keep in mind that it ought to 'be treated with caution, since it is often applied in a more sweeping sense, as a means of disarming reasonable criticism not just of the religion but of any actions taken in its name, even by its most extreme and militant followers' (Jenkins, 2007, p. 236).

[23] Taken in its entirety, Jenkins' (2007) *God's Continent* points toward such a potential outcome.

this moderation were the policies of Mustafa Kemal Atatürk. After assuming power he presided over a (often violent) revolution based on nationalism, secularism and modernisation that in many ways remains unique in the history of Muslim nations. Atatürk pursued a course of action that aimed at the control of Islam, the elimination of its political influence and the minimisation of its visible manifestations.

The simultaneous existence and interplay of additional factors has also contributed to the existence of a more moderate version of Islam in Turkey:

Kemalists and political Islamists in Turkey have been greatly influenced by modern European ideas and practices … [In addition] Islam in Turkey never became an ideological vehicle for nationalist resistance to a Western oppressor … It also missed out on large-scale socio-economic deprivation and frustration that formed a breeding-ground for extremism elsewhere in the Muslim world [and] unlike some other Muslim countries, any existing dissatisfaction could always manifest itself through politics, and government parties and could always be voted out of office (Netherlands Scientific Council for Government Policy, 2004, pp. 56–57).

In recent years, the world has witnessed the rise of political Islam in Turkey. In many ways, however, the electoral victories of Recep Tayyip Erdoğan and his AKP do not represent a theocratic Islamic takeover of the state, but could be seen in the light and tradition of Europe's Christian Democratic parties. Furthermore, some perhaps unexpected developments have also been observed. For example, a study of Muslims in the conservative region of Central Anatolia has concluded that

> [w]ith urbanizations and increased education have come new ideas about the virtues of hard work and entrepreneurship … It appears that a new generation in Central Anatolia has embraced its own peace with modernity. (ESI, 2005, pp. 6, 25)

Despite the significant arguments pointing to the moderation of Islam in Turkey, significant identitarian doubts continue to exist. Some of the more sophisticated should not be ignored or automatically discarded. According to Fouad Ajami (2008),

> [I]n recent years … the edifice of Kemalism has come under assault … The Islamists have prevailed, but their desired destination, or so they tell us, is still Brussels: in that European shelter, the Islamists shrewdly hope they can find protection against the power of the military … I still harbor doubts about whether the radical Islamists knocking at the gates of Europe, or assaulting it from within, are the bearers of a whole civilization. They flee the burning grounds of Islam, but carry the fire with them. They are 'nowhere men', children of the frontier between Islam and the West, belonging to neither. If anything, they are a testament to the failure of modern Islam to provide for its own and to hold the fidelities of the young.

In the final analysis, the stereotypes, fears and suspicion of Islam in Europe and of Muslim Turkey, whether grounded in historical experience, prejudice or prudence, are not likely to vanish in the near future, if at all. As a result, Turkey's accession prospects are seriously imperilled for reasons unrelated to the formal enlargement process and criteria. Popular European perceptions may thus doom Turkey's EU candidacy. The irony of such a likely (but still not certain) outcome should be noted, since the Union's soft power, which is largely culturally based, will be effectively limited by other broadly based cultural concerns. In other words, the EU is about to discover the limits of its enlargement-related soft power. The extent of the Union's soft power will soon be determined.

References

Ajami, F. (2008). The clash. *The New York Times*, 6 January.

Bawer, B. (2006). *While Europe slept: How radical Islam is destroying the West from within*. New York: Doubleday.

Capponi, N. (2006). *Victory of the West: The great Christian-Muslim clash at the Battle of Lepanto*. Cambridge: Da Capo Press.

Duroselle, J. B. (2004). The genesis of the idea of Europe. In R. Olivier (Ed.), *Turkey today: A European country?* (pp. 131–148). London: Anthem Press.

ESI. (2005). *Islamic calvinists: Change and conservatism in Central Anatolia*. Berlin/Istanbul: European Stability Initiative. Available at http://www.esiweb.org/pdf/esi_document_id_69.pdf, September 19.

ESI. (2008). *A referendum on the unknown Turk? Anatomy of an Austrian debate*. Berlin/Istanbul: European Stability Initiative. Available at http://www.esiweb.org/pdf/esi_document_id_101.pdf/, January 30.

Esposito, J. L. (1999). *The Islamic threat: Myth or reality?* Oxford: Oxford University Press.

Eurobarometer. (2006). *Attitudes towards European Union enlargement*. Available at http://ec.europa.eu/public_opinion/archives/ebs/ebs_255_en.pdf/.

European Council. (1993). *European Council in Copenhagen. Conclusions of the Presidency: 21–22 June 1993*. SN 180/1/93 REV 1.

Goodwin, J. (1999). *Lords of the horizon: A history of the Ottoman empire*. New York: Henry Holt and Co.

Gottschalk, P., & Greenberg, G. (2008). *Islamophobia: Making Muslims the enemy*. Lanham: Rowman and Littlefield.

Grabbe, H. (2004). *When negotiations begin: The next phase in EU–Turkey relations*. CER essays. London: Centre for European Reform.

Huntington, P. S. (1996). *The clash of civilizations and the remaking of world order*. New York: Simon and Schuster.

Jenkins, P. (2007). *God's continent: Christianity, Islam and Europe's religious crisis*. Oxford: Oxford University Press.

Jones, L. E. (1987). *The European miracle: Environments, economics and geopolitics in the history of Europe and Asia*. Cambridge: Cambridge University Press.

Jorgensen, K. E. (2007). The politics of accession negotiations. In E. LaGro & K. E. Jorgensen (Eds.), *Turkey and the European Union: Prospects for a difficult encounter*. London: Palgrave Macmillan.

Kotsovilis, S. (2006). Between Fedora and Fez: Modern Turkey's troubled road to democratic consolidation and the pluralizing role of Erdoğan's pro-Islam government. In J. Joseph (Ed.), *Turkey and the European Union: Internal dynamics and external challenges* (pp. 42–70). London: Palgrave Macmillan.

Laqueur, W. (2007). *The last days of Europe: Epitaph for an old continent*. New York: Thomas Dunne Books St Martin's Press.

Leonard, M. (2005). *Why Europe will run the 21st century*. London: Fourth Estate.

Lewis, B. (1993). *Islam and the West*. Oxford: Oxford University Press.

Lewis, L. D. (2008). *God's crucible: Islam and the making of Europe* (pp. 570–1215). New York: W. W. Norton.

Netherlands Scientific Council for Government Policy. (2004). *The European Union, Turky and Islam* (includes the survey, 'Searching for the fault line' by E. J. Zurcher & H. van der Linden). Amsterdam: Amsterdam University Press.

Nye, S. J., Jr. (1990). *Bound to lead: The changing nature of American power*. New York: Basic Books.

Nye, S. J., Jr. (2004). *Soft power: The means to success in world politics*. New York: Public Affairs.

Phillips, M. (2006). *Londonistan: How Britain is creating a terror state within*. London: Gibson Square.

Pocock, J. G. A. (2002). Some Europes in their history. In P. Anthony (Ed.), *The idea of Europe: From antiquity to the European Union* (pp. 55–71). Cambridge: Cambridge University Press and Woodrow Wilson Center Press.

Ruiz-Jimenez, M. A., & Torreblanca, I. J. (2007). *European public opinion and Turkey's accession: Making sense of arguments for and against*. Available at http://www.realinstitutoelcano.org/documentos/289.asp/.

Runciman, S. (1990). *The fall of Constantinople, 1453*. Oxford: Oxford University Press Canto Paperback.

Schrijvers, A. (2007). What can Turkey learn from previous accession negotiations? In E. LaGro & K. E. Jorgensen (Eds.), *Turkey and the European Union: Prospects for a difficult encounter* (pp. 29–50). London: Palgrave Macmillan.

Stenhouse, P. (2007). *The crusades in context*. Available at http://answering-islam.org.uk/Green/crusades-stenhouse.htm/

Tacar, P. (2007). Socio-cultural dimensions of accession negotiations. In E. LaGro & K. E. Jorgensen (Eds.), *Turkey and the European Union: Prospects for a difficult encounter* (pp. 125–146). London: Palgrave Macmillan.

Talbot, M. (2006). The agitator: Oriana Fallaci directs her fury toward Islam. *The New Yorker*. Available at http://www.newyorker.com/archive/2006/06/05/060605fa_fact/, June 5.

Tsoukalis, L. (2003). *What kind of Europe?* Oxford: Oxford University Press.

Tyerman, C. (2006). *God's war: A new history of the crusades*. Cambridge: The Belknap Press of Harvard University Press.

Ye'or, B. (2006). *Eurabia: The Euro-Arab axis*. Madison, WI: Fairleigh Dickinson University Press.

Turkey and European Security

Thanos Dokos

Turkish membership in the European Union has been and, it is safe to assume, will continue to be an issue hotly debated by experts, policymakers and public opinion alike. As argued by EU Commissioner for Internal Market and Services, Frits Bolkenstein, in a view shared by many European officials and a majority of European public opinion, because of Turkey's size, political, economic and social problems and other specificities, Europe would implode should Turkey become a full member. Opponents also argue that expanding the Union's borders to such neighbours as Iran, Iraq and Syria will drag the EU into areas and disputes it could otherwise more easily stay out of (Hughes, 2006). A significant number of European officials and EU member states have a different, perhaps more strategic perspective. They believe that Turkish accession would promote greater stability in its 'near-abroad', ultimately benefiting the EU, and finally dispel Huntington's notion of a 'clash of civilizations' along the cultural fault-lines of Christianity and Islam (Desai, 2005, p. 367).[1]

Indeed, one of the most frequently discussed questions is whether Turkey's EU membership would be an asset for the EU in terms of foreign and security policy. As rightly argued by a Turkish analyst,

> Turkey is being recognized by the EU as an important [pivotal even, by Paul Kennedy's definition (Chase, Hill, & Kennedy, 1996, pp. 33–51)] country, especially from a geographical and geostrategic point of view and this will be Turkey's strongest card in its effort to join the Union or, should negotiations fail, to develop a privileged relationship with the EU (Oguzlu, 2003, p. 288).

Turkey should expect to be scrutinised on several issues (including Home Affairs and Justice) more intensively than any other country wishing to join the EU has ever been or will be, with the exception perhaps of Russia if the two sides ever get to that point. Discussions and consultations will be taking place on a regular basis over the next few years – as long as the negotiations last – in an exercise of mutual learning or, more accurately, mutual understanding, because, although most European countries and Turkey have been allies and partners in NATO, Europe as a political entity

[1] For a full presentation of the pros and cons and of the European debate on Turkey's membership, see High Level Round Table Conference (2003).

C. Arvanitopoulos (Ed.), *Turkey's Accession to the European Union*

clearly is and will remain for some time in a transition phase. The Union is still trying to define its borders and identity and is searching for a regional and global role in a new security environment. In this context, it is trying to strengthen its capabilities in the fields of foreign and security policy[2] and is gradually – and, many would argue, very slowly – evolving into an international actor with a military logic. It is trying to redefine the transatlantic relationship and stabilise its wider neighbourhood; clearly, cooperation between the EU and Turkey – a candidate country unlike any previous one – is essential for a number of obvious reasons.[3]

The European Security Strategy and the new European Neighbourhood Policy (ENP)[4] put great emphasis on the importance of Europe's southern periphery, stressing the need to project stability into the continent's neighbourhood. Proponents of Turkey's accession argue that due to its geostrategic position, Turkey would add new dimensions to the Union's foreign policy efforts in such vitally important regions as the Middle East, Central Asia and the south Caucasus. Furthermore, they argue, Turkey enjoys good relations with both sides (the EU and the United States, despite the relative chilling of relations after 2003) and enjoys credibility in Israel and, increasingly during the past few years, in much of the Arab world (as demonstrated by the recent negotiations between Israel and Syria with Turkey offering its good offices). Its membership would no doubt increase the Union's weight in the Middle East, which could be put to good use in common efforts towards peacemaking and stabilisation in this strategically critical region (Independent Commission on Turkey, 2004, pp. 17–18).

As has rightly been argued, the question 'whether Turkey's EU membership will be a foreign policy asset for the EU will be dependent on a number of developments that will either precede Turkey's entry into the EU or that are partly independent of

---

[2] According to a Turkish analyst, 'there is still a certain lack of cohesion among EU members with regard to the geopolitical and strategic priorities of the Union. In geopolitical terms, it seems that the members, particularly those with an imperial legacy, have more actor-ness than the EU itself as an institution' (Oguzlu, 2003, p. 288).

[3] It has correctly been argued that 'Turkey has aligned itself with many of the EU's common foreign and security policy positions, and it has developed a considerable dialogue with the EU since the mid-1990s on the EU's security and defence policy, including resolving through the Berlin plus agreement the question of how non-EU European NATO members would participate in European security and defence operations. Turkey has participated in international peacekeeping in the Balkans and elsewhere, including Afghanistan. All this means that Turkey is not an unknown quantity for the EU and suggests that its integration into CFSP and ESDP structures could be relatively straightforward' (Hughes, 2006, p. 50).

[4] Based on shared values and common interests in tackling common problems, the ENP is envisaged as a means of working with EU neighbours under the principle of joint ownership:

- To promote prosperity in the EU neighbourhood by supporting the neighbours' economic reform processes and offering significant economic integration;
- To advance freedom and democracy in the neighbourhood by deepening political cooperation, on the basis of shared values and common interests;
- To promote security and stability by working with the neighbours to address development, environment, non-proliferation and counter-terrorism issues – in line with the European Security Strategy (http://ec.europa.eu/world/enp/index_en.htm/).

the latter' (Del Sarto, 2004, p. 138). By the time Turkey joins the EU, EU and Turkish domestic politics and foreign policy, as well as various regions of interest such as the Middle East, are bound to change in unpredictable ways (Everts, 2004, p. 2). The direction of Turkish foreign policy will be another important parameter. As Stephen Larrabee (2008) points out,

> for the first time in decades, Turkey's relations with both Washington and Brussels are strained at the same time. The simultaneous deterioration of relations with the U.S. and the EU has reinforced a growing sense of vulnerability and nationalism in Turkey. Turkey increasingly feels that it cannot count on the support of its traditional allies and must rely on its own devices.[5]

Consequently, there is a perceived need for a new strategic calculus for Turkey (Menon & Wimbush, 2007, pp. 129–144). According to Graham Fuller (2008, p. 174), the 'trend toward an increasingly independent Turkish foreign policy is the most powerful force in Turkey today and is increasingly supported by domestic, regional and global events'.

The logic of the Eurasian strategic alternative has been presented by Ahmet Davutoglou, Prime Minister Erdoğan's main foreign policy adviser. It emphasises the concept of strategic depth, focusing on Turkey's need to have variegation in its foreign policies and a deepening of relations with all states, which in turn would lessen Ankara's vulnerability to great power domination (Fuller, 2008, pp. 168–169). Future foreign policy scenarios include an Ankara-centric foreign policy that stresses independence of outlook and action, that balances cooperative and strategic interactions with a broad range of other powers, and that has a strong Eurasian and Middle Eastern bent (Fuller, 2008, p. 165).

To assess Turkey's compatibility with and contribution to ESDP and European security in general, one would need to compare the views, positions and interests of each side on issues such as threat assessment, strategic culture, terrorism, transnational organised crime, the relationship between NATO and the EU as well as transatlantic relations, peace-support operations and security developments in regions like south-eastern Europe, the Black Sea, the Caucasus and Central Asia and the wider Middle East.

An effort to compare the threat assessment of the EU and Turkey would be a rather complicated exercise. When it comes to the EU's threat assessment, there are disagreements, different national perceptions (one could identify several sub-divisions: big and small countries, north, east and south, 'old' and 'new' Europe) and lack of candour (with more alarmist unofficial threat assessments, very carefully worded official national positions, in a wise effort to avoid offending neighbouring countries and creating self-fulfilling prophecies of clashes of various types, but

---

[5] Larrabee argues that the foreign policy debate in Turkey is much more diverse and fluid today, with more actors influencing policy than in the past. The days when the Turkish military and mandarins in the foreign ministry could control the foreign policy and security debate are over and Turkey's Muslim identity has begun to play a more important role in the self-perception and worldview of many Turks (Larrabee, 2008, pp. ix, 5).

nevertheless not always managing to avoid misperceptions about Europe's actions, especially in its relations with the Muslim world).[6] To the extent, however, that there is a common threat assessment, the main logic is described in the European Security Strategy. Threats to European security include (a) regional conflicts, (b) international terrorism, (c) proliferation of WMD and (d) transnational organised crime and failed or failing states.

Most of the regional conflicts and hotspots (with the exception of Kosovo) are to be found outside Europe (Black Sea/Caucasus, Mediterranean/Middle East, Sub-Saharan Africa), and the two sides (the EU and Turkey) are in most cases equally concerned and have rather similar positions. A quick overview might be useful at this point. Turkey stands on the nexus of a number of important and rather unstable regions, bordering Iran, Syria, Iraq and the south Caucasus, controlling the Bosporus and the upstream waters of the Tigris and Euphrates and 'sharing' the Black Sea with Russia and Ukraine.

In the Black Sea region, regional concerns shared by the two sides include the 'frozen conflicts' (Georgia, Nagorno-Karabakh, Chechnya) and the common objective is to prevent further destabilisation and resolve them in a peaceful manner. There may be a degree of divergence about the Caucasus, due to Turkey's difficult and sensitive relationship with Armenia and its close relations with Azerbaijan, which prevent Turkey from maintaining a reasonably balanced position on the problem of Nagorno-Karabakh. There is also concern about organised crime (especially the trafficking of people, drugs and weapons) and terrorism in the region. With respect to relations with Russia, it is not clear whether the two sides currently have converging views on the matter, due also to the fact that intra-European disagreements have prevented the EU from developing a common strategy on Russia.

Energy security is quickly rising in importance and is already an issue of high priority for Europe. According to Roberts (2004),

> Turkey's role as a gateway through which gas can enter the EU is becoming increasingly important as the EU grapples with the interrelated problems of ensuring energy security and the provision of energy supplies from multiple sources at competitive prices.[7]

---

[6] It should also be mentioned that the post-Cold War global structures are still in a state of flux, especially after 11 September 2001 and the events that followed. Analysts and policy makers are attempting to identify and predict trends as well as recommend policies of adjustment to emerging global and regional patterns.

[7] Turkey is making heavy use of the 'energy argument'. According to the Turkish Ministry of Foreign Affairs, '… Turkey is poised to become a significant energy hub and stands as an important energy partner for Europe and its energy strategy is consistent with the EU's energy security policy. Turkey's objective to become Europe's fourth main artery of energy supply following Norway, Russia and Algeria, overlaps with the EU's energy supply security policy and opens a new avenue for cooperation between Turkey and EU that will also reinforce Europe's ties to Asia' (Turkish Ministry of Foreign Affairs, 2008). Furthermore, 'Turkey's geopolitical position and close links with tens of millions of Turkic people in neighbouring countries could help secure European access to the enormous wealth of resources in Central Asia and regions of Siberia, making Turkey a vital factor for Europe's security of energy supplies coming from the Middle East, the Caspian Sea and Russia' (Roberts, 2004, p. 19).

There is cooperation in the energy sector with Azerbaijan, Greece and Italy (Turkey–Greece–Italy/TGI pipeline) and Ankara has expressed its readiness to participate in the Nabucco pipeline (currently under discussion); but at the same time Turkey is the recipient of Russian natural gas through the Blue Stream pipeline and has signed an important natural gas agreement with Iran.

In the Middle East,[8] both sides share the general interest to contain and manage instability. It is argued that engagement, not containment or pre-emption, would be the most appropriate mechanism for dealing with those regimes (Oguzlu, 2003, p. 297). In the case of Syria, for example, both Turkey and the EU argue against a destabilisation campaign and forced regime change unless there is a clearly viable alternative, strongly supported by domestic political forces. Regarding Iraq, both sides support the need to preserve the territorial integrity of that country and to avoid the further destabilisation of the Gulf region and the spread of Islamic terrorism. The AKP government has adopted a more active and balanced policy vis-à-vis the Middle East, maintaining good working relations with Israel (under pressure from the Turkish military) but clearly and frequently distancing itself from Israel's handling of the Palestinian problem. Turkey has expressed its willingness to contribute to the resolution of the Palestinian problem and has played an important intermediary role in recent talks between Syria and Israel and a secondary role in efforts to stabilise Lebanon.

In the Balkans, there is good transatlantic cooperation with common efforts to further stabilise the region. There are no major problems or disagreements, with both sides sharing the objective of avoiding a change of borders through the use of force. Turkey participates in international peacekeeping forces in Bosnia-Herzegovina and Kosovo.

Europe is concerned about WMD proliferation, not necessarily as a direct threat, but more because of the possible domino effect and the resulting erosion of the international non-proliferation regime. It is also quite worried about non-state actors acquiring WMD. Turkey is also concerned about WMD proliferation as it actually borders potential proliferating countries. Both sides share a preference for a diplomatic solution to the crisis caused by the Iranian nuclear programme.

[8] Stephen Larrabee paints a rather pessimistic picture of Turkey's neighbourhood and security challenges, arguing that the 'locus of threats and challenges to Turkish security has shifted. Turkey faces a much more diverse set of security threats and challenges: growing Kurdish nationalism and separatism; increasing sectarian violence in Iraq that threatens to spill over and draw in outside powers; an increasingly assertive Iran that may acquire nuclear weapons; and a weak, fragmented Lebanon dominated by radical groups with close ties with Syria and Iran. Most of these threats are on Turkey's southern periphery. As a result, Turkish attention today is focused much more intensely on the Middle East than in the past. This is where the key challenges to Turkish security are located' (Larrabee, 2008, pp. ix, 3).

On international terrorism the two sides do not necessarily see eye to eye on all aspects of the issue. Europe is concerned about Islamic terrorism. Turkey is worried about two types of terrorism: (a) Islamic (the Al-Qaeda network, which may have links with local Turkish organisations, e.g. Hezbollah) and (b) the activities of separatist organisations, namely the PKK.[9] There is extensive scope for cooperation in the first field. Disagreements have been observed on the second, as many Europeans view this as an issue of human or minority rights etc. There is rather frequent criticism of the policies of Turkish governments. Europeans are not sympathetic to the PKK's methods, but neither are they happy with Turkey's handling of the problem. On the other hand, according to a moderate Turkish view,

> if the Turkish policymakers failed to distinguish between the PKK separatists and supporters of Kurdish cultural rights, EU policymakers in many capitals failed to see or acknowledge the difference between terrorists on the one hand, and activist supporters of human rights in Turkey on the other. (Evin, 2004, p. 131)

The PKK – and militant Kurds in general – is an issue where Turkey and Iran (as well as Syria) have common interests; this often leads to active cooperation, to the dismay of the United States, which is trying to keep Iran isolated and under pressure.

There is mutual concern about organised-crime activities in the Balkans and the Black Sea region, as well as about failed or failing and weak or dysfunctional states in Africa and other neighbouring parts of the world (even in the Middle East, should the worst-case scenarios about Iraq, Palestine and Lebanon materialise). Turkey, as is the case with a number of other countries in the region, is both a source of organised crime and a transit route for illegal activities. Cooperation is essential for all sides involved. Turkey is rapidly becoming part of Europe's first line of defence against organised crime[10] and the two sides need to discuss and agree on ways to increase efficiency.[11] Although both sides understand that cooperation in Justice and Home Affairs (JHA) will be mutually beneficial and that this is basically a one-way street, it has rightly been pointed out that for Turkey to take

---

[9] See, for example, the official website of the Turkish Ministry of Foreign Affairs (2008), where it is argued that 'In the context of the required international solidarity in the fight against terrorism, the decision of the EU in May 2002 to include PKK, a separatist/terrorist organization and the extreme leftist DHKP-C in the list of terrorist organizations, followed by its decision in April 2004 to include KADEK and KONGRA-GEL, both aliases of PKK in the said list, constituted a positive development'.

[10] In this context, it is argued that leaving Turkey outside the EU and treating it as a barrier against soft (more dangerous) and hard (less dangerous) security threats will not work in today's environment because of the global and trans-regional nature of security issues in this part of the world (Oguzlu, 2003, p. 296).

[11] It has been argued that the Turkish International Academy against Drugs and Organized Crime (TADOC) is already a valuable professional institute for the entire region (Emerson & Tocci, 2004). For a detailed discussion on JHA, see also Apap, Carrera, and Kirişci (2004, p. 30).

on the entire EU *acquis* in the areas of freedom, security and justice will be a lengthy, difficult, sensitive and even costly process (Hughes, 2006, p. 51).[12]

On should also examine Turkey's national threat assessment, where it is explicitly mentioned that there are significant internal and external challenges to Turkish security and prosperity: economic and social development, the EU accession course and new, asymmetric, as well as more traditional security threats, especially on Turkey's eastern borders (which prompted a re-orientation of Turkish security policy, as demonstrated – at least on the verbal level – by the reported changes in the most recent Defence White Paper). According to press reports (unconfirmed, as this is a classified document), the White Paper adopts the position that Turkish national security is threatened by the Islamist and separatist problems. Greece is one of the second-tier threats. For Greece, Turkey remains the only threat to its national security. This is both awkward and costly in many ways (human lives have been lost on both sides, in addition to the financial burden). It is also a paradox to have a geopolitical rivalry (sometimes turning into military confrontation, although bilateral relations have considerably improved since 1999) and *casus belli* statements by one member against another member of the same alliance (NATO) and future partners in the context of a political union, the EU.[13] As Kirsty Hughes (2006, p. 52) put it very succinctly,

> [t]he EU in general expects candidate countries to have good or at least normalised relations with neighbouring countries, in particular with existing EU member states. This means that Turkish accession does imply a settlement of the Cyprus problem and further development of relations with Greece leading to a settlement of disputes over borders in the Aegean.

The situation in northern Iraq and the re-emergence of the Sèvres syndrome (the fear of territorial dismemberment as a result of some form of foreign intervention), which makes Turkey suspicious of Western countries, further complicate the situation, as they contribute to a weakening of Turkey's self-confidence. As long as Turkey is unstable, lacks self-confidence and feels insecure, the whole neighbourhood will feel the consequences. The role of the Turkish military in shaping threat assessment, drafting national security policy and making major decisions on weapons procurement is quite exceptional and a factor not to be underestimated. It is not unusual for large bureaucratic organisations to use various means to retain and increase, if possible, their role and influence. It cannot be

---

[12] Obviously, a rejected Turkey would also be likely to prove a much less cooperative partner on issues concerning border security, illegal migration and international crime.

[13] Overall, bilateral relations between Greece and Turkey are much better today than they were nine years ago. Having said that, it should be emphasised that the two countries have not moved from their firm positions regarding issues of 'high politics'. Greece and Turkey continue to perceive each other through a Hobbesian prism. The Cyprus problem and issues related to the Aegean Sea, most of which are perceived by Greece as unilateral Turkish revisionist claims, are nowhere near resolution. The next phase of Greek–Turkish conflict resolution efforts will be a much more difficult and complicated endeavour (Dokos, 2005).

a priori excluded that 'discovering' new threats or exaggerating existing ones is part of an effort to preserve the Turkish military's special role and influence[14] and sizeable share of government expenditures.

As for whether the refusal of some European countries to offer military support to Turkey during the Iraq War,[15] combined with the considerable chilling of Turkish–American relations after 2003, has left any scars, the answer should be given by the Turks themselves.[16] It is, of course, understandable that Turkey, as explained elsewhere in this essay, will be thinking hard about its future relations with and reliance on NATO and the EU. Barring unforeseen developments, it will try to maintain a good working relationship with both major Western powers – although a return to a strategic alliance with the United States cannot be taken for granted at this stage – without alienating, when possible, important regional powers such as Russia and Iran.

The question also needs to be asked whether Turkey has a strategic culture profoundly different from the EU's. Ian Lesser (2005) correctly points out that Turkey retains a relatively traditional, military-centric view of security policy – a natural approach, perhaps, for a state with a large standing army, a wide range of 'hard' security risks on its borders and a guardianship role for the armed forces.[17] The EU's approach on security issues can clearly be described as post-modern, with emphasis on soft power and integration processes. Although many analysts

[14] The acknowledged custodial role of the Turkish Armed Forces is part of the culture of the army. Society at large accepts the legitimacy of a dominant political role for the TAF (Cizre, 2003, p. 215).

[15] At the time of the 1991 Gulf War, some European allies questioned whether the commitment would apply in the event of an Iraqi attack against Turkey in retaliation for coalition air strikes from Turkish territory. When Turkey requested deployment of part of the Allied Command Europe (ACE) Mobile Force, in response to threats on its eastern border, NATO agreed. But there was a vigorous debate in various European capitals and national parliaments, including the German Bundestag, as to whether Turkey had brought the threat upon itself.

[16] It is possible that it did, but one needs to also ask the questions: Was there at the time any real threat to Turkish security? Was the refusal by the Europeans directed against Turkey or against US policy? Regarding the consequences of that incident, it has been argued that 'the fact that putting Article V into practice did not turn out to be a 'smooth and automatic' process led some Turkish policymakers to perceive this hesitance as indicative of the EU's perception of Turkey as a 'burden' and not an 'asset' for building security in Europe' (Bilgin, 2001, p. 41).

[17] Turkish scholar Ahmet Insel has observed that the national security regime is founded on the notion that there are constant and imminent threats to the regime and that Turkey is plagued by internal and external enemies. According to this view, Turkey's unique geopolitical position – between East and West, and in the midst of conflicting and 'dangerous' ideologies – makes it a country whose very existence is under ceaseless attack. Externally, all neighbours, as well as the West, are viewed as potential enemies that would like to see a weaker Turkey. Internally, the threats are various, although political Islam and ethnic separatism – threatening secularism and national unity, the two sacred pillars of Kemalism, respectively – are considered the main enemies of the state. The fear of ever-present enemies bent on carving up Turkey gives the military the mandate it needs to stay involved in Turkey's political affairs (quoted in Akkoyunlu, 2007, p. 23). See also Faltas and Jansen (2006), Cizre (2006).

would agree, using the terminology of Robert Kagan, that 'most Turks have been like Americans, from Mars, while Europeans are from Venus' (Everts, 2004, p. 3), it is now argued that Turkey has started to 'adopt the EU's distinct foreign policy "style" of promoting security through multilateral mechanisms and institutional integration'.[18] The EU-linked socialisation process, a by-product of being a candidate and subsequently a member of the EU – clearly observed in, for example, the case of Greece – can safely be expected to further strengthen this process of change.

Turkey's potential military contribution to the ESDP is another important issue. The arguments regularly put forward by Turkish officials and analysts are that (a) the proximity of Turkish military bases to the potential crisis areas and its military infrastructure would be assets for the EU; (b) Turkish armed forces have had considerable experience in peacekeeping in several countries, ranging from Somalia to Bosnia and (c), unlike most European armies, the Turkish army has actively been engaged in fighting against PKK guerrillas for extended periods. For these technical and political reasons, it would be useful to fully integrate Turkey into the mechanisms of the ESDP (Cayhan, 2003, p. 46).

Although the EU is still debating the type of missions that will be carried out in the context of the ESDP, one can safely assume that there will be a need for agile, deployable and interoperable forces. Although the size of the Turkish Armed Forces is quite impressive (510,600 men), the Turkish military is trained, equipped and deployed as a territorial defence and not an expeditionary force and its power projection capabilities are quite limited. This is, of course, the case with all European countries, with the partial exception of Britain and France.

Despite its generally low usability rate, the Turkish Armed Forces possess quite useful units (such as five battalions of Special Forces with combat experience from the war against the PKK) and military equipment (such as fifty S-70B transport helicopters, thirteen C-130B/E Hercules and forty-six CN-235 transport aircraft, seven KC-135R Stratotanker refuelling tankers and three modern amphibious ships, with the Gendarmerie[19] having another thirty-three transport helicopters: fourteen S-70A and nineteen Mi-17 Hip H). There is considerable interoperability in the context of NATO and Turkey has a strong presence in several peacekeeping missions (ISAF/Afghanigtan, 1,220; EUFOR/Operation Althea, 253; KFOR/Kosovo, 940; UNIFIL/Lebanon, 746, including a frigate and a patrol boat).

[18] Perhaps because it feels less like an 'abandoned' country that must guarantee its own survival in an anarchic world, Turkey's behaviour has become more balanced and sophisticated. Turkish officials and leaders are still keen defenders of their national interests. But they have started to moderate their inclination to think mainly in zero-sum terms, acknowledging the possibility of win-win solutions (Everts, 2004, pp. 3–4).

[19] Turkish gendarmerie units are mobile forces with military characteristics and have contributed to missions in Hebron (Israel) TIPH, Bosnia-Herzegovina (SFOR), Kosovo (KFOR) and Afghanistan (ISAF) (Hursoy, 2005, p. 406).

As Stephen Larrabee argues, the fact that Turkey is not a member of the EU – and is not likely to become one in the near future – also influences its approach to cooperation between NATO and the EU over crisis management (an issue already difficult and delicate for a number of reasons). While in principle not opposed to the expansion of the EU's role in security and defence matters, Turkey does not want this to weaken NATO's role because this would reduce Turkey's ability to influence European security issues. Ankara has sought assurances that it will be involved in the planning and decision-making in EU crisis management operations, especially those that directly affect its own security interests, and has vetoed any joint activity in which the participation of the Republic of Cyprus has been envisaged (Larrabee, 2008, pp. ix, 22).

In conclusion, in many areas Turkey has evolved into a security producer and provider, not merely a security consumer. It has been a frequent participant in peace-support operations under the aegis and operational command of both the UN and NATO. There are, as is to be expected, significant similarities and substantial differences between the threat assessments of the EU and Turkey and relations have often been characterised by a pattern of considerable unease between the EU and Turkey. The two sides do not share identical views on a number of foreign policy issues, although increasing convergence can be observed in several areas. In the future, it will be necessary to have regular consultations and frequent assessment processes on the EU side in a rapidly changing security environment, with evolving institutional mechanisms and evolving national perspectives in the context of the EU.

European perceptions, as well as the actual impact of Turkey's contribution to the Common Foreign and Security Policy, which remains at a relatively early stage of development, will largely be determined by the future vision of the EU regarding its own regional and global role: if an inward-looking, defensively-oriented, 'fortress Europe' mentality prevails, then Turkey's potential contribution will be viewed as negative, bringing the EU much closer geographically to unstable and unfriendly regions. Should a more outward-looking and active policy be adopted by the EU in an effort to stabilise and re-shape its wider neighbourhood, then Turkey will most likely be considered an asset. Of course, developments inside Turkey and the pace of evolution in EU–Turkey relations will also be important factors in shaping Turkey's relationship with and contribution to the EU's efforts to develop an effective foreign and security policy.

References

Akkoyunlu, K. (2007). *Military reform and democratisation. Turkish and Indonesian experiences at the turn of the millennium*. Adelphi Paper No. 392. London: International Institute for Strategic Studies.

Apap, J., Carrera, S., & Kirişci, K. (2004). *Turkey in the European area of freedom, security and justice*. CEPS EU-Turkey Working Paper No. 3, Brussels.

Bilgin, P. (2001). Turkey and the EU: Yesterday's answers to tomorrow's problems. In G. P. Herd & J. Huru (Eds.), *EU civilian crisis management*. Sandhurst: Conflict Studies Research Centre, Royal Military Academy.
Cayhan, E. (2003). Towards a European security and defence policy: With or without Europe. *Turkish Studies*, *4*(1), 35–54.
Chase, R., Hill, E., & Kennedy, P. (1996). Pivotal states and U.S. strategy. *Foreign Affairs*, *75*(1), 33–51.
Cizre, U. (2003). Demythologizing the national security concept: The case of Turkey. *Middle East Journal*, *57*(2), 213–229.
Cizre, U. (Ed.). (2006). *Almanac Turkey 2005: Security sector and democratic oversight*. Istanbul: TESEV-DCAF.
Del Sarto, R. (2004). Turkish membership: An asset for the EU's policy towards the Mediterranean and the Middle East. In N. Tocci & A. Evin (Eds.), *Toward accession negotiations: Turkey's domestic and foreign policy challenges ahead*. Florence: European University Institute.
Desai, S. (2005). Turkey in the European union: A security perspective – risk or opportunity? *Defence Studies*, *5*(3), 366–393.
Dokos, T. (2005). Greek–Turkish relations as a variable in the Mediterranean and transatlantic equations. In *Greek–Turkish Relations*. Bologna: Johns Hopkins University.
Emerson, M., & Tocci, N. (2004). Turkey as bridgehead and spearhead: Integrating EU and Turkish foreign policy. *Turkey in Europe Monitor*, *7*(3).
Everts, S. (2004). *An asset but not a model: Turkey, the EU and the wider Middle East*. London: Center for European Reform.
Evin, A. (2004). Turkey and the Middle East: Antecedents and precedents. In N. Tocci & A. Evin (Eds.), *Toward accession negotiations: Turkey's domestic and foreign policy challenges ahead*. Florence: European University Institute.
Faltas, S., & Jansen, S. (Eds.) (2006). *Governance and the military: Perspectives for change in Turkey*. Harmonie papers. Groningen: Center for European Security Studies.
Fuller, G. (2008). *The new Turkish republic. Turkey as a pivotal state in the Muslim world*. Washington, DC: USIP.
High Level Round Table Conference. (2003). *Turkey and the EU. From association to accession?* Amsterdam, November 6–7.
Hughes, K. (2006). *Turkey and the EU. Four scenarios: From train crash to full steam ahead*. Brussels: Chatham House, Friends of Europe.
Hursoy, S. (2005). A Regional dimension to peace operations: European contributions to the UN and implications for Turkish co-operation and co-ordination. *Defence and Security Analysis*, *21*(4), 399–412.
Independent Commission on Turkey. (2004). *Turkey in Europe: More than a promise*. Available at http://www.independentcommissiononturkey.org/pdfs/english.pdf.
Larrabee, F. S. (2008). *Turkey as a U.S. security partner*. Santa Monica, CA: Rand Corporation.
Lesser, I. (2005). *The evolution of Turkish national security strategy*. (Mimeo).
Menon, R., & Wimbush, S. E. (2007). The US and Turkey: End of an alliance. *Survival*, *49*(2), 129–144.
Oguzlu, H. T. (2003). An analysis of Turkey's prospective membership in the European Union from a 'security perspective'. *Security Dialogue*, *34*(3), 285–299.
Roberts, J. (2004). The Turkish gate. *Turkey in Europe Monitor*, *11*(2).
Turkish Ministry of Foreign Affairs. (2008). *Synopsis of Turkish foreign policy*. Available at http://www.mfa.tr/.

Is Turkey Still an Asset for European Security?

Can Buharalı

The Cold War was a period when the roles and duties of the security and defence structures in Western Europe were well defined. The lead role was with NATO, which bound together both sides of the Atlantic and gave a strong and unitary message to NATO's adversaries. With the end of the Cold War, however, threat perceptions on both sides of the Atlantic started to diverge, particularly with regard to the central security issues. As a result, some European actors not only started to distance themselves from more militarist United States attitudes, but also came forward with ideas for more independent action on the European side. This approach entailed the use of European soft power, relying on soft power with civilian aspects more than military intervention. However, change does not occur quickly in a difficult and cumbersome area like security; European security structures have been in constant evolution since the end of the Cold War. Moreover, it is taking time for all the European actors to converge around the new ideas and new structures.

The aim of this chapter is to provide an understanding of the recent developments from the perspective of Turkey, a long-time European ally that more and more feels itself pushed aside.

1 Turkey's Perspective of Multilateralism in Security

Turkey has been an active member of the European security system for a long time. Turkey's contribution to security has not been limited to its membership in NATO – it has been a member since 1952 – but has also been demonstrated through its participation in peacekeeping operations all around the world. Ambassador Uğur Ziyal, former Undersecretary of the Ministry of Foreign Affairs, makes reference to Turkey's contribution in the following quotation:

> As one of the founding members of the UN, Turkey has always been committed to upholding the universal goals and principles enshrined in the UN Charter. It has a formidable record in active contribution to the preservation of regional and global peace and stability. Turkey's commitment to international stabilisation efforts dates back to the Korean War ....

C. Arvanitopoulos (Ed.), *Turkey's Accession to the European Union*

> Currently Turkey takes part in several UN peacekeeping operations. It has participated in numerous operations and missions, notably in Somalia, Bosnia and Herzegovina, Kosovo, Georgia, East Timor, North Korea, Sierra Leone and the Democratic Republic of Congo … [and] assumed the leadership of ISAF for 8 months in Afghanistan …. (Ziyal, 2004)

This description of Turkey is that of a country committed to 'multilateralism', one which 'works with partners' and one 'active' in the preservation of peace and stability around the world.

Europe's security and defence concepts and structures have gone through radical changes since 1989, first as a consequence of the collapse of the communist regimes in Central and Eastern Europe and then because of the dissolution of the Soviet Union. As the dangers confronting Europe became less clearly defined and the territorial threats disappeared, Turkey's contribution to Europe's security has been recognised less and less.

On many occasions, therefore, Turkey's representatives and even Turkish scholars have felt it necessary to remind particularly their Western European counterparts of Turkey's contribution to European security, and also how relevant and important it is that this contribution continue. Particular emphasis is regularly placed on the actual and potential role of Turkey in confronting the new challenges. This common line of argumentation became more widespread after the 9/11 attacks in the United States, and its use has not been limited only to Turkish scholars. The aim was obviously to convince the other participants, opinion leaders and decision makers of Turkey's strategic importance. After all, Turkey and the EU share common threat perceptions in relation to the emergence of the new challenges that were outlined in the 'Solana document' (i.e., terrorism, weapons of mass destruction, regional conflicts, state failure and organised crime).[1] All these key threats are equally central to Turkey's threat perceptions; Turkey often confronts the risk of standing between the source of these threats and Western Europe. The Solana document states that the EU needs to be more active, more capable and more coherent in order to tackle the challenges.[2] It is not difficult to argue that the same is also valid for Turkey. It is worth noting that Turkey and a large majority of EU member states have developed a harmonised working dynamic as a result of the integrated command system of NATO. As a result, the troops and the command structures are working well together. This obviously facilitates the aim of being more capable, at least at the operational end. Moreover, this shared experience is not limited to security matters but is valid also for foreign policy issues. It is worth mentioning that Turkey's alignment with Common Foreign and Security Policy (CFSP) statements and positions stands at 92%. This is significant in demonstrating that there is already a lot of common ground should the parties choose to cooperate more actively.

When discussing potential contributions to international security, there appear to be two sets of complimentary capabilities: military and civilian. It is generally

---

[1] For more details, see *A secure Europe in a better world – The European security strategy*. 12 December 2003.

[2] For a more elaborate analysis see Buharalı (2004).

understood that military interventions cannot create long-lasting stability and security if not supported by civilian tools that eventually create a civil society capable of managing the country in the aftermath of the international mission. On the other hand, it is sometimes impossible to interject the civilian contribution without having credible military capabilities deployed in the theatre of operation to control the chaos and stop or prevent the bloodshed.

The EU should be ready to deploy both types of capabilities. A European defence policy is needed as part of an effective CFSP. The 'Proposal for a White Paper' on European defence published by the EU Institute for Security Studies makes reference to the need for, on the one hand, mobile, flexible and rapid forces for expeditionary intervention and, on the other, peacekeeping forces that can be sustained for long periods of time for crisis management (Gnesotto et al., 2004). There may be cases where both are needed as part of a single military operation. In order to answer these different and extensive military needs, Europe must bring together its collective capabilities. Turkey, which has the largest army of the European states, has quite a lot to offer to the EU in these areas. Indeed, Turkey's past and present contribution to peacekeeping operations around the world is witness to this fact.

The present writer tends to think, however, that it is no longer the duty of Turkish scholars or representatives to mention Turkey's role in and importance for European security, for this has been explained at length on various occasions. It is the duty of the representatives and scholars of the EU member states to argue for or against this assumption 'if they were so to choose', in security jargon, to make matters clear. After all, if Turkey is contributing to the peace and security of Europe, this would need to be first felt and then endorsed by the representatives of other European states. The atmosphere prevailing today in some EU member states looks rather different; Turkey's contribution to European security is treated as almost obligatory or is, on most occasions, taken for granted.

2 Turkey's Status in European Security Risks Being Eroded

If we take stock of the developments since 1989 it should be no secret that Turkey's status within the European security architecture has seen serious erosion over the last two decades.

First, associate membership in the Western European Union (WEU) was less than what Turkey had expected. This decision was particularly disconcerting since Greece was admitted as a full member to the WEU. So, for a first time in post-World War II European history, Turkey and Greece were treated separately in the security arena. In other words, Turkey's experience within the new European security architecture began rather badly.

In time, however, Turkey managed to regain its profile within the WEU despite some difficulties. The fact that it was an associate member remained true on paper, but thanks to its participation and its contribution, Turkey began to be treated almost as a full member within the WEU Council. For instance, Turkey's contribution to the

WEU police mission in Albania was more substantial than that of most full members, including that of Greece. The 'WEU at 18' thus started working effectively. One must admit that the operational link created between NATO and the WEU, with the powers it transferred from NATO, helped Turkey regain its status.

Nevertheless, the WEU's new lease on life was cut short at St Malo in December 1998, when the French and the British agreed on a new way forward. This new approach set aside the structures established by the WEU and made way for a new role for the EU. Following that historic moment, the EU has developed new structures by way of the Nice Treaty, which have completely closed the doors to non-EU European allies. As a result, the seat created for Turkey at the WEU became meaningless. This has increased the feelings of bitterness in Turkey.

Turkey's concern at that stage was limited to interest in its own fate; in other words, concern over its role in European security structures until it achieved membership in the EU. Turkey wanted to associate itself with the new structures created in the EU in the long interim period until its membership. However, the institutional rigidities created in the EU, and the unwillingness of some member states to think constructively about finding solutions, have pushed Turkey further outside of ESDP structures.

The erosion in Turkey's status attained even greater dimensions when Cyprus joined the Union as a full member. Cyprus's membership harmed the security relations in two different ways. First, it blocked Turkey's involvement in security structures such as the European Defence Agency (EDA). The EDA was established with the aim of coordinating and planning Europe's military spending in accordance with its collective needs. Turkey, with its large army and defence spending, is in a better position to contribute to this aim than are many of the current members. Moreover, the EDA does not comprise only EU member states. Norway, which shares the same institutional status with Turkey (a member of NATO but not the EU), has become a member of the EDA. In other words, there are no institutional obstacles to Turkey becoming a member of EDA, if Cyprus stops blocking it.

Second, the Cyprus problem has started to undermine the trust between Turkey and the EU. In accordance with the principle of community solidarity, the EU has become a party to the Cyprus problem rather than contributing to its solution. The most important cause of the mistrust between Turkey and the EU happens also to be the cause of the difficulties surrounding the NATO–EU relationship. Neither the 'Berlin Plus' agreements dating back to the Washington Summit in 2001 and the following agreement reached on its modalities (the Nice implementation document) vis-à-vis the rights and participation of non-EU European allies in EU-led operations using NATO assets and capabilities, nor the joint institutional mechanisms (NAC-PSC) for a strategic partnership between NATO and the EU are in force. The main reason for this state of affairs is Cyprus's membership in the Union in 2004, prior to the final solution of the island's status. This remains a serious obstacle to sincere and genuine cooperation between these two important organisations on issues like Kosovo, energy security or any strategic exchange of opinion at the institutional level. For instance, the EU is preparing to send a rule-of-law mission to Kosovo, which would include police and civilian resources (EULEX). At the same time, NATO is active in Kosovo, with KFOR maintaining peacekeeping activities with over 15,000 troops. Under normal conditions the EU and NATO forces should be able to act together and fulfil the needs of a strategic partnership. This requires, however, that the North Atlantic Council (NAC) and the EU Political and Security Committee (PSC) work together, including holding joint meetings. This, on the other hand, cannot be realised since Turkey sees Cyprus's participation in these meetings as opposed to the spirit of the Berlin plus and strategic partnership agreements reached in Washington. In other words, the Washington decisions are interpreted differently by the different parties. This is obviously not a desirable situation in a delicate area like security and defence.

This erosion has led to a 'confidence vacuum', particularly on the Turkish side. Security is a very particular domain, in which lack of confidence may have serious repercussions. If Turkey has so far managed to live with that confidence vacuum, this is so for two primary reasons:

1. Turkey is a candidate country destined to join the EU, with accession negotiations advancing despite various ups and downs and difficulties.
2. The role of the EU in security is still limited; NATO is the primary organisation in that domain and Turkey is an important member of the latter.

On the other hand, it is now common knowledge that the first point is being seriously questioned, particularly by some EU member states reluctant to admit Turkey for various reasons (be it domestic and thus tactical or else related to the EU's future and thus strategic). The reluctance or even opposition of some member states leaves the EU as an institution in a difficult position as well. This hesitant approach of the EU inevitably creates opposition in Turkey to its present course and the continuation of the reforms required for membership, particularly in nationalist circles not yet ready to accept pooling some of Turkey's sovereignty with the EU.

Turkey's accession negotiations, under present circumstances, are advancing slowly and remain subject to further problems. It seems that so long as the institutional setup of the EU following the enlargements is incomplete, the EU's soul-searching exercise will not achieve much. We can only hope that the ratification of the Lisbon Treaty will lead to a happy outcome in that regard. But as long as this soul-searching exercise continues, the EU's future and Turkey's place within that future will remain unknown. This, in turn, will not facilitate a solution to the Cyprus problem, for the parties directly involved are unable to bring it to an end without international support. An EU busy defining its own future and its own role in international relations will not be able to positively contribute to a solution for the island. To the contrary; as things stand right now, the EU has become a tool for those unwilling to promote a solution to the Cyprus problem. Moreover, increasingly it risks becoming a party to the problem, instead of contributing to efforts under UN auspices. The EU's potential contribution would require a strong political will to tackle the problem, as well as objectivity, particularly among the leading member states active in international relations. Furthermore, it would eventually require a decision opening the way for Turkey's pending EU membership. A lasting solution will, in the end, be tied to Turkey's membership in the EU, as indeed was suggested in the Annan Plan. The necessary political will has not yet emerged. To the contrary, the prevailing opinion is that some member states are hiding behind the Cyprus question or even manipulating it in order to slow down – if not to fully stop – Turkey's accession negotiations. On the other hand, we can hope that the recent elections in Cyprus will break open the deadlock created by the rejection of the Annan Plan and that a solution is near.

The emergence of a strong and credible ESDP would be a bright prospect for the role of the EU in security matters, and one could argue that Turkey has a rightful place within that ESDP. A more active and capable EU in foreign and security policy would help in the creation of a better neighbourhood. This is necessary for the overall balance in world politics. Nevertheless, the problem is found right at this point. The EU has not yet been able to demonstrate credible intentions in this regard. Indeed, the views of EU member states vary as to the role of the EU in security matters. It would not be wrong, however, to state that their views converge at least around the concept of soft power. The Solana document is, in a way, a demonstration of this consensus. Still, in the EU's case, words do not often match deeds. American political scientist Joseph Nye defines 'soft power' in the following terms: 'The ability to get what you want by *attracting* and *persuading* others to adopt your goals' (Nye, 2003). As things stand right now, it is not easy to argue that the EU is either 'attracting' or 'persuading' on the regional or international scale in matters related to security. At most, it could be said that its role in contemporary regional issues remains limited. Its influence beyond the European continent does not match its economic power or its contributions in financial aid (e.g., to Palestine). The war in Iraq and the differences of opinion between member states, and statements about 'old Europe' versus 'new Europe', have not positively contributed either.

However, the changes in world politics and balances of power require the EU to play a larger role, particularly in sharing its wisdom and in extending the stability it has created in Europe. Europe's experiences after the Second World War and the culture of consensus creation within the EU are indeed valuable tools in preserving and developing security in our neighbourhood. Nevertheless, these experiences cannot achieve much on their own. They require the necessary decision-making mechanisms and operational tools, as well as political will. On this particular point, Turkey has a great deal both to gain and to contribute to the development of a sound security policy within the EU. It is with this understanding that Turkish governments have in principle been supportive of the development of an ESDP, despite the institutional difficulties it created for Turkey. Again, this understanding has been the basis of Turkey's past and present operational contribution to peacekeeping or police operations as carried out by the EU: Concordia and Proxima (in the former Yugoslav Republic of Macedonia), EUFOR (in the Democratic Republic of Congo), Althea (in Bosnia), EUPM (in Bosnia) and EUPOL (in Kinshasa). Turkey is also aiming to participate in the EU-led Kosovo police mission.

It must be admitted, however, that if Turkey's EU membership prospects were not there, it would have been very difficult to follow the same path. After all, any organisation that Turkey could not be a member of would, over the medium term, run the risk of undermining Turkey's role and its 50-year-long contribution to

European security. Moreover, Turkey and Greece, two neighbouring countries, have a great deal to gain from the enlargement of this security and stability zone. The development of this stability zone would offer grounds for cooperation as well as commercial and financial gains. Security now needs to be a domain where the two countries cooperate and from which they would thus benefit. The Franco-German example stands before us as an example how things could develop. It should, therefore, be in the interests of both Turkey and Greece to keep Turkey's accession negotiations on track. Moreover, ways to strongly associate Turkey with the CFSP/ESDP structures, even prior to accession, would help overcome the existing 'confidence vacuum' in the relationship. The following would be positive steps in that direction:

- fully associating Turkey with the planning and implementation of EU-led missions as opposed to asking for its contribution if and when needed and after the political and technical planning phase is completed;
- paying particular attention to consultations when the EU envisages action in the proximity of Turkey or in areas of strategic interest to Turkey (as indeed was agreed to in the Nice implementation document);
- increasing bilateral contact between Turkey and the EU on crisis management;
- convening the Committee of Contributors[3] at a higher level with more frequent updates from the Operation Commander to the Committee, so as to enable a direct and timely information flow to Turkey;
- a Turkish presence in EU headquarters for operations where Turkey contributes;
- membership in the EDA (Ülgen, 2008).

The present unwillingness among some member states and the current institutional rigidities constitute a genuine obstacle to these suggestions. However, the security zone cannot be enlarged with half-hearted promises.

References

A secure Europe in a better world – The European security strategy. 12 December 2003. Available at http://www.consilium.europa.eu/uedocs/cmsUpload/78367.pdf/

Buharalı, C. (2004). Turkey's foreign policy towards EU membership: A security perspective. *Turkish Policy Quarterly*, *3*(3), 95–114.

Gnesotto, N. et al. (2004). *European defence – A proposal for a white paper*. Paris: European Union Institute for Security Studies, May.

Nye, J. (2003). Propaganda isn't the way: Soft power. *International Herald Tribune*, 10 January.

Ülgen, S. (2008). *The evolving EU, NATO and Turkey relationship: Implications for transatlantic security*. EDAM Discusion Paper Series 2008/02. Istanbul: Centre for Economics and Foreign Policy Studies, March.

Ziyal, U. (2004). Re-conceptualization of soft security and Turkey's civilian contributions to international security. *Turkish Policy Quarterly*, *3*(2), 1–9.

[3] The Committee of Contributors is the civilian entity overseeing the joint EU–NATO operation.

The Emergence of New Security Threats to the EU and Their Implications for EU–Turkey Relations: The Case of Illegal Migration

Özgür Ünal Eriş

Relations with the European Union have triggered the radical reforms undertaken recently in Turkey in several areas – improvement of its policies towards the illegal migrants within the country being one of the most important. In this context, this chapter contends that new security threats to the EU (independent variable) have led to the strengthening of its justice and home affairs policies (intervening variable), which, in turn, have led Turkey to modify the migration policies it applies (dependent variable). This hypothesis will be tested in the three sections that follow. In the first section, the concept of new security threats will be dealt with and a brief definition will be given in order to clarify their importance for the EU. In the second section, the emergence of new security threats within the European arena will be described and there will be an analysis of how these threats influence the direction of the EU and the changes in the *acquis communautaire*. In the last section, the whole problem will be analysed in the context of the relations between the EU and Turkey. One aspect in particular of the new security threats will be dealt with – given its crucial effect on EU–Turkey relations – and that is illegal migration.

1 The Emergence of New Security Threats

With the end of the Cold War, the notion of security is no longer restricted to military security – as was the case during the Cold War. Security now includes a range of non-military factors, such as economic, political, environmental and societal factors. In other words, security is no longer equated only with nation states and their territories and arms, but also includes people and their development. A pilot study undertaken in 1999 (Kirchner & Sperling, 2002)[1] identified 12 conceivable security

[1] This study was based on government documents, the academic literature and the response of 42 leading European and North American security experts to an extensive questionnaire. The individuals surveyed for this project were mainly security and defence policy experts and were asked for their perceptions with regard to the definition of new security threats as they appear in two different time periods: 1999 and 2010.

C. Arvanitopoulos (Ed.), *Turkey's Accession to the European Union*

threats to the European security space after the end of the Cold War: biological/chemical attack, nuclear attack, the criminalisation of economies, narcotics trafficking, ethnic conflict, macroeconomic destabilisation, general environmental threats, specific environmental threats, cyber warfare or cyber vandalism against commercial structures, cyber warfare against defense structures, terrorism against state structures and migratory pressures. All these threats are outcomes of global developments in the fields of technology, communications, economics and finance, the environment, human rights etc. and their impact on countries and regions. Those specifically connected with terrorism, environmental degradation, migration or ethnic conflict cannot be contained beyond the borders of the state and can be described as global threats (Kirchner & Sperling, 2002).

As the distinction between domestic and international politics has blurred and threats are classified as global or transnational rather than as national, the effectiveness of strictly national policy instruments has decreased considerably as well. Given the trans-boundary nature of the threats, dealing with them will require a *coordinated* and *cooperative* approach. Thus there was a consensus among the respondents to Kirchner and Sperling's survey that states are more likely to fight the new security threats *as part of*, rather than *outside of*, multilateral institutions. Specifically, the EU was seen as the institution most capable of responding to these threats; it was seen as more adequate than, for example, NATO. Given the global range of its commercial, financial and political activity, the EU possesses more numerous and varied instruments of influence within the framework of technical aid and assistance programmes, political and military cooperation schemes and intensive diplomatic relations (Kirchner & Sperling, 2002, p. 36).

2 Developments within the EU against New Security Threats

The end of the Cold War exacerbated the new security threats. The possibility of an increase in the problem of transnational crime as a result of the opening of the borders among the EC members helped provide the impetus for the creation of the 'third pillar', Justice and Home Affairs, in the European Union, created by the Maastricht Treaty in 1991. However, as the original third pillar limited the role of the Commission and largely restricted authority to the intergovernmental Council in which individual member states had a potential veto over decisions, progress on JHA was quite slow (Kirchner & Sperling, 2002, p. 202).

As enlargement to the CEECs looked increasingly likely from the mid-1990s on, it was assumed that their accession would only add to the EU's existing problem of dealing with shared borders. The prospect of adding new members and expanding the Schengen free-travel area provided additional impetus for the EU to increase its cooperative efforts on JHA; hence a desire to reform the third pillar. The Seville European Council Summit of June 2002 was important for the fact that it adopted conclusions on a number of immigration and asylum issues. These conclusions concentrated on joint management of migration flows and compulsory readmission in the event of illegal migration, offering financial assistance to third-party states to assist with the readmission of their own and other countries' nationals.[2]

3 Why Illegal Migration?

The globalisation of economic activities and technological advances have increased the mobility of people in various forms, ranging from the migration of documented labour to illegal flow of labour including illegal migrant smuggling and trafficking. Studies show that many illegal migrants who choose a clandestine route to work abroad feel compelled to leave their home communities because of unemployment, the risk of hunger and economic crisis. There are other complementing factors as well that lead to cases of illegal migration: including political conflict, ethnic persecution and the fear of rape at home in the case of many ethnic minority women (Kyle & Koslowski, 2001).

Human smuggling is also very much related to illegal migration. Human smuggling is the procuring of illegal entry of a person into a state of which the person is not a national or permanent resident, in order to obtain a financial or other material benefit. Again, as with illegal migration, economic discomfort and political persecution are the most important factors driving people to seek the assistance of smugglers who can move them to developed countries through the use of clandestine routes and illegal methods when legal means are unavailable (CNN News, 3 May 2002).

Human smuggling has become complicated and costly, as there is the need to arrange convoluted travel arrangements, falsified documents and safe houses. This is where organised crime networks move in, with past experience in transporting drugs and other contraband.[3] This is also an area where fines and prison sentences are often weak or non-existent, overburdened legal systems do not give high priority to tough prosecution, potential witnesses are frequently considered first and foremost to be deportable aliens and are deported before trials take place and the potential seizure of assets has not been the type of threat it poses, for example, to drug traffickers.[4] The smuggling of human beings, in other words, can be considered a relatively low-risk, high-gain activity and has today become the preferred trade of a growing number of criminal networks and, worldwide, a multi-billion dollar business. Human smuggling and organised crime are very much intertwined.

---

[2] For more details see Peers (2003).

[3] 'Transnational Organised Crime is a crime committed by an organized criminal group, which is planned or committed in more than one state, or has substantial effects on more than one state, or is committed by a group which commits crimes in more than one state. An organized criminal group is a structured group existing for a period of time and acting in concert, with the aim of committing one or more crimes for financial or other material benefit' (United Nations Convention Against Transnational Organised Crime, 2000).

[4] For more details, see Narli (2002/2003).

The problem of irregular migration is closely associated with the problem of trafficking in human beings. Human trafficking is the recruiting, transporting, transferring, harbouring or reception of persons for the purpose of exploitation (Friebel & Guriev, 2002). Unlike the previous groups, who are smuggled at their own request, these are people who are being *forced* across frontiers against their will. Among them are young women who have been lured to accept work abroad and instead find themselves forced into prostitution and trapped in the hands of organised crime, or children who are used in the sex trade.

What is needed to fight the problem of human smuggling and trafficking is a comprehensive and global approach that is a part of managing illegal migration. Addressing one aspect of it at a time, in isolation, and with a focus on the short-term fix is unlikely to have much success.

As stated before, the growing influence of the new security threats, specifically illegal migration, on the internal security of the EU has influenced the evolution of the EU *acquis communautaire*. This inevitably influences the relations between Turkey and the EU, as the EU attaches special importance to the candidate country fulfilling the JHA *acquis*. Turkey is a country that is faced with new security threats, especially with regards to its role both as a source and host of illegal migration.

4 The Fight against New Security Threats: Illegal Migration, the Case of Turkey

Turkey has long been a country of emigration; there are currently close to 3.5 million Turkish citizens living in the EU. Still, it would not be correct to identify Turkey only as a sending country in terms of international migratory flows. Since the mid-1980s, Turkey has become both a receiving and a transit country and a major destination for asylum seekers. There are two factors that explain why Turkey has increasingly become a transit zone and a host country for the large numbers of people who enter Turkey, legally or illegally, from the South and East.

First, political turmoil and regime changes. Events such as the Iranian revolution in 1979, wars and civil wars and the numerous conflicts in the Middle East, such as the Gulf War, and wars in several countries in Africa, have led to a substantial flow of people away from these regions. In addition, developments after the collapse of the Soviet Union, the conflicts in the Balkans and the Caucasus – in Chechnya, especially – have forced refugees, transients and all types of migrants into the country in search of security, protection from persecution and a better life. Turkey shares borders with many of the countries in the Middle East, the Caucasus and the Balkans, and also has cultural and ethnic ties with many of them. These ties generate human channels for illegal migrants who already have geographical access to Turkey.

Second, Turkey's geographical location between East and West and the South and North has made the country a *transit zone* for many migrants intending to reach western and northern countries. Turkey has received migrants from the Middle

East, the former Soviet Union, and the Balkans and Africa; but mainly those from Afghanistan, Pakistan, Iran, Iraq and Bangladesh who wish to reach Europe.

Some of these people enter the country with legal documents, seeking shelter on a temporary basis in order to move to another country. Some of the illegal migrants choose Turkey as a place to work and live. These people usually overstay their visa and work in the black market. Romanians, Russians, Moldovans, Ukrainians and some Iraqis have come to Turkey to work illegally. For example, between 1988 and 1991, approximately 600,000 Iraqis, mostly Kurds, poured into Turkey. Despite the fact that a large number of them returned home, a residual group has remained in Turkey. Many were brought by human smugglers who have benefited from this illicit trade (İçduygu, 2005).

Approximately 25,000 Bosnians also sought refuge in Turkey from 1992 to 1994. While the majority of them considered Turkey a transit country, some of them stayed and started businesses. The other flow from the Balkans was the migration of Albanians caused by the Kosovo crisis in 1999. They entered Turkey with valid passports and visas. It was not hard for them to find lodging and jobs since they had many relatives and pre-established networks, just as the Bosnians had.

As we have already pointed out, there is a relationship between organised crime and the illegal movement of humans: including the illegal migration of labour, illegal migrant smuggling and human trafficking. The smugglers are often part of larger organised crime networks already involved in drug trafficking and the illegal arms trade. In Turkey, human smuggling is coordinated both by organised crime networks operating in Turkey and in the Balkan countries, and by the terrorist groups who need money to finance their activities. During the 1990s, this was a major security concern; government officials have always had an interest in at least trying to stop illegal migration and human trafficking. This often failed, however, to translate into actual concerted action against preventing irregular migration. The reasons for this are as follows.

Insufficient funds allocated to the police are an important cause. Police officers complain that at times they find themselves having to meet the basic needs of illegal migrants from their own meagre salaries or to seek donations from the public. Moreover, it is often much easier for police officials to let illegal migrants pass than face the bureaucratic hassles of intercepting, apprehending and deporting them. They have also complained that, compared to drug trafficking, the penalties for human trafficking are very low and the profit for the risk is very high (Kirişci, 2003).

Turkey is also a country of asylum, receiving people from neighbouring countries undergoing political chaos and conflict. The origins of Turkey's current asylum policies can be traced to the early years of the Cold War, to 29 August 1961, when Turkey adopted the 1951 Geneva Convention on the Status of Refugees. However, Turkey inserted a geographic reservation under Article 42 of the Convention and indicated that it would admit only aliens from Europe seeking asylum in Turkey. Partly as a consequence of anti-Communist policy during the Cold War, this meant that Turkey would grant refugee status only to people coming from Eastern Europe and the Soviet Union, but would not accept any obligations for non-European refugees.

There were several reasons for the application of geographic limitations to the 1951 Convention. One issue was whether Turkey had the capacity to carry out the tasks associated with such changes. Turkey does not have the economic base and resources to sustain a support system for asylum seekers and refugees that would meet the requirements of the Convention. Also, under the current system, again often because of a lack of funds, Turkey does not have the resources to pursue for deportation asylum seekers who have had their cases rejected. Such persons often remain in Turkey illegally and/or pursue alternative ways of seeking asylum or migration to a third country. Thus the question of asylum is very closely related to the issue of illegal migration.

5 How Has Turkey Adapted Itself to the Progress of the EU on This Issue?

As was shown in the previous section, illegal migration is a serious problem for Turkey as a country located between Europe and the unstable Middle East and Central Asian regions. Thus this issue, as well as other challenges that may be considered as new security threats and fall under the category of the so-called Justice and Home Affairs policy of the EU, is also quite important for Turkey–EU relations. Clearly, if Turkey wishes some day to achieve full EU membership, it has to embark upon a variety of reforms. These include the need to harmonise its visa policy with the Schengen visa regime, sign readmission treaties and improve control over its eastern borders. Furthermore, if Turkey were admitted to the EU, it would become, in accordance with the existing EU *acquis*, a country of first asylum and hence have to process these claims itself (Kirişci, 2003).

In January 1998, after a series of ships had arrived in Italy carrying illegal Kurdish migrants, mostly from Iraq but also some from Turkey, the General Affairs Council adopted an Action Plan. The plan, which placed heavy emphasis on efforts to stop unauthorised migration, was to provide assistance to Turkey to improve conditions for illegal migrants being detained prior to removal, and to provide training for the Turkish police in screening asylum seekers. Unfortunately the plan was not implemented in a systematic manner, although the EU has provided funding for training seminars run by the United Nations High Commissioner for Refugees (UNHCR) focusing on separating genuine asylum seekers from irregular migrants.

The Budapest Process has become the major multilateral forum where most of the cooperation in Europe on irregular migration takes place. This process has become a consultative forum of more than 40 governments and 10 international organisations aiming to prevent irregular migration.[5]

[5] See the Policy Paper drafted by the Secretariat at the International Centre for Migration Policy Development for the purpose of the twelfth meeting of the Budapest Group of Senior Officials (ICMPD, 2004).

One of the critical issues that has come up at the Budapest Process is the question of readmission agreements.[6] It was expected that Turkey would sign these readmission agreements but so far Turkey has resisted doing so. A major concern of Turkish officials is the fear that Turkey would become a dumping ground for irregular migrants apprehended in Europe. They also argue that in implementing the readmission agreements the EU is not giving sufficient attention to the root causes of migration. People usually decide to leave a country because of limited economic opportunities or a threat posed by conflict or human rights abuses. As long as the large economic gap between Europe and the countries of the region remains, people who are returned to their country of origin will be back in another effort to reach Europe. Hence the current police measures are not adequate. The tight visa regime prevailing in Europe aggravates the situation by forcing people to try illegal means to reach Europe.

Turkey's asylum policies were strongly criticised by Western governments as well. As a result, Turkey implemented new regulations on asylum seekers, entitled 'Regulations on the Procedures and the Principles Related to Mass Influx and the Foreigners Arriving in Turkey or Requesting Residence Permits with the Intention of Seeking Asylum from a Third Country'. These regulations include the right to determine the status of asylum seekers under the control of the Turkish government and also introduced strict regulations governing access to the asylum procedures. These too attracted serious and concerted criticism. Critics argued that Turkey was violating the rights of asylum seekers and refugees by denying them access to asylum procedures or failing to provide them with adequate protection (Kirişci, 2003).

The most intense criticism from European governments as well as from refugee advocacy and human rights groups, however, was directed at the geographic limitations to the asylum policies of Turkey. It was only after 1999, when the EU made it clear that adopting the EU *acquis* on asylum should be an integral part of Turkey's accession process, that Turkey finally accepted the lifting of the geographic limitation.

As Turkey's efforts to harmonise with the EU *acquis* on JHA issues proved quite slow, the country received a warning from EU leaders, who had placed illegal migration at the top of their agenda at the EU Council Summit in Seville in June 2002.

The first concrete step Turkey has taken towards harmonising its legislation with that of the EU was ratifying the UN Convention of 2000 against transnational organised crime (the Palermo Convention) in March 2003; the additional Protocol to prevent, suppress and punish trafficking in persons, especially women and children; as well as the Protocol against the smuggling of migrants. The Turkish Criminal Code was amended in August 2002 to align it with the Palermo Convention by classifying smuggling of and trafficking in human beings as crimes. These articles have introduced heavy deterrent penalties for human smugglers and traffickers and

[6] Readmission agreements are the standard method of ensuring that persons are expelled from member states individually or from the EU as a whole. Since 1995 the EU has inserted clauses into a number of its association and cooperation agreements insisting that the other country readmit its own citizens whenever an EU member state requests that it do so (Peers, 2003).

also led to stricter controls at borders and ports. An interministerial working group to combat human trafficking was set up in October 2002 under the coordination of the Foreign Ministry.[7] Furthermore, there have also been the following developments:

- In February 2003 the Turkish Parliament passed legislation on foreign nationals' work permits that allows only the Ministry of Labour and Social Security to issue work permits for foreign nationals entering Turkey legally – rather than a series of different bodies. The new Act allows foreign nationals to work on the same basis as Turkish nationals, which was not possible under the earlier legislation. It also aligns Turkish law with the provisions concerning refugees in the 1951 Geneva Convention.
- The Turkish Nationality Act was amended in June 2003 to outlaw marriages of convenience.
- In January 2004 a unit specialising in human trafficking was set up in the Interior Ministry. Its role is to improve dialogue and coordination between the police and other authorities. A directive ordering health care to be provided free of charge for victims of traffickers was also issued. A refuge to accommodate them was opened in Istanbul in August 2004.
- Protocols on cooperation and information exchange to combat human trafficking were ratified with Kyrgyzstan and Moldova.
- In June 2004 Turkey ratified the International Convention on the Protection of the Rights of All Migrant Workers and Members of Their Families.
- Turkey has also continued to participate in the early warning system of the Centre for Information, Discussion and Exchange on the Crossing of Frontiers and Immigration.

There has also been progress regarding the treatment of refugees:

- An interministerial crisis centre was established under the auspices of the Prime Minister, and provisional shelters were set up for refugees near the border with Iraq.
- Asylum requests began to be processed in conjunction with the UNHCR. Although the material needs of non-European refugees and asylum seekers are mostly looked after by the UNHCR, Turkey provides direct assistance (food, clothing, healthcare, heating fuel etc.).
- Training schemes have been established for officials on asylum matters in cooperation with the UNHCR.
- The situation has improved as regards schooling for refugees and the children of asylum seekers.

Turkey is still having difficulties with signing readmission agreements, specifically with Greece. Given the problems encountered, the two sides decided in 2004 to take measures to ensure that the Protocol was implemented more efficiently. In March 2004 Turkey agreed to start negotiations with the EU on a similar agreement.

[7] For more details, see http://europa.eu.int/scadplus/leg/en/lvb/e22113.htm.

A readmission agreement was signed with Romania and Syria. Negotiations are under way with Pakistan, Sri Lanka, Jordan, Lebanon, Libya and Uzbekistan.

Some progress has been made with regard to visa policy:

- Since 2002 visas have been required for nationals of Bahrain, Qatar, the United Arab Emirates, Kuwait, Saudi Arabia and Oman.
- In 2003 nationals of thirteen other countries were exempted from the visa requirement.
- Turkey has pursued its efforts to align its blacklist with the EU list.
- The Turkey–Brazil visa exemption agreement entered into force in July 2004.

Some progress has also been made regarding the Schengen *acquis*. In March 2004, Turkey set up a national bureau in the Interpol department of its directorate-general for security that will act as the central authority for Schengen purposes and as the Europol and OLAF (Office Europées de Lutte Antifraude/European Commission: European Anti-fraud Office) contact.[8]

A meaningful reform process on asylum law would mean lifting the geographic reservation to the Geneva Convention. Thus the Turkish government adopted an Action Plan for Asylum and Migration, which came into force on 25 March 2005. The Action Plan is a detailed document, and contains a description of existing legal practices as well as the mid- and long-term goals to be achieved by 2012. The process of comprehensive codification, comprising the Law on Asylum and the Law on Aliens, should be concluded by 2012. The adoption of these two codes would not only bring Turkish legislation into line with the European *acquis*, but also establish a more effective legal framework for asylum and migration issues, which are currently regulated by various pieces of legislation (Kirişci, 2005).

6 Conclusion

Within the context of the EU, an impressive *acquis* has been developed in the area of Justice and Home Affairs, to which the new members have had to adjust their law accordingly. Protecting the EU from unregulated movements of people is the central aspect of the enlargement process. Turkey is under pressure to follow suit. The EU will be very careful in assessing Turkey's capacity to live up to the standards of the Union; Turkey's geographic position especially will make these issues all the more sensitive for the EU.

From the perspective of the EU, a key objective is to prevent irregular migration through Turkey from becoming a path for those seeking asylum in the EU. In this respect Turkey faces an important challenge; it is expected not only to stop irregular transit migration, but also to distinguish between potential asylum seekers and economically motivated illegal migrants, and to process their applications accordingly.

[8] For more details, see European Commission (2005).

Turkish legislators have demonstrated their commitment to controlling illegal migration by including provisions to combat illegal migration in the most recent set of reforms, and the government has also made considerable efforts to limit transit migration. Since the changes in the Turkish legislation came into effect, there has been a sharp decrease in transit migration and attempts at illegal migration have also declined. The authorities have pointed out that, following stronger efforts and initiatives to combat illegal migration, international migration routes have begun to change from Turkey to a southern route – Iraq, Syria and Lebanon – and a northern route – Iran, Caucasus and Ukraine. Changes have also occurred in the routes used by ships carrying illegal migrants from African countries to Italy and France and also from Sri Lanka and India – through the Suez Canal directly to Cyprus, Greece and Italy. This progress has been acknowledged in the Progress Reports prepared by the European Commission since 2004.

In the past, Turkey's asylum policy has been criticised from a human rights perspective. As a result, Turkey agreed to eventually lift the geographic reservation to the 1951 Geneva Convention Relating to the Status of Refugees in its Action Plan for Asylum and Migration. This is a significant and revolutionary change, specifically because of the fact that it shows the improvement in asylum practice in Turkey and the growing influence of a human rights agenda.

Turkish officials recognise that harmonising their law on these issues with the EU *acquis* is imperative for the smooth progress of the accession process. Assistance from the EU will be critical, however, as will additional economic and political changes in Turkey. For example, lifting the geographic reservation to the 1951 Geneva Convention would result in Turkey's becoming a safe third country according to the practice of EU member states. Turkey is concerned that it may be forced to bear all of the responsibility for assessing the applications of all asylum seekers passing through Turkey. In the absence of the support mechanism in the EU, taking on such responsibility raises burden-sharing concerns for Turkey. Thus the progress made in this reform is strongly linked to the negotiations between the European Commission and the Turkish government on burden sharing and this is why Turkey has postponed the adoption of the Asylum Bill until 2012 (European Commission, 2005). As already noted, Turkey has also begun revising its visa policy as it prepares to adopt the Schengen visa system. This will mean that the entry of nationals from a large number of countries will become more strictly controlled. Some experts believe that this may actually become an additional factor causing an increase in illegal migration and, possibly, the number of asylum applications (Kirişci, Apap, & Carrera, 2004).

It is clear that Turkey is on the verge of overhauling its whole asylum, visa and immigration policies. In this way, after having served as the bastion of Western Europe's defence during the Cold War against the Soviet Union, thanks to its geo-strategic location, Turkey may now serve as a buffer zone for keeping some of the unwanted and uncontrolled movement of people into the EU at bay.

If Turkey is to successfully perform this task, however, there will have to be very close cooperation between Turkey and the EU. EU officials will need to be sensitive to the relatively unique geographic location of Turkey in terms of refugee movements as well as to the expectation of Turkish officials that there will be a close, convincing and generous commitment to burden-sharing.

Unfortunately, many Turkish officials feel that they are not receiving the recognition they deserve for the energy and resources currently being channelled into combating irregular migration. Furthermore, they feel that Turkey is being treated differently from other candidate states, which, for example, signed readmission agreements *after* the start of accession talks, and then only on a bilateral basis. This difference is a major source of contention, which is exacerbated by what Turkish officials consider a lack of burden sharing. They complain that Turkey is basically left to its own devices to combat irregular migration and to arrange for the return of illegal migrants to their countries of origin (European Commission, 2005).

This fact leaves Turkey facing difficult dilemmas. The cost of meeting EU requirements in asylum and illegal migration policy is economically as well as bureaucratically, socially and politically significant. Yet, at the same time, Turkish decision makers may ask themselves whether, after all these adjustments, Turkey might still not be admitted as a member of the EU. This could leave the country facing major difficulties on its own without any benefits of EU membership and, more importantly, without any sense of the security that comes with that membership (Kirişci, 2005).

In addition to this, Turkish officials feel that no matter how hard the EU tries, the dynamics of migration will remain as intractable as before unless the root causes of migration are solved. North–South inequalities in wealth, development and opportunities still continue. Thus there has to be better reflection, analysis and effort on how to manage integration, solve the problem of illegal migration and ultimately stop the effect of the new security threats on the internal security of EU member states. The whole process necessitates the inclusion of Turkey; but only as a fairly treated, equal partner with the EU.

References

Buzan, B., Waever, O., & de Wilde, J. (1998). *Security: A new framework for analysis*. London: Lynne Rienner.

Erder, S., & Kaska, S. (2003). *Irregular migration and trafficking in women: The case of Turkey*. Geneva: International Organisation for Migration (IOM) Report.

European Commission. (2005). *Enlargement strategy paper*. Brussels: COM 561 Final, 9 November.

Friebel, G., & Guriev, S. (2002). *Human trafficking and illegal migration*. Working Paper. Stockholm: Stockholm School of Economics.

İçduygu, A. (2005). Turkey: The demographic and economic dimension of migration. In P. Fargues (Ed.), *Mediterranean 2005 report*. European University Institute, European Commission and EuropeAid Co-operation Office.

ICMPD. (2004). *The development of the Budapest process since the Rhodes Ministerial Conference*.

IOM. (1995). *Transit migration in Turkey*. International Organisation for Migration, Migration Information Programme.

Kirchner, E. J. (2003). European security trends. *Jean Monnet/Robert Schuman Paper Series*, *3*(6).

Kirchner, E. J., & Sperling, J. (2002). The new security threats in Europe: Theory and evidence. *European Foreign Affairs Review*, *7*(4), 423–452.

Kirişci, K. (2002). *Justice and home affairs issues in Turkish–EU relations*. Istanbul: TESEV Publications.

Kirişci, K. (2003). The question of asylum and illegal migration in European Union–Turkish relations. *Turkish Studies*, *4*(1), 79–106.

Kirişci, K. (2005). Turkey: The political dimension of migration. In F. Philippe (Ed.), *Mediterranean 2005 report*. European University Institute, European Commission and EuropeAid Co-operation Office.

Kirişci, K., Apap, J., & Carrera, S. (2004). *Turkey in the European area of freedom, security and justice*. EU–Turkey Working Paper No. 3. Brussels: Centre for European Policy Studies.

Kyle, D., & Koslowski, R. (2001). *Global human smuggling: Comparative perspective*. Baltimore: Johns Hopkins University Press.

Narli, N. (2002/2003). Human smuggling and migration of illegal labour to Turkey. In *Crushing crime in south east Europe: A struggle of domestic, regional and European dimensions* (pp. 61–88). Vienna: National Defence Academy of Vienna and Institute for Peace Support and Conflict Management. Available at http://www.bmlv.gv.at/pdf_pool/publikationen/crime_narli.pdf/

Occhipinti, J. (2004). Justice and home affairs. In N. Neill (Ed.), *European Union enlargement*. Hampshire: Palgrave.

Peers, S. (2003). Readmission agreements and EC external migration law. *Statewatch Analysis*, *17*. Available at http://www.statewatch.org/news/2003/may/readmission.pdf/

Tokuzlu, L. (2005). Turkey: The legal dimension of migration. In F. Philippe (Ed.), *Mediterranean 2005 report*. European University Institute, European Commission and EuropeAid Co-operation Office.

United Nations. (2000). *United Nations Convention against transnational organised crime*. Available at http://www.unicri.it/wwd/justice/docs/TransnationalCrime/2000_UN_Convention_Transnational_Crime.pdf/

United Nations Development Program. (1994). *Human development report*. New York: Oxford University Press. Available at http://hdr.undp.org/reports/global/1994/en/

How Can the European Union Transform the Greek–Turkish Conflict?

Panayotis J. Tsakonas

1 Introduction

A certain amount of optimism was expressed by most analysts of the Greek–Turkish dispute after the European Union summit in Helsinki in December 1999. Because of Turkey's candidacy and potential accession to the European Union, it was thought that Greece and Turkey would seek ways of resolving their longstanding territorial dispute. It seems, however, that the European Union itself is a contentious issue between Greece and Turkey so long as Turkey is still generally seen as being a long way from full membership. By implication, then, the Greek–Turkish dispute is a hard case when assessing the impact of the EU on conflict transformation, not to mention resolution.

By bridging rational-institutionalist and constructivist accounts, this chapter aims to explore the impact the European Union has had and, most importantly, is expected to have, on the management and/or transformation[1] of the long-standing Greek–Turkish territorial dispute.[2] The main argument is that the EU can play a promising role and change the interests, or the identity scripts, of the parties in conflict only if two particular conditions are fulfilled. The first condition is the strength of the norms the EU exerts on the parties in conflict and the legitimacy and credibility the EU enjoys vis-à-vis these parties. The second is the type of socialisation the EU mechanisms produce. In other words, it does matter whether the institutional mechanisms – by which EU seeks to attain domestic salience and legitimacy – are directed at the elites of the parties in conflict only or at the elites as well as the public and the society. A thorough internalisation of the institutional rules and norms, and not solely an elite-driven one, is a crucial determinant of the positive

[1] The literature distinguishes between 'conflict management' (regulation of conflictual relations) and 'conflict transformation' (the transformation of subject positions from incompatibility/antagonism to compatibility/tolerance).

[2] From a theoretical point of view, rational and constructivist efforts have so far generated some promising propositions to better specify the mechanisms of institutional effects and the conditions under which international institutions are expected to lead to the internalisation of new roles or interests from their member states, but much less has been done on the role institutions play as facilitators of cooperation and conflict management or transformation.

C. Arvanitopoulos (Ed.), *Turkey's Accession to the European Union*

transformation of the Greek–Turkish dispute. Simply put, what matters for an institution to have a transformative impact on an interstate conflict is not only 'what it does' (the type of norms it exerts on the parties in conflict) but also 'how it does it' (the type of socialisation its mechanisms produce).

After a brief review of the relevant literature on the role of international institutions in interstate conflict and a summary of the research efforts undertaken so far in investigating whether and how the EU matters in managing and/or transforming the Greek–Turkish conflict, the analysis turns to empirically testing whether the fulfilment of the aforementioned interrelated conditions can impact the strategies of the parties in conflict towards cooperation and conflict transformation.

2 Institutions and Interstate Conflict: The EU and the Greek–Turkish Dispute

Neoliberal institutionalist accounts of how international institutions may promote peaceful relations argue that institutions can shape state strategies by conveying information, reducing transaction costs – especially those associated with bilateral negotiation, monitoring and verification – providing opportunities for side payments, linking issue-areas, increasing the level of transparency, attenuating the fear of unequal gains, raising the price of defection, discouraging cheating and thus fostering cooperative ventures (Keohane, 1984, pp. 146–147, 1986; Kupchan & Kupchan, 1991).

For constructivists, institutions not only can affect the behaviour or strategies of states, they can also alter their identities by promoting a collective security identity. By providing legitimacy for collective decisions, international institutions – according to constructivist premises – transmit, through the 'process of socialization' (Schimmelfennig, 2000), their norms and rules to their members as well as to prospective member states (Finnemore, 1996; Finnemore & Sikkink, 1999). Motivated by ideational concerns to join international institutions, namely the legitimisation of their national identity (Hurd, 1999), states gradually define their national identities and interests by taking on each other's perspectives, thus building a shared sense of values and identity (Wendt, 1994; Wendt & Duvall, 1989).

Based on both institutionalist and constructivist premises, most recent studies have tried to better specify the mechanisms through which institutions are able to socialise states and states' agents as well as the conditions under which institutions are expected to internalise new roles and interests (Checkel, 2005). More specifically, these studies have suggested that particular socialisation mechanisms are usually at work (e.g., strategic persuasion and/or normative suasion) and have linked them to particular state behaviour or policy (Gheciu, 2005; Schimmelfennig, 2005).

Building on various theoretical strands, research into the effects of the EU on the strategies of Greece and Turkey regarding cooperation and positive identification and, more specifically, into the transformation of their conflict has shown that these institutions matter and, more importantly, how they matter. From a constructivist perspective, and through a case study of Greek–Turkish relations in the period

1995–1999, it was shown how – by situating Greece and Turkey in different and also liminal positions with respect to 'Europe' – the community-building discourse of the EU reinforced and legitimised the two states' representations of their identities as different from and also as threatening to each other, thus allowing for the perpetuation of their conflicts (Rumelili, 2003).

Most recent studies exploring the impact of the EU on the Greek–Turkish conflict, however, suggest a rather promising role for the EU in bringing about a positive transformation of the long-standing dispute. Indeed, these studies argue that the EU, especially after 1999 when Turkey was recognised as a membership candidate, can have a positive transformative impact on a series of border conflicts (the Greek–Turkish being one) through four particular pathways (Celik & Rumelili, 2006; Diez, Stetter, & Albert, 2006, pp. 563–593).

It is worth noting that these studies view the European Union both as a framework that can eliminate the bases of interstate conflicts in the long run through democratisation and gradual integration, and as an active player that can impact border conflicts (also in the short run) in direct and indirect ways. Thus the EU appears as a (necessary) condition that can have a direct (compulsory or connective) as well as an indirect (enabling or constructive) impact on the strategies of the disputants – especially on Turkey – in the direction of cooperation and, by implication, on the positive transformation of the conflict between the two states.

3 Assessing the EU's Performance with Respect to the Conflict

3.1 'What you do' Matters: Strong Norms, Legitimacy and Credibility

With regard to the conflict between Greece, a full member since 1981, and Turkey, an aspirant country since the early 1960s, the European Community (EC) approach towards the resolution of the conflict has been hesitant, if not indifferent (Stephanou & Tsardanides, 1991). Mainly concerned with keeping both Greece and Turkey anchored in the West, the EC has purposely kept out of the conflict, thus leaving some space for intervention either to the US or to the isolated diplomatic activities of some of its members (Meinardus, 1991). Not surprisingly, the indifference of the EC to the resolution of the conflict has been viewed, interpreted and dealt with differently by the disputants.

Greece's membership in the EC, though largely economically motivated, was also meant to bolster the existing Greek government and, more importantly, to strengthen the country's international position, especially its deterrent capability against Turkey.[3] Enjoying a comparative advantage as a full member of the EC,

---

[3] In the words of a senior Greek official: 'Turkey would thus think twice to attack an EU member state', see *The Economist*, 26 July 1975 and *The Guardian*, 19 May 1976 (as quoted in Valinakis, 1997, p. 279).

Greece tried to use the latter as a diplomatic lever against Turkey. As Greek and Turkish analysts argue, the EC's collective approach towards the conflict was greatly influenced, if not determined, by Greece's views and desiderata on Cyprus and Greek–Turkish relations (Couloumbis, 1994; Guvenc, 1998/1999). Indeed, successive Greek governments have shown remarkable continuity in using the Cyprus issue to block EU–Turkey relations since the 1980s (Kramer, 1987; Stephanou & Tsardanides, 1991).[4] At the same time, any advancement in relations between the EC and Turkey has remained linked to the exercise of Greece's veto power, unless Turkey first meets particular criteria – related mainly to the state of democracy and the respect for human rights – and abandon its revisionist policy in the Aegean.[5]

Unsurprisingly, the EU was perceived by Turkey as just another platform through which Greece, taking full advantage of its position as a member, could exert pressure on Turkey and pursue its national agenda with respect to Turkey. Furthermore, the perception of an EC held hostage by Greece was negatively interpreted as a reflection of European reluctance to accept Turkey into Europe (Ugur, 1999). This reluctance in turn fuelled a long-standing conviction in Turkish political culture, namely the 'Sèvres syndrome', or the fear of dismemberment as a result of a Western conspiracy (Kirişci & Carkoglu, 2003). It is thus evident that by choosing to keep out of the Greek–Turkish dispute, the EC was exerting weak norms over the disputants with respect to the management and resolution of their conflict. Indeed, the hesitancy or indifference of the EC to intervene in disputes over national issues had negatively affected the EC's third-party capacity as well as its credibility to act as an honest broker for the resolution of the Greek–Turkish dispute and, overall, its ability to have a positive impact on the conflict.

Interestingly, the institutional strengthening of the EC and its transformation into the European Union was not followed by a more credible stance towards the Greek–Turkish conflict. Following the Imia crisis in January 1996, some normative pressure was applied on the aspirant Turkey by the EU Commission, Parliament

[4] It was not until March 1995 that Greece decided to lift its veto of the EU–Turkey customs union agreement. In exchange for the lifting of the Greek veto on the customs union, accession negotiations between the EU and Cyprus would begin in March 1998. Cyprus would thus be included in the next round of enlargement accession negotiations. With regard to Turkey's European orientation, decisions made in Luxembourg and Cardiff, in January and June 1998 respectively, further burdened the already tense and fragile Greek–Turkish security agenda, as the postponement of Turkey's accession negotiations remained linked to Greece's deliberate policy of keeping the doors of the EU closed.

[5] In 1986, Greece vetoed the resumption of the Association relationship between Turkey and the EC and the release of frozen aid to Turkey. A year later, when Turkey applied for EC membership, Greece was the only member that openly opposed referring the application to the EC Commission for an opinion (Guvenc, 1998/1999). It is characteristic that even up to the EU–Turkey Association Council in April 1997, Greece maintained its veto and continued blocking EU aid to Turkey worth 375 million ECUs. As explained by the then Greek Minister of Foreign Affairs, Theodoros Pangalos, the veto would be maintained until Turkey stopped disputing Greek sovereignty in the Aegean (Athens News Agency, 30 April 1997).

and Council,[6] but the result was a further strengthening of the reigning perception among the Turkish elite, namely, that the EU was held hostage by Greece (Rumelili, 2004b, p. 13). Unsurprisingly, the 1997 European Council decisions in Luxembourg – which introduced the conditionality factor in the EU's intervention in the Greek–Turkish conflict – were also interpreted by Turkey as a policy of conditional sanctions imposed by Greece on an ambivalent, if not reluctant, EU with regard to Turkey's membership (Rumelili, 2004b, pp. 17–18).

The parochial impact of the EU on the transformation of the Greek–Turkish conflict prior to late 1990s should not be attributed only to the EU's hesitant, if not indifferent, stance towards the dispute. More importantly, the EU's impact on the transformation of the Greek–Turkish conflict remained dependent on the weak norms the EU had been exerting since the early 1990s towards the disputants and on its low level of credibility, as the few initiatives taken did not incorporate any membership carrot for the aspirant country and served only to reinforce the latter's perception that the EU's initiatives towards the settlement of the conflict were controlled by the disputant who happened to be a member of the EU.

Things seemed to change dramatically in the late 1990s, however, especially prior to the EU's 'big bang', namely, its enlargement to the east. Particularly the EU's enlargement process has been widely legitimised by the argument that it will bring peace and stability to a part of Europe that would otherwise be in danger of returning to violent conflict, with possible spill-over to the old member states. Built on core principles, values and norms, the EU sought to export its success story to those who were willing and could meet the criteria. Pursuing its enlargement task, the new post-Westphalian European Union demanded that candidate countries undergo a radical transformation process by following certain principles and adopting the EU Community Law in earnest. These characteristics were reflected in the norms and conditions promoted by the European Union in states that sought to become members, such as one of the disputants, namely Turkey.

Indeed, prior to the enlargement, the norms and conditions promoted by the EU were both constitutive (i.e., democratisation, the rule of law, respect for minority and human rights, the role of the military in politics etc.) and regulative (i.e., certain economic and administrative adjustments to harmonise the state's internal structures with European standards etc.). Moreover, by strengthening its normative ability to determine the confines of appropriate state behaviour in the European theatre, the EU asked the states that sought to become members to organise their domestic and foreign policies on the premises underlying liberal-pluralistic democracy. Especially

[6] The EU Commission expressed the EU's solidarity with Greece and warned Turkey that its relationship with the EU had to take place in a context of respect for international law and the absence of the threat or use of force. The European Parliament expressed its concern over Turkey's territorial demands vis-à-vis an EU member and the EU Council of Ministers issued a statement in July 1996 urging Turkey to appeal to the International Court of Justice (ICJ) over Imia, to show respect for international law and agreements as well as for the EU's external borders, and to declare its commitment to the aforementioned principles (General Affairs and External Relations Council, 1996).

with regard to the Greek–Turkish conflict, at the 1999 EU Council in Helsinki, the EU's role and credibility concerning the positive transformation and resolution of the dispute were tremendously enhanced.[7] What seemed to make the difference in the EU's transformative ability with regard to the conflict was a series of factors that may be put under the same heading: the exertion of strong norms and positive conditions.

First of all, the EU decisions at Helsinki established the peaceful resolution of outstanding border disputes as a community principle (Rumelili, 2004a, p. 9). This in turn meant that the EU was not interested in providing a patchwork solution that would either settle for short-term solutions or consolidate the status quo that was unacceptable to both sides. Instead, for the first time in the history of the conflict between the two states, there was a clear reference[8] to the final forum and mechanism that the two states should use for resolving their long-standing conflict. By imposing a particular time-frame and by indicating the final forum to which the disputants should refer for a resolution to their conflict (i.e., the ICJ), the EU succeeded in encouraging and, moreover, facilitating substantive and long-term solutions, instead of offering short-run and ad hoc ones.

Second, in the Helsinki decisions, progress on Turkey's candidacy for membership in the EU was linked to the resolution of its border disputes with an EU member. What is of particular importance here is that the strong carrot of candidacy for membership was linked to a positive condition. Thus, the EU's stance towards the conflict was viewed, especially by the Turkish elite, as a policy of conditional rewards, and not – as had been the case in the past – as a policy of conditional sanctions. The incentives for the disputants to find a better way of resolving their conflict were thus also enhanced.

Third, the resolution procedure adopted in Helsinki by the EU, namely, a two-step compromise structure involving, first, negotiations on all issues followed by adjudication of unresolved issues, reflected a compromise proposal, allowing the disputants to perceive the EU's influence not as an imposition but as a deal struck on a balanced distribution of gains.[9] It should be stressed at this point that besides the EU Council, the European Commission and the European Parliament also contributed, especially after 1999, to the mitigation of the distributional conflicts

[7] Turkey's eligibility for EU membership after Helsinki depended on resolving two issues: its border conflict with an EU member state, Greece, and the Cyprus issue. With regard to Greek–Turkish relations, Helsinki made it clear to Turkey that it had four years (until 2004) to resolve the conflict with neighbouring Greece before the critical review that would assess Turkey's path towards the European Union (European Council, 1999).

[8] Both the Helsinki Conclusions and the provision on Greek–Turkish relations, in the medium-term priorities of the Accession Partnership, do refer to the resolution of the outstanding border disputes between the two states.

[9] For this remark see Rumelili (2004b, p. 14). The approach adopted by the EU in the Helsinki Summit is indeed different from past approaches. For example, the EU Council of Ministers stated in July 1996 (after the Imia crisis) that 'the cases of disputes created by territorial claims, such as the Imia islet issue, should be submitted to the International Court of Justice'. Similarly, the Luxembourg Council decisions of December 1997 urged 'the settlement of disputes, in particular, by legal process, including the ICJ'.

by keeping account of deals struck, compromises made and gains achieved. For examples of effective mechanisms for resolving distributional conflicts one may refer to EU Commission Reports and EU Summit and Council Conclusions where the progress achieved in Greek–Turkish relations since Helsinki are recorded.[10] Particularly with regard to the conflict between a member state and a candidate state, the EU emphasised the flexibility of the *acquis* in order to accommodate special concerns arising between the disputants. In this manner, disputes, perceived by the European Commission as a 'series of issue conflicts', were translated into possible solutions through pragmatic approaches.[11]

The 1999 EU summit in Helsinki was a breakthrough in the way the EU had intervened in the Greek–Turkish conflict. By applying strong and convincing norms and conditions to a particular interstate conflict, the EU succeeded not only in strengthening its ability to be viewed as a framework with potential positive effects in the long run, but also as an active player, able to impact the conflict in a plethora of ways.

Unfortunately, the EU's ability to apply strong norms and, hence, its credibility to positively affect the conflict, were severely damaged at the 2004 EU summit in Brussels; the EU Council's decision that EU–Turkey accession negotiations would start on October 2005 meant that an issue of paramount importance for the resolution of the conflict was set aside.[12] More specifically, the EU decided – obviously with Greece's concurrence – that the Helsinki timetable, urging the two countries to solve their bilateral differences or else agree, by December 2004, to refer them to ICJ, should be withdrawn. Turkey – in addition to the Copenhagen criteria – was now asked by the EU simply to commit to good neighbourly relations and resolve any outstanding border disputes in conformity with the principle of the peaceful settlement of disputes in accordance with the United Nations Charter, *including if necessary jurisdiction of the ICJ*. By implication, progress on Turkey's membership would no longer be linked to the resolution of its dispute with Greece, with an obvious decrease in the incentives for both disputants, especially Turkey, to find a way of resolving their conflict. It thus seemed that a resolution of the Greek–Turkish conflict should, for the immediate future, be sought outside the EU context and be achieved some time in the distant future by a hesitant Greece and a – hopefully – increasingly Europeanised Turkey en route to Brussels.

---

[10] Commission discourses also include references to the continuous improvement in relations between Greece and Turkey. The evolution of Turkish foreign policy and perception of security interests towards EU standards have also been recorded, although the Greek–Turkish dispute remains unresolved. See the plethora of examples cited in Pace (2005).

[11] According to the EU Commission discourse, the Greek–Turkish conflict appears as a series of 'issue conflicts', whereas the use of carrot and stick to promote political reforms in Turkey could be seen to have a multi-channel impact on the Greek–Turkish conflict. See Pace (2005).

[12] The Greek government that emerged from the parliamentary elections in March 2004, burdened with the rejection of the Annan Plan by the Greek Cypriots and hesitant to pay the cost that a compromise settlement with Turkey before the Helsinki deadline (i.e. the end of 2004) would entail, opted to postpone the resolution of the dispute to the future. For an analysis of Greece's socialisation strategy vis-à-vis Turkey prior to Helsinki and after it, see Tsakonas (forthcoming).

3.2 *'How you do it' Also Matters: The Type of Socialisation*

As suggested by the relevant literature, institutions exert their norms and, more importantly, impact the domestic landscape of the states to be socialised through a series of mechanisms (cognitive, normative, rhetorical and/or bargaining) and by following particular socialisation policies.[13] A useful categorisation of the domestic impact distinguishes between normative effects and the depth of internalisation (Schimmelfennig, 2002, pp. 9–10). The former refers to the kind of institutional impact,[14] and the latter, also known as 'norm salience' (Cortell & Davis, 2000, pp. 70–71), to the extent that the international norm has been transposed into a state's domestic political institutions and culture. By implication one may refer to degrees or levels of internalisation and salience (high/intermediate/low internalisation or high/moderate/low degree of salience). Needless to say, different kinds of normative effects (formal, behavioural, communicative) may be detected at different levels of internalisation or norm salience.

The good news about the potential impact of the EU on the transformation and resolution of the Greek–Turkish conflict is that the exertion of the EU's strong norms and positive conditions since the Helsinki Summit have started producing some promising results with regard to changes in the strategies and interests of the disputants towards cooperation and positive identification. Indeed, at Helsinki the EU put into motion a mix of cognitive, normative, rhetorical and, more importantly, bargaining mechanisms for internalising a set of strong norms and rules in the domestic agenda of the disputants (Tallberg, 2002). Thus the EU has actively promoted Turkey's democratisation by asking it to proceed with a 'small revolution' internally in order for the European *acquis* to be internalised. The bad news is that this process seems to have been seriously damaged by the watering down of the norms, rules and conditions related to the resolution of the Greek–Turkish conflict decided at the 2004 EU summit in Brussels.

It is worth noting that the new EU policy of conditional rewards was received positively by the Turkish elite, who began reconsidering past views that the decisions of the EU are held entirely hostage by Greece.[15] Almost all EU Summit and Council Conclusions and decisions from Helsinki onwards have established certain procedures and mechanisms to monitor Turkey's progress in fulfilling the

[13] For the various mechanisms that institutions use to exert their norms – either following the logic of appropriateness or the logic of consequentiality, see Schimmelfennig (2002, pp. 12–13) and Checkel (1999).

[14] It includes the formal conception of norms (mainly seen in the transfer of institutional norms to domestic laws or in the creation of formal institutions that enforce the institutional norm), the behavioural conception of norms (measured by the extent the behaviour of the states under socialisation is consistent with the behaviour set by the institutional norm) and the communicative conception of norms (related to the ways the communication or discourse among the domestic actors is being affected).

[15] On elite receptivity as a factor essential to the socialisation process, see Ikenberry & Kupchan (1990, p. 284).

conditions set by the EU.[16] Moreover, the EU compliance system was perceived to be operating through a combination of enforcement and management mechanisms in applying norms, which contributed to the EU's ability to combat detected violations, thereby reducing non-compliance to a temporal phenomenon. By implication, the use of a carrot and stick approach by the EU to promote political reforms in Turkey seemed to be having a multi-channel impact on the Greek–Turkish conflict.

An examination of Turkey's internalisation of the European *acquis* after its EU candidacy in 1999 reveals that a thorough adoption of the EU's legislation, norms, rules and requirements was put into effect[17] with the participation of, and legitimacy provided by, several political and social actors, beyond those in government. More specifically, these normative and internalisation effects of the EU on Turkey took place on a series of levels, namely on the domestic institutions level, the elite level and the societal level.

Various EU Council Conclusions ask that certain EU norms and rules (in the form of conditions) be enmeshed into domestic institutions. Indeed, from 2001 to 2004 various political reform packages were adopted in order to fulfil the Copenhagen political criteria that resulted in deepening Turkey's Europeanisation process (Bac, 2005, p. 21). Turkey has so far taken some big steps forward in order to fulfil these conditions and thus has managed – inter alia – to regulate the constitutional role of the National Security Council as an advisory body and in accordance with the practice of EU member states,[18] to fulfil certain economic and legal conditions (e.g. harmonisation of the country's legislation and practice with the European *acquis*) and to extend in practice the cultural rights of minority groups (allowing mother tongue broadcasting and education as well as the liberalisation of laws restricting freedom of speech and association).

At the elite level, the formal conception of norms (the transfer of EU norms to national laws) had, in turn, certain internalisation effects (constitutive effects) on the basic political actors in Turkey. Especially the civil–military elite, which functions as the primary securitising actor, able to define the internal and external threats to the state, and for whom EU membership is a primary objective, has slowly, painfully, but steadily entered a process of de-securitisation. It was the EU, especially through the *acquis communautaire*, which increased the chances of successful de-securitisation by providing a reference point to legitimise conflict-diminishing policies.

One should at this point stress the change in the interests of Turkey's elite over the Cyprus issue due to the EU-membership incentive and the EU's normative impact on Turkey's political elite (Tsakonas, 2001). Indeed, despite strong reservations about the role of the EU and veiled threats to EU members that either the

[16] After Helsinki and in order to prepare Turkey for membership, the Accession Partnership called upon Turkey to prepare a National Program for the Adoption of the Acquis (NPAA) that would be compatible with the priorities established in the Accession Partnership.

[17] For a good account of the political and legal reforms that have been stimulated since Turkey's EU candidacy, see Bac (2005).

[18] A development that has had certain repercussions for the ability of the Turkish military to alone define the issues that concern the country's national interest.

self-proclaimed Turkish Republic of Northern Cyprus would be integrated into Turkey or Turkey would withdraw its own candidacy if the Greek–Cypriot administration was accepted as a full member before the Cyprus problem was solved, nothing happened. Quite the contrary, it seemed that there was a general understanding among the Turkish elite that the Cyprus issue had to a great extent been Europeanised and that Turkey would need to reach acceptable compromises with Greece, the Greek Cypriots and the European Union should it aspire to join the EU. Particular credit should be given to the Turkish government, which first neutralised and finally replaced the intransigent Turkish–Cypriot leader Rauf Denktash in order for the Greek–Cypriot community to support the Annan Plan for the reunification of the island. Ironically, the EU had a less positive impact on the Greek–Cypriot elite and the Greek–Cypriot public, which rejected the UN Secretary's plan for the reunification of the island.

More importantly, at the societal level Turkey's EU candidacy has empowered domestic actors in both Greece and Turkey and has given significance, urgency and, most importantly, legitimacy to official and private efforts to promote Greek–Turkish cooperation. Thus, after 1999 a pro-EU coalition (bolstered by the EU's combined strategy of conditions and incentives) emerged that gradually and steadily gained ground over another, vocal, anti-EU coalition (Öniş, 2003). In addition, Turkey's EU candidacy has resulted in funding for civil society efforts directed towards Greek–Turkish cooperation. The effectiveness of the EU in promoting Greek–Turkish cooperation has thus stemmed not so much from its direct interventions as from the success of various domestic actors in using the EU as a funder, a symbol and a source of legitimation (Rumelili, 2005).[19]

In a general sense, the more democratisation has taken root, the more diverse societal and political groups have challenged the primacy of the Kemalist understanding of foreign policy. It seems therefore that the ongoing democratisation process in Turkey is having a continuing impact on the process, style and content of Turkey's foreign policy, leading towards a more rationalised and multilateralist stance and a gradual re-definition of Turkey's national interest that is closer to European rules and norms of behaviour.[20]

An overall assessment of the normative and internalisation effects of the EU on Turkey suggests that the degree of salience or the level of internalisation could be

[19] Especially after 1999, again slowly but steadily, one could notice, within both Turkey and the self-proclaimed Turkish Republic of Northern Cyprus, the emergence of numerous political parties, business associations and civil society organisations that have challenged the orthodox, well-established Turkish policy on Cyprus and started demanding that Turkey and the self-proclaimed Turkish Republic of Northern Cyprus cease adopting a sceptical view of the EU and the accession of the island to the EU.

[20] Our focus on the institutional effects on Turkey's foreign policy behaviour is mainly related to the fact that, as theory suggests, convergence effects appear when institutions exert their greatest influence on precisely those states whose behaviour deviates substantially from institutional norms (Martin & Simmons, 2001). In the Greek–Turkish dyad, Turkey is undoubtedly the disputant whose behaviour deviates more from institutional norms. Hence the assessment that the EU's ability to exert its normative and internalisation effects on Turkey's foreign policy is limited.

characterised as moderate to high. Indeed, although norms appearing in the domestic discourse have produced some changes in Turkey's national agenda as well as on its institutions, countervailing institutions, procedures and normative claims are still present. However, although for some norms and rules the domestic discourse still admits exceptions, reservations and special conditions, it seems that gradually a legitimisation of alternative policies at the elite level has been taking place and the activities of civil society and norms retain more and more salience as a guide to behaviour and policy choice.

At the 2004 summit in Brussels, however, there was a setback in the EU's willingness to actively contribute to the resolution of the Greek–Turkish conflict. As noted above, the EU decided, with Greece's concurrence, to withdraw the Helsinki timetable, which had set December 2004 as a deadline for the resolution of the conflict either through an agreement between the disputants or via the compulsory reference of the Greek–Turkish dispute to the International Court of Justice. The 2004 Brussels decision thus had certain consequences not only for the credibility of the EU as an active player in the resolution of the Greek–Turkish conflict but also for its ability to be viewed as a framework with potential positive effects in the long run.

Indeed, from 1999 to 2004 the EU made the long-term goal of the resolution of the conflict a community principle and exerted clear and strong rules and norms on the disputants. Most importantly, the strong norms the EU exerted after 1999, which were supported and complemented by a mix of cognitive, normative, rhetorical and bargaining mechanisms, managed to result in a moderate degree of internalisation by Turkey, the disputant whose behaviour deviated more from institutional norms. It would seem that by delinking progress on Turkey's membership from the resolution of its dispute with Greece, the 2004 EU summit decreased the incentive for both disputants, but especially for Turkey, to search for a solely bilateral compromise solution.

Even worse, a series of other developments may further exacerbate the EU's ability to constructively intervene and contribute to the resolution of the Greek–Turkish conflict. Indeed, in the years to come the resolution of the Greek–Turkish conflict is expected to become even more secondary to the EU's priorities in its enlargement policy (Celik & Rumelili, 2006, p. 208). Moreover, portrayals of Turkey as 'non-European', especially after the rejection of the European Constitution by France and the Netherlands, have resurfaced in many EU countries, Greece included, as the European identity discourse began to emphasise the 'non-European' characteristics of Turkey. Such developments may move Turkey back to an ambiguous, if not threatening, institutional position in relation to the EU and thus have detrimental consequences for the resolution of its conflict with Greece.

4 In Lieu of Conclusions

Building on various theoretical strands, research on the effects of the EU on the strategies of Greece and Turkey in the direction of cooperation and positive identification and, more specifically, on the transformation of their conflict has shown whether and mainly how it matters. A certain amount of optimism has been expressed in the relevant literature, especially after 1999, for a promising EU role in the transformation of the Greek–Turkish dispute. Through an assessment of the empirical records of EU performance in the transformation of the Greek–Turkish conflict, this chapter has argued that two interrelated conditions seem to account most for the EU's promising role in the Greek–Turkish conflict.

The first is related to the strength of the norms the EU exerts on the two parties, while the second concerns the type of socialisation or the depth of internalisation the EU mechanisms produce. Interestingly, the fulfilment of the two interrelated conditions highlighted in this chapter also demonstrates the limits to the EU's potential role in the positive transformation of the Greek–Turkish conflict. Indeed, as the EU case demonstrates, international institutions should – apart from fulfilling the aforementioned conditions – also be careful to promote the right mix of conditionalities and incentives to the disputants in order to positively contribute to the transformation of an interstate dispute.

References

Bac, M. M. (2005). Turkey's political reforms and the impact of the European Union. *South European Society and Politics, 10*(1), 17–31.

Celik, B. A., & Rumelili, B. (2006). Necessary but not sufficient: The role of the EU in resolving Turkey's Kurdish question and the Greek–Turkish conflicts. *European Foreign Affairs Review, 11*(2), 203–222.

Checkel, J. (1999). *Why comply? Constructivism, social norms and the study of international institutions* (Working Paper No. 24). Oslo, Norway: ARENA.

Checkel, J. T. (Ed.) (2005). Special issue on international institutions and socialization in Europe. *International Organization, 59*(4), 860–1079.

Cortell, P. A., & Davis, W. J. (2000). Understanding the domestic impact of international norms: A research agenda. *International Studies Review*, *2*(1), 65–87.

Couloumbis, T. (1994). Introduction: The impact of EC membership on Greece's foreign policy profile. In P. Kazakos & P. C. Ioakimidis (Eds.), *Greece and EC membership evaluated* (pp. 189–198). London: Pinter Publishers.

Diez, T., Stetter, S., & Albert, M. (2006). The European Union and border conflicts: The transformative power of integration. *International Organization, 60*(3), 563–593.

European Council. (1999). *Helsinki European Council: Presidency Conclusions* (SN 300/99), 10–11 December.

Finnemore, M. (1996). *National interests in international society*. Ithaca, NY: Cornell University Press.

Finnemore, M., & Sikkink, K. (1999). International norm dynamics and political change. In P. J. Katzenstein, R. O. Keohane, & S. D. Krasner (Eds.), *Exploration and contestation in the study of world politics*. Cambridge, MA: MIT Press.

General Affairs and External Relations Council. (1996). *The declaration adopted by the fifteen ministers of foreign affairs of the EU* (SN 3543/96). Brussels, Belgium, 15 July.

Gheciu, A. (2005). Security institutions as agents of socialization? NATO and the 'New Europe'. *International Organization, 59*(4), 973–1012.

Guvenc, S. (1998/1999). Turkey's changing perception of Greece's membership in the European Union. *Turkish Review of Balkan Studies, 4*, 103–130.

Hurd, I. (1999). Legitimacy and authority in international politics. *International Organization, 53*(2), 379–408.
Ikenberry, G. J., & Kupchan, A. C. (1990). Socialization and hegemonic power. *International Organization, 44*(3), 283–315.
Keohane, R. O. (1984). After hegemony: *Cooperation and discord in the world political economy*. Princeton: Princeton University Press.
Keohane, R. O. (1986). Reciprocity in international relations. *International Organization, 40*(1), 1–27.
Kirişci, K., & Carkoglu, A. (2003). Perceptions of Greeks and Greek–Turkish rapprochement by the Turkish public. In B. Rubin & A. Carkoglu (Eds.), *Greek–Turkish relations in an era of détente*. London: Frank Cass.
Kramer, H. (1987). Turkish application for accession to the European Community and the Greek factor. *Europa Archiv, 42*(10), 605–614.
Kupchan, A. C., & Kupchan, A. C. (1991). Concerts, collective security and the future of Europe. *International Security, 16*(1), 114–161.
Martin, L., & Simmons, B. (2001). Theories and empirical studies of international institutions. In L. Martin & B. Simmons (Eds.), *International institutions*. Cambridge, MA: MIT Press.
Meinardus, R. (1991). Third-party involvement in Greek–Turkish disputes. In D. Constas (Ed.), *The Greek–Turkish conflict in the 1990s: Domestic and external influences* (pp. 157–163). New York: St Martin's Press.
Öniş, Z. (2003). Domestic politics, international norms and challenges to the state: Turkey–EU relations in the post-Helsinki era. *Turkish Studies, 4*(1), 9–34.
Pace, M. (2005). *EU policy-making towards border conflicts*. University of Birmingham, Department of Political Science and International Studies, Working Paper Series in EU Border Conflicts Studies, 15. Retrieved from http://www.euborderconf.bham.ac.uk/publications/files/WP15_EU.pdf.
Rumelili, B. (2003). Liminality and perpetuation of conflicts: Turkish–Greek relations in the context of community-building by the EU. *European Journal of International Relations, 9*(2), 213–248.
Rumelili, B. (2004a). *The European Union's impact on the Greek–Turkish conflict: A review of the literature*. Working Paper Series in EU Border Conflicts Series, 6.
Rumelili, B. (2004b). *The microprocesses of hegemonic influence: The case of EU and Greece/Turkey*. EUBORDERCONF Project, Boğaziçi University, Turkey.
Rumelili, B. (2005). Civil society and the Europeanization of Greek–Turkish cooperation. *South European Society and Politics, 10*(1), 43–54.
Schimmelfennig, F. (2000). International socialization in the new Europe: Rational action in an institutional environment. *European Journal of International Relations, 6*(1), 109–139.
Schimmelfennig, F. (2002). Introduction: The impact of international organizations on the Central and Eastern European States – Conceptual and theoretical issues. In R. Linden (Ed.), *Norms and nannies: The impact of international organizations on the Central and East European States*. Lanham, MD: Rowman & Littlefield.
Schimmelfennig, F. (2005). Strategic calculation and international socialization: Membership incentives, party constellations, and sustained compliance in Central and Eastern Europe. *International Organization, 59*(4), 827–860.
Stephanou, C., & Tsardanides, C. (1991). The EC factor in the Greece–Turkey–Cyprus triangle. In D. Constas (Ed.), *The Greek–Turkish conflict in the 1990s: Domestic and external influences* (pp. 207–230). New York: St Martin's Press.
Tallberg, J. (2002). Paths to compliance: Enforcement, management, and the European Union. *International Organization, 56*(3), 609–643.
Tsakonas, P. (2001). Turkey's post-Helsinki turbulence: Implications for Greece and the Cyprus issue. *Journal of Turkish Studies, 2*(2), 1–40.
Tsakonas, P. (forthcoming). *The incomplete breakthrough in Greek–Turkish relations: Grasping Greece's socialization strategy*. Basingstoke: Palgrave.

Ugur, M. (1999). *The European Union and Turkey: An anchor/credibility dilemma*. Aldershot, UK: Ashgate.

Valinakis, Y. (1997). *With vision and program: Foreign policy for a Greece with self-confidence*. Thessaloniki, Greece: Paratiritis [in Greek].

Wendt, A. (1994). Collective identity formation and the international state. *American Political Science Review, 88*(2), 384–396.

Wendt, A., & Duvall, R. (1989). Institutions and international order. In E. Czempiel & J. Rosenau (Eds.), *Global changes and theoretical challenges: Approaches to world politics for the 1990s*. Lexington, MA: DC Heath.

Whither Turkey? Greece's Aegean Options

Kostas Ifantis

On 3 October 2005, Turkey turned a corner in its bid to join the European Union, with the opening of accession negotiations. Although Turkey's long-term prospects for EU membership remain rather uncertain, the accession talks have already put Ankara's orientation, as well as the EU's role and identity, in a new perspective. To become a member, Turkey must meet all the criteria and requirements laid out in the Negotiating Framework adopted in September 2005. On the political level, Turkey must create stable institutions that guarantee democracy, the rule of law, human rights and respect for minorities. It should also unequivocally commit itself to good neighbourly relations and to the peaceful solution of border disputes according to the UN Charter and international law. In the economic field, the EU expects Turkey to create a functioning market economy and to adopt the *acquis communautaire*. All these will require Turkey to reform itself drastically to adopt, implement and enforce European principles and values.

However, the accession talks are taking place against the backdrop of a very sceptical EU public as well as an elite majority that is less welcoming of Turkey's European prospects. Old prejudices against Turkey, based mainly on religion and history, are still very present and are reinforced by more pragmatic concerns related to the basic arithmetic of EU functioning: the number of votes in the Council, European Parliament seats, funding and subsidies etc. And it is true that the thorniest issue in the whole process is the EU's capacity to absorb Turkey. Financially, Turkey's integration can happen only after an overhaul of the EU's budget and redistribution mechanisms. The institutional changes required are fundamental.

All of the above are reasons why Turkey negotiates its European future under the most stringent terms any candidate has ever had to endure in the history of European integration. That is why, to have any chance for success, Turkey will have to win the hearts and minds of EU citizens (Akcapar & Chaibi, 2006, p. 53), and this must be done by a country in a time of peril. Domestic developments in Turkey seem to be of a structural nature that threaten age-old certainties in the country.

For Greece, the challenge is enormous as well. Since the early 1960s, Turkey has been the main concern of Greece's security policy and the driving force behind most foreign policy decisions. In fact, Turkey has dominated Greek security thinking and the identification of its strategic needs and priorities. The 1974 Cyprus crisis was regarded as the major turning point in post-WW II Greek security considerations.

C. Arvanitopoulos (Ed.), *Turkey's Accession to the European Union*

For the vast majority of the Greek elite and for the public at large, the Cyprus crisis was a traumatic experience; but it was also a basis for 'new thinking' in security policy.

1 The Greek Policy Shift

The 1974 Cyprus crisis led to, among other things, the realisation that NATO was of limited value, as was dependency on the US as a security asset against perceived Turkish 'revisionism'. Therefore the quest for the adoption of a more sophisticated 'external balancing' strategy became, in the minds of Greek policy makers, the only way to enhance Greek deterrence. To this end, full participation in the European integration project appeared to be the most appropriate instrument for the country's external balancing initiatives vis-à-vis Turkey. The primary goal was to use the EU's assets: a system of political solidarity and security provisions, capable of applying diplomatic and political pressure to deter Ankara from potential adventures in the Aegean. For more than 25 years, this policy was expressed with a series of Greek vetoes of any policy designed to establish a more institutionalised EU–Turkish relationship.

Following a number of bilateral crises in the 1990s over the Aegean and Cyprus, Athens became conscious of the fact that this policy could not work in the face of the recurring turbulence and that tension could not easily be kept to manageable levels. The potential for unwanted escalation was high, as the 1996 crisis over the islets of Imia demonstrated. Moreover, by placing Greece's quest to meet EU economic prerequisites at the top of the national agenda, Athens started to question the basic determinant of Greek–Turkish competition, namely the existing, intensifying arms race. Greek defence expenditure – the highest among EU member states – constituted a heavy burden for the Greek economy, especially at a time when Greece was completing the implementation of an economic austerity programme in order to fulfil the criteria for membership in the European Monetary Union.

Thus, Greece was facing the difficult 'guns or butter' dilemma. The dilemma came down to Greece's ability to sustain an adequate deterrence capability while at the same time advancing to the inner circle of European integration. Both goals were considered essential for the country's future. To achieve them both, Greece had to undertake a series of initiatives that would convey to those responsible for the cost/benefit strategic calculus on the Turkish side that cooperation would be far more beneficial for Turkey.

Efforts to effectively balance the Turkish threat without undermining Greek strategic priorities had to move towards a new position, where credible military deterrence would be coupled with engaging Turkey in a context where Greece enjoyed a comparative advantage, namely the EU. In the minds of the Greek foreign and security policy elites, the EU was the best available forum for setting priorities and enforcing prerequisites in accordance with European principles and standards on those countries that wish to become members. The conviction was that the strengthening of Turkey's European orientation would engage her in a medium- and long-term process that would eventually lead to the adoption of a more cooperative attitude. This was clearly reflected to the 1999 European Council decision at Helsinki to grant Turkey EU candidate status, but with two major conditions attached: first, Turkish claims concerning 'grey zones' in the Aegean and the dispute over the delimitation of the continental shelf had to be submitted to the International Court of Justice if all other efforts failed; and, second, the accession of Cyprus to the EU would not be conditional on the resolution of the Cyprus problem (Tsakonas & Dokos, 2004).

At Helsinki, the EU acknowledged the link between Turkey's orientation, the resolution of the Greek–Turkish conflict over the Aegean issues and the solution to the Cyprus problem. Thus, Greece managed to confine both the Cyprus and the Aegean disputes within the EU context, and to closely link them with Turkey's path to accession. In addition, Greek policy-makers estimated that Turkey's integration into the EU would eventually entail certain costs for Turkey, especially at the domestic level. By strengthening the drive to democratisation, it was expected that the civil-military establishment would be put under pressure to make a more rational distribution of the country's assets. Moreover, the military would be put under civilian control, the process of elite circulation would be accelerated and a new state elite would eventually be forced to start searching for new definitions of 'national interest' that would be founded on European norms and contexts.[1] This has been the rationale behind Greece's sincere support for not just a virtual or sui generis but a real candidacy for Turkey. For Greece, the embedding of Turkey in European norms and values has been a grand strategic decision.

But how do Greeks perceive Turkey's adjustment to Europe? Beyond issues related to the technical aspects of the *acquis* or issues pertinent to the domestic reform of Turkish democracy, the paramount perception in Greece is that adjustment is an urgent strategic imperative. At Greek and Greek-Cypriot insistence, the 'Helsinki context' has been transferred to a very demanding Negotiating Framework, where the Copenhagen criteria have been complemented with a very specific set of requirements: unequivocal commitment by Turkey to good neighbourly behaviour and to the peaceful settlement of disputes; continued support for efforts to achieve a comprehensive settlement of the Cyprus problem within the UN framework and in line with the principles on which the EU was founded; normalisation of bilateral relations with Cyprus; etc.

Real progress by Ankara in this context would 'anchor' Turkey ever more closely in Europe and lend greater stability to Greek–Turkish relations, leading eventually to a full normalisation between the two countries and the withdrawal of the Turkish troops from northern Cyprus. The mainstream argument in Greece is that there is a need – for both countries – for a more 'strategic' approach towards each other. Both countries have a long-term strategic interest in seeing Turkey's EU vocation succeed. Turkey's successful adjustment to Europe has the potential to

[1] For a Turkish view, see Ozel (2003).

alter Greece's perception of threat, and to foster political and economic reform in a Turkey reassured about its place in Europe.

However, the challenge for Turkey is enormous and this is something that at least the Greek elites are conscious of. This is the first time that Turkish elites have had to think differently about the nature of the state in a modern democracy. EU candidacy – let alone full membership – implies a great deal more institutionalised scrutiny, convergence and compromise. From the more mundane political issues (e.g., food regulations) to high politics, a closer relationship with formal EU structures will pose tremendous pressures on traditional Turkish concepts of sovereignty at many levels and will severely challenge (and has already done so) the role of the military in Turkish politics (Rumelili, 2003).

For an EU member state, pursuing nationalist options outside the integration context has become extremely difficult and costly if not impossible. For Turkey, the accession process, however long, will almost certainly reinforce the democratic dynamics already unleashed in the 2000s, even if there will occasionally be setbacks and slowdowns. The social contract between the state and the status quo–oriented middle class seems to have weakened. As a result, the drive towards an accountable, transparent and efficient government ruled by law can go forward on a stronger social basis than ever before. Initial resistance and a nationalist backlash notwithstanding, the conviction in Greece is that membership would become all the more prized as an aid in the cause of transforming the culture of the Turkish state. The EU accession process would be instrumental for attracting much-needed foreign direct investment, achieving better and more efficient government, securing the rule of law and realising the prospects of wide-ranging modernisation (Öniş, 2005).

However, the relative stagnation in EU–Turkish relations following the 2004 EU decision to start accession talks has contributed to a sense of disappointment and uncertainty, and has made Turkish behaviour in general more unpredictable and perhaps harder for the West to control. If Turkey cannot strengthen its relationship with the EU – in the context of future membership – it cannot successfully pursue its legitimate foreign policy goals. For the EU it would be a disaster to 'lose' Turkey, but how properly to bind it to Europe seems not very clear. EU–Turkish relations have always been complex. For many decades, Turkey has been a critical part of the European system; that is, part of the pattern of European political, economic and security relations. The question of whether Turkey is part of the European integration project is far less clear. 'Despite a strong preference for a European orientation since the founding of the Republic, Turkey's own sense of identity in this regard has varied with time' (Khalilzad, Lesser, & Larrabee, 2000, p. 2). The sense of ambiguity and ambivalence in EU–Turkish relations remains and raises as many questions as it resolves. In the context of this chapter, the most important question is whether Turkey is really prepared for the enormous sovereignty compromises that integration implies, especially during a period of significant domestic turbulence.

Turkish society, politics and economics have evolved substantially since the early 1990s. The pace of this change has increased in recent years, and has included the rise of a much broader and more active debate on all aspects of public policy and socio-political development. The period since 1999 can been seen as 'the formative years' of a new domestic landscape, in which the drive for modernisation seems to be reshaping traditional perceptions and Manichean principles of socio-political formation.

2 Turkey: The End of Domestic Certainties?[2]

The 1999 general elections produced a nationalist coalition of the right and the left, with a sharp decline in support for centrist parties and for Islamic political agents. The consolidation of military influence in defence of the secular state, which began with the removal of the Welfare Party from power and its banning from Turkish politics, also meant that the Turkish military remained a key interlocutor in foreign and security policy issues at the time. Three years later, the Turkish general election of 3 November 2002 transformed the country's political landscape dramatically. None of the members of the outgoing governing coalition won seats in the new Parliament. The Justice and Development Party (Adalet ve Kalkinma Partisi, AKP), formed in mid-2001, came to power with 34.3% of the vote and a massive majority of 363 seats in the 550-member Parliament. The centre-left CHP, after its disastrous performance in the 1999 election, emerged as the second party with 19.4% of the vote and 178 seats. Another nine seats were won by independents, with all other political parties failing to cross the 10% threshold.[3]

The indications that the transition would be turbulent were strong. The transition culminated in a confrontation with the powerful Turkish military, backed by the secular establishment, over who should be the country's next President, and led to the early elections of 22 July 2007. The AKP was returned to office after it won a landslide victory. The elections were marked by a turnout of 84% when a record number, 42.5 million voters, cast ballots. Out of 550 parliamentary seats, 341 went to the ruling party, 112 to the CHP, 71 to the far-right MHP and 26 to the independents, most of whom are Kurds. The AKP increased its share of the national vote from 34.3% to 46.7%. The CHP, which campaigned on the threat to secularism, won 20.9% of the vote, while the MHP won 14.3% (Oktem, 2007).

The AKP won in all but a few coastal provinces in the west. Even in traditional bastions of Kemalism like Izmir, the CHP narrowly escaped defeat, while in Antalya, the home province of CHP leader Deniz Baykal, the AKP won. In the predominantly Kurdish southeast, the ruling party doubled its share from roughly 26% in 2002 to 53%. The CHP, despite its merger with the Democratic Left Party,

[2] The following two parts draw from Ifantis (2007).

[3] The three parties in the coalition government saw their total vote fall to 14.7% from 53.4% in 1999. Additionally, the opposition leaders were voted out. Tansu Çiller's True Path Party won just 9.6% of the vote as compared to 12% in 1999 (Jenkins, 2003). For further details, see Carkoglu (2002).

fared well only in some western provinces, while it fell below 10% in the southeast. The MHP succeeded in doubling its vote, doing especially well in western and southern Turkey. Undoubtedly, the MHP benefited from the rise of nationalism in Turkey stemming from disenchantment with the long drawn-out process of joining the EU, increasing opposition to membership from countries such as France and the resurgence of terrorism by the PKK.

According to Kerem Oktem, the AKP succeeded in establishing itself in the societal centre. Moreover, it has now emerged as the only political party that enjoys strong backing across Turkey, and has a legitimate claim to represent both Turks and Kurds, a substantial proportion of the Sunni Alevi community and virtually all social classes.[4] At the same time, the CHP – the oldest Turkish political party, whose logo consists of the six arrows which represent the foundational principles of Kemalist ideology: republicanism, nationalism, statism, populism, secularism and revolutionism – has practically ceased to be a national party that enjoys support across the regional and ethnic divide. Instead, it has become 'a regional party rooted in Turkish identity politics' (Oktem, 2007).

Moreover, the results of the 2007 elections indicate that patrician loyalty to modernisation as a top-down process 'has outlived the ability to impose such a Jacobin trajectory'. What is emerging is a country 'less beholden to the military-civilian elite that drove modernisation from above, but is more diverse, more inclusive and, dare one say it, more modern' (Oktem, 2007).

3 Modernisation the Islamic Way?

The past five years have revealed a very interesting trajectory in the evolution of political Islam in Turkey and the friction between secular and religious outlooks within the Turkish society. Key elements of the Kemalist tradition that guided Turkish perceptions and policies since the foundation of the Republic – secularism, statism and orientation to the West – have come under severe strain. This was particularly evident in the events that led to the 22 July general election. Two aspects of domestic change are particularly important: the rise of Turkish nationalism and the polarisation of 'secular' and 'religious' elements in Turkish society.

As far as nationalism is concerned, a strong sense of it has always been imbedded within Kemalist culture, and has traditionally supported the process of Turkey's modernisation and Westernisation. The fundamental assumptions underpinning Kemalism have been widely shared among Turkish elites. However, a more vigorous nationalist sentiment has been visible in Turkish society and the body politic since the end of the Cold War. The emergence of independent Turkic republics in Central Asia and the Caucasus stimulated a lively debate in Turkey over the prospects for

[4] Surveys show that around half of the voters in the lower- and middle-income groups supported the AKP, while around 35% percent of upper middle class and 23% of upper-income groups did likewise. See Oktem (2007).

new ties based on ethnic affinity. This pan-Turkic potential was taken up by elements of the nationalist right and was embraced in a milder form by mainstream parties as well as Turkey's active business community (Khalilzad et al., 2000, p. 2). At the same time, the violent Kurdish insurgency in south-eastern Turkey, led by the PKK, and a more general rise in Kurdish political activism provoked a nationalist reaction across the political spectrum.

This reaction continues today; the nationalist impulse has been reinforced by thc post-Iraq War experience and the very disquieting prospects of an autonomous Kurdish state/province in Northern Iraq backed by the US. Even in moderate circles, this residual concern encourages the view that, without considerable vigilance, Turkish sovereignty and national interests may be 'sold out', even by strategic partners in the West (Akcakoca, 2006, p. 24).

At the same time, the flux in Turkey's relations with the EU and the stalling of the EU accession-talks process in December 2006 have contributed to the rise of nationalism. Although the AKP was able to establish a national consensus around EU accession with a high level of support among the population, public opinion began to shift as Turkey entered the accession-negotiations phase in 2005, for a number of reasons. First, the anti-Turkish mood in many European quarters, expressed in the continued talk of a 'privileged membership' as an alternative to full membership, open-ended talks or eventual 'safeguard clauses', came as a shock to many Turks. Second, the European perspective has not so far resolved Turkey's basic nationalist dilemma. A Turkish elite and public that have grown accustomed to a more vigorous assertion of Turkish nationalism – often in opposition to European preferences – found themselves facing an enormous challenge. Never before have Turkish elites had to confront the dilemma posed by a strong nationalist tradition and a powerful attachment to state sovereignty, on the one hand, with the prospect of integration in a sovereignty-diluting EU, on the other.

Both issues have contributed to declining public support for the accession process. Nationalists in Turkey have been quick to capitalise on this growing public disenchantment with the EU, and some political parties that previously saw EU membership as a crucial part of Turkey's democratisation and modernisation development have joined the Euro-sceptic camp. The national consensus has been fading away, with every reform being portrayed as a concession to an insincere, hostile, not-to-be-trusted Europe.

At the level of public discourse, the nationalist reaction was led by a coalition of anti-liberal forces, made up of retired generals and their civil society organisations, elements of the security services and far-right groups. The nationalist counter-movement was not confined to symbolic politics but expressed itself violently with assassinations – most notably the murder of the Turkish-Armenian journalist and activist Hrant Dink in January 2007 – and mob attacks. Parallel to these tactics, a wave of prosecutions was mounted against public intellectuals such as Orhan Pamuk, Elif Shafak, Ragip Zarakolu and Baskin Oran to name but a few.

The constitutional crisis of summer 2007 showed that although a lot has changed in Turkey in the 2000s, the mindset of the secular establishment has not followed (Chislett, 2007b, p. 3). This was due also to some steps taken by the

AKP government, which have not helped the party's image with secularists: the effort in 2005 to outlaw adultery, the attempts by some mayors to create alcohol-free zones, the issue over the Islamic headscarf and, most importantly, the policies to create loopholes allowing students at the *imam-hatip* schools (IHS) to transfer to academic high schools before graduation, thus granting them preferential treatment when going on to non-theology majors in university (Cagaptay, 2007, p. 4).[5]

The secular elite feared that if the AKP controlled the presidency as well as the Parliament and government, the system of checks and balances that guarantees the secular character of the state would disappear (Chislett, 2007a, p. 2).[6] That is why, since 1972 and the entry into the Parliament of the MSP, the secular block and/or the military has constantly intervened with successive bans. Successive bans that have had no effect, however. Indeed, quite the reverse, as the 2007 election results show. What the secular establishment failed to comprehend is that Turkey's Islamism is more a movement than a party and, as such, has managed to sustain political momentum despite the bans. As Chislett has noted (p. 2), 'the AKP is a bottom-up movement which has successfully challenged the authoritarian, centralized top-down paternalism of the political system'. Traditionally, Islamism in Turkey was built on and legitimised by a strong anti-Western attitude. In the late 1990s, however, the AKP realised that they needed the West in order to confront the Kemalist tradition. They acquired systemic legitimacy by engaging in democratic and human-rights discourse and began to challenge the secularist elite (Devrim, 2007, p. 4). At the same time, secularism, while the bedrock of the Republic founded in 1923 by Atatürk, is equated more with westernisation and modernity than with democracy. Kemalism was a state-centred, elite-defined and illiberal modernisation project. Secularism and liberal democracy are not viewed by the Kemalist establishment as necessarily complementary, as they are in the West. The military, in particular, in their self-perceived role as the guardians of the secular and unitary state, occupy the paradoxical position of 'safeguarding' democracy while at the same time being the major impediment to Turkey's true democratisation.

This was more evident in the events following the summer 2007 crisis and the election of Abdullah Gül as President of the Republic. The election of Abdullah Gül constituted a serious setback for the military, which – unusually – had remained silent. For the first time, the military had to accept a President from an Islamist tradition, with a wife wearing the Islamic headscarf. However, what followed shows that the crisis is much deeper than some believe.

[5]Since the rise of the AKP government, however, the number of IHS students has increased. In 2005, 108,064 students attended the IHS.

[6]The President, who swears an oath of allegiance to the 'secular nature of the Republic', is Commander-in-Chief of the armed forces, responsible for the appointment of judges, top members of the administration and university rectors and has a veto power over laws approved by parliament.

The Turkish Parliament's landmark decision to change the constitution and lift the ban on Islamic headscarves in the universities represents a symbolic watershed in the history of the Turkish republic. It has polarised Turkey as perhaps never before and plunged the country into a crisis from which it will be extremely difficult to extricate itself without deep convulsions. The constitutional amendment was apparently the trigger for the appeal by the Chief Prosecutor to the Constitutional Court, seeking the closure of the AKP. The appeal requested the banning of Prime Minister Erdoğan, President Gül and dozens of other AKP members from politics, on account of subverting the secular order.

The widespread perception is that the real force behind the case was the military. Indeed, this perception appears to be dominant in the AKP as well. It was probably no coincidence that on the same day that the Chief Prosecutor was to deliver his oral argument in the case to the constitutional court, the government ordered the arrest of two dozen suspects, including two former four-star generals, in an investigation directed at militant secularist groups allegedly conspiring to undermine the government.

What this sequence of events suggests – in particular the Ergenekon arrests – is that Turkey finds itself in a novel situation, without historical parallel. The AKP is not only resisting the secular establishment's attempt to safeguard the Republic's secular system; it is actively fighting back against the secular establishment, including the military. At the end of the day, the events since the summer of 2007 show the intensity of the struggle for power by an old guard that is tied to the establishment and threatened by the new forces of the AKP, whose growing power is leading to the transformation of Turkey's social and political character. The outcome is not easy to predict.

Turkey has by all accounts reached a critical point in the contest between Islam and secularism. The country could drift towards growing authoritarianism, be it of a religious or a secular nature. Meanwhile, the democratic third way appears increasingly squeezed between the two extremes. The AKP's policies seem to offer justification to all those who suspect it of a secret Islamicisation agenda. As far as the secular camp is concerned, it has once again resorted to a countermeasure that will find few supporters internationally, and that will further contribute to the ideological isolation of Turkish secularism from the West. The problem is that Turkey's secular tradition has historically been the vector of Turkey's Westernisation, and thus of its democratisation. The current and very peculiar situation, whereby Turkey's moderate and centrist secular forces lack strong representation in the political spectrum, and where traditionally pro-Western, secular forces are increasingly tempted by an isolationist neo-nationalism, raises the critical question whether or not a secular Turkey can reconnect to the West.

Ultimately, the future of Turkish democracy depends on a societal consensus being reached between the secular and conservative halves of the country. By exacerbating existential tensions – about religion, lifestyle and identity – the AKP has reduced the likelihood of such a consensus. The negative impact on a sustainable democratic process at this critical juncture of Turkish political development cannot be underestimated.

4 Conclusion: Qualifying the Future

Greece and Turkey share common land and sea borders and they both have extensive coastlines along the Aegean Sea. The geographic imperatives of both countries can moderate actions as well as provoke them. These imperatives are long term and can transcend governments and ruling elites. They are also interconnected, so that if one imperative is altered it will probably affect others. A sincere and viable rapprochement between Turkey and Greece can only be the outcome of a novel bilateral structural arrangement that would include two fundamental elements: first, there should be a gradual and constant redefinition of the two countries' national interests, which would allow a historic convergence of interest-based strategies. This process is possible considering the current power locations of the two actors, as well as the interplay of their respective domestic publics. In other words, the presence of large socio-political majorities that favour the current process is vital and must be sustained at any cost. Second, it is imperative that for at least as long as the process of rapprochement remains fragile and weak, a 'healthy', transparent and thus stabilising balance of power should remain the overarching principle of the bilateral structure. Such a structural constraint would, above all, make the cost even of an accidental clash extremely high, while adding, at the same time, value to the hard effort of rapprochement.

What makes the Greek–Turkish conflict appear intractable is, above all, its subjective dimension, namely the incredible psychological barrier resulting from years of antagonism and enmity. Like most ethnopolitical conflicts, the Greek–Turkish conflict is characterised by a total lack of mutual confidence, suspicion bordering on paranoia and demonisation of the 'other'. In the final analysis, the state of relations between Greece and Turkey is a product of the attitudes and perceptions of ruling elites and the general public operating within global and regional settings. However, developments of the past decade show that historic patterns can change.

Overall, the two countries are much better off today in terms of bilateral relations than they were a few years ago. Under the – delicate – spirit of rapprochement currently reigning between the two countries, the prospects for a crisis or increased tension have been drastically curtailed and new, uncharted territory for peaceful coexistence, transactions and communication has opened. Having said that, it should not be forgotten that there has been no real attempt to address the fundamental differences between the two countries. This situation is unsustainable in the longer run. The longer that bilateral relations remain uncertain, the easier it becomes to return to the dangerous pre-1999 status of protracted tension. The difficult issues that continue to divide and haunt both countries should be addressed, sooner or later. It should be noted, however, that good planning and patience are vital prerequisites. Nobody should expect that decades of animosity and hatred will easily be overcome. Perceptions need to change, but this will happen gradually. Trust must be built up, and bureaucracies and populations must be prepared for change. Nobody should forget that these are not issues for interested parties to experiment with, and it is counterproductive to pressure either country into taking too many risks without having a good expectation of the outcome. Stable relations do not mean abandoning or compromising national interests.

The process has been rather cost-free so far, but in a well-planned and sincere strategic interaction, real progress could be forthcoming.

Rapprochement is intimately linked to the positive development of the relationship between Ankara and Brussels. Stagnation of or deterioration in the EU–Turkey relationship would almost definitely complicate and perhaps threaten the Greek–Turkish rapprochement. With Ankara's candidacy confirmed, Turkey's relations with the EU have become less uncertain. At the same time, however, they have moved into a more highly structured and legalistic pattern, with fixed criteria and fewer opportunities for arguments on strategic grounds. While joining the EU increasingly emerges as Turkey's best strategic option, for most Greeks, Europe is the only actor powerful enough to transform Turkey into a modern democratic state.

Greece has an overwhelming stake in a positive outcome for Turkey's EU accession process. A collapse in Turkey–EU relations, unlikely but not inconceivable, would overthrow the strategy of engagement and 'anchoring' vis-à-vis Ankara, and could revive traditional sources of bilateral tension in the Aegean and Cyprus, putting Turkish contingencies back at the top of the Greek defence agenda, with all that this would imply for national budgets, political energy and interests elsewhere. To most Greeks, future developments will be dependent upon the following:

First, the preservation of the prospect of full membership for Turkey. Other options short of full membership would undermine the strategic depth of the Greek engagement strategy of Turkey. A privileged partnership scheme would most probably result in removing from the EU–Turkish agenda all those issues that have made the Turkish accession process strategically attractive to Athens (human and minority rights, normalisation of relations with Cyprus, pressure on the Aegean issues etc.). It would satisfy some parts of the 'old' elites in Turkey, and the 'Turkosceptic' coalitions in Europe but it would be a bargain that would not confer any real gain for Greece. On the contrary, it would result in the neutralisation of its EU bargaining chips vis-à-vis Ankara. Such a development, without prior settlement of the Greek–Turkish disputes, would most probably be perceived by Athens as highly unattractive, even damaging, and it would result in a return to the 'age of veto'.

Second, Turkey's ability to positively respond to Greek 'openings'. It should not escape us that most of the changes have come on the Greek side. There has been no major shift in Turkish policy. Without a Turkish gesture to match Greece's lifting of its veto on Turkey's EU candidacy and its subsequent support for such a candidacy, it may prove difficult for Athens to maintain domestic support over the long run. Indeed, the Greek government operates with the benefit of the doubt even within its own party.

Third, Turkey's willingness to fully adopt the *acquis* and structurally internalise the changes that it entails. The first step is to realise that the accession negotiations are not the place to bargain. There is no choice but to proceed decisively with full implementation of all the changes required.

Fourth, the Cyprus issue. Without progress based on the reality of Cyprus being a sovereign member of the UN and a full member of the EU, the current rapprochement will be hard to sustain over time.

Finally, Turkish domestic developments. From the perspective of Greek–Turkish as well as EU–Turkish relations, three aspects of domestic change are particularly significant: (1) the rise of Turkish nationalism; (2) the polarisation of 'traditional' and 'modern' elements in Turkish society; and (3) the emergence of a more dynamic private sector and a new constellation of interlocutors for continuing engagement with the EU (and Greece).

References

Akcakoca, A. (2006). *EU-Turkey relations 43 years on: Train crash or temporary derailment?* (Issue Paper 50). Brussels, Belgium: EPC, November.

Akcapar, B., & Chaibi, D. (2006). Turkey's EU accession: The long road from Ankara to Brussels. *Yale Journal of International Affairs, 1*(2), 50–57.

Cagaptay, S. (2007). *How will the Turkish military react?* (Europe-ARI 80/2007). Madrid, Spain: Real Instituto Elcano, July 16.

Carkoglu, A. (2002). The rise of the new generation pro-Islamists in Turkey: The Justice and Development Party phenomenon in the November 2002 elections in Turkey. *South European Society and Politics, 7*(3), 123–156.

Chislett, W. (2007a). *Turkey's military throw down the gauntlet* (Europe-ARI 51/2007). Madrid, Spain: Real Instituto Elcano, 7 May.

Chislett, W. (2007b). *Turkey's election: Islamists deal a blow to the secular establishment* (Europe-ARI 86/2007). Madrid, Spain: Real Instituto Elcano, 24 July.

Devrim, D. (2007). *Blockade of the Turkish presidential elections: A clash of wills between moderate Islamists and the secular establishment* (Europe-ARI 59/2007). Madrid, Spain: Real Instituto Elcano, 28 May.

Ifantis, K. (2007). Turkey in transition – Opportunities amidst peril. *Journal of Southern Europe and the Balkans, 9*(3), 223–231.

Jenkins, G. (2003). Muslim democrats in Turkey? *Survival, 45*(1), 45–61.

Khalilzad, Z., Lesser I. O., & Larrabee, S. (2000). *The future of Turkish-Western relations: Toward a strategic plan.* Santa Monica, CA: RAND.

Oktem, K. (2007). Harbingers of Turkey's second republic. *Middle East Report Online.*Retrieved from http://www.merip.org/mero/mero080107.html/, 1 August.

Öniş, Z. (2005). *Turkey's encounters with the new Europe: Multiple transformations, inherent dilemmas and the challenges ahead.* Unpublished paper presented at UACES Conference, Zagreb, Croatia.

Ozel, S. (2003). After the tsounami. *Journal of Democracy, 14*(2), 80–94.

Rumelili, B. (2003). Liminality and perpetuation of conflicts: Turkish-Greek relations in the context of community-building by the EU. *European Journal of International Relations, 9*(2), 213–248.

Tsakonas, P., & Dokos, T. (2004). Greek-Turkish relations in the early twenty-first century: A view from Athens. In L. G. Martin & D. Keridis (Eds.), *The future of Turkish foreign policy.* Cambridge, MA: MIT Press, pp. 101–126.

Greek–Turkish Peace Processes as Autopoietic Systems

Eugenia Vathakou

1 Introduction

This chapter examines the Greek–Turkish peace processes attempted from the aftermath of the crisis of 1996 until the earthquake of 1999. These are peace initiatives undertaken by governmental organisations – of the two countries or of third parties such as the EU or the US – and non-governmental organisations. More specifically, the focus here is on the emergence and development of peace processes involving negotiation and mediation, peaceful conflict resolution workshops and conferences bringing together Greek and Turkish academics, journalists and other professionals.

The relevant literature on Greek–Turkish relations is confined mainly to the analysis of initiatives undertaken by governmental agents and places the emphasis mostly on bargaining processes. It does not ask how – if at all – these processes are connected with each other and with their environment – that is, the society within which they emerge and develop. It does not pose the question how it can be that several peace initiatives have been launched over the last few years but no progress has been made with regard to the issues of the conflict. The literature has not questioned what practitioners say in unguarded moments – namely, that an important obstacle to the success of governmental peace initiatives is the resistance of the Greek and Turkish societies to accepting a compromise with regard to the issues of the conflict.

The chapter explores the emergence and development of governmental and nongovernmental initiatives, considering them to be essentially similar in terms of their constitutive elements, their nature and their potential to bring about a change in the conflict. Accordingly, peace processes are approached as highly complex social systems of interaction constituted on the level of communication. They come about through the a-causal synchronisation of parallel ongoing processes – multiple connections among selective occurrences of communication. The task, from a second order perspective, is to disentangle these connections. In other words, this chapter explores the semantics with which various systems refer to the system/environment distinction and how these semantics affect the information processing of these systems; that is, their orientation towards peace

C. Arvanitopoulos (Ed.), *Turkey's Accession to the European Union*

and cooperation. The chapter makes a contribution to the overall theme of the book inasmuch as it provides important analytical insights into the potential impact that progress in Turkey's European integration may have on Greek–Turkish relations. It is demonstrated that the impact of Turkish integration can contribute to the dynamics of communication directed to cooperation and peace as well as to conflict, independently of the resolution of the issues of the conflict itself.

This chapter is divided in two main parts. The first describes various Greek–Turkish peace processes. The second part analyses them using Luhmann's modern systems theory. The chapter is based on fieldwork conducted in Turkey and Greece and involves primary source material gathered through more than 20 interviews with Greek and Turkish politicians, diplomats, academics, journalists and civil society representatives.

2 Greek–Turkish Peace Processes as a Field of Experimentation

This section explores the emergence and development of several Greek–Turkish peace processes launched by governmental and civil society organisations after the crisis of 1996.

The crisis of 1996 served as a stimulus; it increased the complexity of the conflict and motivated politicians, scientists, businessman and civil society organisations to undertake various initiatives, such as negotiation, mediation, problem-solving conflict resolution workshops (PSWs) and academic conferences, that could improve communication between Greeks and Turks.

Nevertheless, it is argued here that these peace processes were not the result of a rational decision-making process nor were they motivated only by one objective, such as peace. They emerged and developed through the a-causal synchronisation of parallel ongoing recursive processes of communication in the course of society's autopoiesis.

2.1 Governmental Initiatives

The crisis of 1996 was the stimulus for the peace initiative launched by Turkish Prime Minister Mesut Yilmaz in a press conference on 24 March 1996. Yilmaz invited Greece to enter into negotiations with Ankara on all the outstanding issues between the two countries, without preconditions. Additionally, he stated that Turkey was ready to 'discuss with good will, appropriate third-party methods of settlement' and would not, 'from the beginning, exclude any method of settlement including third party arbitration' (Syrigos, 1998, p. 365). This latter part of the statement marked an important change in the traditional Turkish stance, which had sought resolution solely through bilateral negotiations – that is, through political and not judicial means.

The emergence of this initiative reflects the perception of Yilmaz and his advisors that after the Imia/Kardak crisis a basis of support for a peace initiative had been formed among a broad constituency in Turkey.[1] This was also in accordance with what they perceived to be the background of the emergence of the crisis. Yilmaz himself criticised both former Prime Minister Tansu Çiller and the Turkish bureaucracy for escalating the Imia/Kardak crisis for political reasons. Finally, the Turkish leadership had to deal with the repercussions of the crisis and Turkey's failure to gain EU funds due to a post-crisis Greek veto.

Nevertheless, this initiative failed to bear fruit. At first sight it seems that the Greek government rejected it (Athens News Agency Daily Bulletin, 26 March 1996). However, the Greek Prime Minister, Costas Simitis, sent a message through Turkish businessman Sarik Tara to Yilmaz, saying that he could not undertake any action prior to his impending party congress, which was to take place in June.[2] When Simitis was ready, following his election as president of his party, Tansu Çiller had already succeeded Mesut Yilmaz to the Turkish Premiership. It was no surprise that there was no follow up by Çiller to the initiative; Çiller had accused Yilmaz, when the latter announced this initiative, of making concessions contrary to Turkey's national interests.[3]

On the other hand, the Greek answer to Yilmaz's initiative reflected its perception of its environment in the aftermath of the crisis of 1996. When the Turkish Prime Minister made this proposal, Simitis was under pressure from the opposition parties, as well as from opposition within his own party, which accused him of yielding to Turkey during the Imia/Kardak crisis. Journalists and analysts argue that if Simitis had shown signs of reconciliation with Turkey three months before his party's congress, he would have committed political suicide, because the anti-Turkish wing of PASOK had been strengthened following the crisis.[4] The selection of an unofficial envoy to communicate with Yilmaz demonstrates acknowledgement by the Greek Prime Minister of the existing 'boundaries' within Greek society.

Another effort was made on 27 April, when the Greek and Turkish Ministers of Foreign Affairs met in Bucharest. There, they agreed to explore the possibility of

---

[1] Interview with Ambassador Yalim Eralp, who was Yilmaz's advisor at that time, Istanbul, 4 May 2002.

[2] Interview with Ambassador Yalim Eralp, Istanbul, 4 May 2002.

[3] According to people who were close to Tansu Çiller, she wanted to present a similar proposal to Greece should she become Prime Minister. Nevertheless, when Yilmaz launched this initiative she took the opportunity to attack him for not protecting Turkey's interests. Interview with Ambassador Yalim Eralp.

[4] Interviews with the Greek journalist Nikos Georgiadis, Chief Editor, *Exousia*, Athens, 15 March 2001 and Alkis Kourkoulas, *Athens News Agency*, Istanbul, 5 October 2001. See also Athanassopoulou (1997).

bilateral negotiations and arranged to meet in May in Berlin. These hesitant steps were to be reversed after the Gavdos crisis.

This crisis emerged during the planning meetings in Naples, on 30 May, for the military exercise 'Dynamic Mix', when the Turkish representative to NATO suggested that Turkey considered the island of Gavdos to be a disputed area and for that reason it should not be included in NATO's operational planning. The island of Gavdos is located hundreds of miles away from Turkey, south of Crete. According to Article 4 of the London Peace Treaty of 1913, Turkey renounced all sovereign rights over Crete and Gavdos.

It is important here to explore the connection between the claims of the Turkish officer and the peace process that was underway. Discussions with Turkish officials and a careful reading of the relevant evidence demonstrate that these claims had not been preceded by preparation within the Turkish Foreign Ministry. In fact, Turkish officials, caught by surprise, tried to play down this incident.[5] The Foreign Minister made a statement maintaining that 'the Turkish representative at the NATO meeting had not made a political statement but a technical announcement' (Turkish Daily News, 6 June 1996).[6] Nevertheless, when these claims were disseminated in Greece through the news media, to an audience particularly sensitive to these kinds of claims, they immediately gained the kind of publicity connected with the themes of Turkish expansionism and the plans of the Turkish military against Greek sovereignty. The Greek government had to demonstrate its determination to protect Greek national interests, which it in fact did by expressing a strong reaction and pulling out of the talks. Furthermore, it used this episode to expose Turkey within the international community as aggressive and not respectful of international law and the agreements it had signed.[7]

The crisis in Kosovo, which escalated with NATO's military intervention in March 1999, offered an opportunity for close cooperation between the then newly appointed Greek Foreign Minister, George Papandreou, and the Turkish Foreign Minister, Ismail Cem. The stream of refugees fleeing Kosovo towards the neighbouring countries was a motivation for cooperation between the two countries. The two Ministries coordinated their activities regarding refugee camps and the dispatching of aid to refugees, as neighbours to the crisis and members of NATO.

---

[5] That this incident was not planned by the Turkish Ministry of Foreign Affairs was also confirmed by people within the Ministry in interviews with the author. See also the newspaper article regarding this issue written by the retired Turkish Ambassador to Washington, S. Elegdag. 'Every time there is a political vacuum in Turkey, and governments do not inspire respect and confidence in the military, there emerges a diarchy' (*Milliyet*, 17 June 1996).

[6] See as well as the written statement of the Turkish Foreign Minister, Emre Gonensay, that the Gavdos issue was a 'military technical' matter and not a political one (*Turkish Daily News*, 6 June 1996).

[7] Ambassador Elegdag, in his article in *Milliyet*, writes as follows: 'Our position on the issue of Gavdos was wrong and cost Turkey a great deal. Not only did we give the advantage to our adversaries but we created a situation that could harm our interests in the Aegean dispute and could mar the image of Turkey … The only viable move left to us would have been to recall our representative at the headquarters of NATO in Naples, saying that "he transgressed his orders" and definitively close this matter' (*Milliyet*, 17 June 1996).

Apart from initiatives undertaken by the two governments, several initiatives were also launched by other states within the parameters of international organisations like the EU and NATO. Hans Van Mierlo, President of the EU Council of Ministers and Dutch Foreign Minister, proposed the establishment of a 'Committee of Wise Men' to resolve the Greek–Turkish differences. The proposal was made in April 1997 in the Maltese capital, during the Euro-Mediterranean Conference.

The European initiatives for facilitation of a Greek–Turkish rapprochement should be examined in the context of the implications Greek–Turkish relations have for the three-way Greek–Turkish–EU relations.[8] As Greece's policies towards Turkey often appear to conflict with the interests of the European Union, the EU countries have tried to facilitate a rapprochement, which would ease the tension between the two countries.[9]

This initiative too was never pursued. Its development is described by Professor Couloumbis, a member of the Committee, as follows: 'It was December 1997, just prior to our first meeting, which was meant to be a discussion on procedural matters. At that time, the Luxemburg Summit was convened. The decisions of the 15 about Turkey were a real blow to Turkey'.[10] On 16 December 1997, the EU made it clear that Turkey was not on the list of the countries with which the EU would initiate membership talks. Meanwhile, it confirmed that negotiations on the accession of Cyprus to the European Union were to start in 1998. 'The Turkish Ministry of Foreign Affairs, reacting to that decision, intervened in the process of the Committee. It asked for the activation of the committee of "Wise Men" between the two governments and their Embassies, not through the "evil" EU. The Greek government did not reject this proposal but it replied that this was an initiative undertaken by the EU. Finally the Committee was never activated'.[11]

2.2 Civil Society Initiatives

The term 'civil society initiatives' refers here to PSWs, as well as to conferences and meetings among journalists, academics, business people and other professionals organised by non-governmental agents. The undertaking of the examination of PSWs together with other civil society initiatives might appear unconventional to the reader of conflict resolution literature. Mainstream theory discusses PSWs separately from initiatives like conferences, for example, because it is argued that the rules of

[8] The German Foreign Minister Claus Kinkel, in an article he wrote for *Frankfurter Allgemeine Zeitung*, underlined that the key to Turkey–EU relations was Greek–Turkish relations (*Ta Nea*, 16 February 1998).

[9] See the statements by Commissioner Van den Broek concerning this development, where he pointed out that the release of the MEDA funds for Turkey was considered very important for the relations of the EU with Turkey, the economic interests of the EU as well as for the problems in the Aegean and Cyprus (*Eleftherotypia*, 23 October 1996).

[10] Interview with Professor Theodore Couloumbis, Athens, 3 September 2001.

[11] Interview with Professor Theodore Couloumbis, Athens, 3 September 2001.

organisation and conduct applied to the workshop are specific. This distinction is not followed here. From the social systems perspective, these rules are considered to be social structures, part of the complex environment of the interaction, that guide the selections of psychic and social systems and constrain infinite complexity.

As will be demonstrated below, this approach is also justified by the results of empirical research. Indeed, most of these meetings, whether they were called PSWs or whether they were conferences among academics or meetings of organisations like the Journalists for Peace in the Aegean and Thrace or WINPEACE, involved elements of PSW theory. That means that either the organisers invited a facilitator from a conflict resolution institution to facilitate the meeting or that the meeting was organised by one of the big conflict resolution institutions and/or the participants had experience with these kinds of workshops and applied these rules. On the other hand, the name of the workshop – specifically a PSW or more generally a meeting among Greeks and Turks – or the name of the organiser should not be considered as an indicator of the rules finally applied. It seems that even meetings organised by reputable conflict resolution institutions do not always follow the rules of contact that every basic conflict theory handbook includes. Some of the workshops were not successful in terms either of facilitation or of organisation. Among the complaints often raised by Greek and Turkish participants to several PSWs is that these rules were disregarded. For example, participants felt they were rushed to sign a document that would ultimately justify the role of the organisers.[12] Evaluations show that lack of preparation, which is often reflected in the choice of participants, was another factor contributing to the failure of several PSWs among Greeks and Turks.[13]

In what follows, civil society initiatives are explored as enforced selectivity towards cooperation. Furthermore, their development depends on their complexity and the complexity of their environment.

2.2.1 Helsinki Citizens Assembly[14]

The Greek HCA was the first civil society organisation to undertake a peace initiative in the aftermath of the crisis of 1996. The Greek branch of the organisation contacted the Turkish HCA and together they organised a conference, which was attended by about 50 Greek and Turkish opinion leaders, politicians, retired diplomats, journalists and academics in March 1996.

[12] Interviews with the President of the Greek HCA Paulina Lampsa, Athens, 19 February 2001; Ambassador Costas Zeppos, Athens, 14 September 2001; Gülden Ayman, Assistant Professor of International Relations, Marmara University, Istanbul, 29 June 2003.

[13] Interviews with Nimet Beriker, Assistant Professor of International Conflict Analysis, Sabanci University, Istanbul, 14 March 2002; Costas Zeppos, retired Ambassador and member of the Greek–Turkish Forum, Athens, 14 September 2001; Paulina Lampsa, Athens, 19 February 2001.

[14] The Helsinki Citizens Assembly (HCA) is an institution born in Prague in 1990 out of the euphoria that developments in Eastern Europe had generated. It has national branches in Europe aiming to promote European integration and to serve the causes of democracy and human rights by reinforcing civil society initiatives.

The President of the Greek HCA, Paulina Lampsa, explained the rationale for this initiative as follows:

> [U]ntil that time [the crisis of 1996], Greeks and Turks were cooperating in the framework of the international organisation, HCA, at the level of civil society, basically in multiparty activities. We had neither thought about nor aimed to promote some kind of bilateral activity. This may be because the nature of the problems were technical and gave the impression they required specialised knowledge or that some problems were frozen between the two countries.... When the crisis of 1996 happened, some of us thought the frozen problems were not only the concern of the governments and the military, but that these were problems that concern our personal, everyday lives, and our interests, the interests of ordinary citizens. We could not stay indifferent, especially because of the way the crisis happened in Imia. It was not a crisis where a military aircraft enters and violates the national airspace and there is a quarrel, which is somehow clearly military. It was a crisis caused partly by journalists and the mayor of Kalymnos, people who belong to civil society. And we realised that this concerns us and we could not leave it there without any reaction. It could be the starting point for more systematic contact between people who shared the same thoughts.... We believed that a strong, public reaction was required or things were at risk of getting much worse. Bridges would be broken and that would be very dangerous at the official level.[15]

This narrative demonstrates that the cooperation/conflict difference found connections on the side of cooperation in the semantics of the role civil society had played and should play in the developments between the two countries. The existing structures of the HCA organisation, with its institutionalised cooperation with the Turkish branch of the HCA, further enabled the realisation of this conference, constraining complexity towards the direction of cooperation. The Greek HCA contacted the respective Turkish organisation because, as Lampsa says, 'we cooperated with them in the past and we trusted them.... They made the choice of the Turkish participants'.[16]

Nevertheless, the HCA did not continue its activities after the meeting in Nauplio because, despite the efforts the Turkish HCA made, they could not find the resources to organise a meeting in Turkey.[17]

2.2.2 Journalists for Peace in the Aegean and Thrace

The movement Journalists for Peace in the Aegean and Thrace was initiated in February 1996 and has, since its foundation, a long history of meetings and contacts between the two sides of the Aegean Sea. These contacts are not confined to journalists, as the name of the organisation might suggest. The movement has developed a network of people and organisations working for the promotion of cooperation and friendship in the region of the Aegean Sea and Thrace.

---

[15] Interview with the President of the Greek HCA, Paulina Lampsa, Athens, 1 September 2001.

[16] Interview with the President of the Greek HCA, Paulina Lampsa, Athens, 1 September 2001.

[17] Interview with the President of the Turkish HCA, Professor Murat Belge, Istanbul, 27 September 2001.

The idea for this initiative was conceived by two Greek journalists, Stratis Balaskas from the island of Lesvos and Giannis Tzoumas from the island of Chios; the two islands are located opposite the Turkish coasts.

After living through the crisis of 1996, Balaskas and Tzoumas were concerned by the developments in Greek–Turkish relations, both as journalists and as islanders. They were concerned as journalists, because it was the first time they realised journalists were not only reporting but creating events. They were also concerned as islanders living on the borders with Turkey. Suffice it to refer to Balaskas's words: 'the night of the crisis we were called on by the army and dressed in a military uniform. Although the next morning we were dismissed, this was enough. If I am to die, I want to know why. For what should I die?'[18]

This initiative also reflects the perception the founders of the organisation had of their local environment. Balaskas explains that they knew the geography and the history of the region and met people from both sides. They believe that Turks and Greeks have a similar mirror image of the enemy that does not reflect reality.

The stimulus for this initiative was an article in the Greek newspapers about a statement made by Turkish journalists, condemning the attitudes of some of their colleagues during the Imia/Kardak crisis.[19] After they read this article they sent a fax to the *Yeni Asir*, a newspaper published in Izmir, the biggest city on the Turkish coast opposite their islands. The person who received their fax

> [w]as the best possible person to receive that letter, Suleyman Yonsel. Yonsel is a descendant of Turks from Crete. His origins and his family's memories motivated him to learn more about Greek–Turkish relations. He had lived in Athens for some time in the past where he learned Greek. Additionally, he had conducted research on the co-existence of Greeks and Turks during the nineteenth century.[20]

After Yonsel's positive reply, the organisation was set up and many Greek and Turkish journalists soon joined. One of them was Ioannis Tzanetakos, who became the Director of the Greek State Radio Station in 1998. After his appointment, he launched an initiative for cooperation among journalists in the Balkans, making Greek–Turkish cooperation an important part of this project.[21]

In the case of this initiative, the difference cooperation/conflict continuum found points of connection in the journalist's professional code of conduct, the sudden awareness of the possibility that a journalist might be forced into the role of soldier and the background of a culture of peaceful conflict resolution and cooperation.

Research on the development of this movement demonstrates that it was also dependent on its own complexity and that of its environment. For example, its annual meeting, planned to take place in Komotini at the end of January 1999, was postponed several times. Initially, it was postponed until April, after the organisers received warnings from hard-liners, a car bomb destroyed the car of one of the organisers and another bomb was placed opposite the General Consulate of Turkey

---

[18] Interview with Stratis Balaskas, *Eleftherotypia*, Athens, 20 September 2001.

[19] Interview with Stratis Balaskas, *Eleftherotypia*, Athens, 20 September 2001.

[20] Discussion with Süleyman Yönsel, Komotini, 27 March 2002.

[21] Interview with Ioannis Tzanetakos, Athens, 7 March 2002.

in Komotini.[22] The climate of tension the Öcalan crisis created in mid-February 1999 led to a further postponement of the meetings of this NGO, this time without a future date being fixed.

2.2.3 Businessmen

Business leaders have always been at the forefront of efforts to improve Greek–Turkish relations. The reason for this is that there are great opportunities for economic cooperation between the two countries and thus for making profits. Nevertheless, this is conditional on a stable political climate (Tsardanidis, 2000).

The crisis of 1996, in particular, endangered the plans business leaders had made for the immediate future. The Customs Union Agreement signed between Turkey and the EU in 1995, which should have come into force after 1 January 1996, raised high expectations for joint ventures and economic cooperation, which would increase profits for business leaders on both sides. The crisis of January 1996, however, created a climate unfavourable to any entrepreneurial activity.[23]

Business leaders' reaction to this situation was a series of meetings to discuss ways to overcome the seemingly endless political obstacles to the development of trade and economic relations (Athens News Agency Daily Bulletin, 10 December 1996; *Radikal*, 11 December 1996). Apart from their capacity for lobbying and their efforts to enhance cooperation in the economic field, they also financed many academic conferences, scholarship programmes, meetings of journalists and research programmes. The structural couplings among different systems such as the system of the economy, the system of education and the system of media through these activities enabled new possibilities of communication and increased the rate of structural change.

Nevertheless, the development of this process was also dependent on its environment, as were the other processes. In February 1999, the President of the Turkish side of the Greek–Turkish Chamber of Commerce, Rahmi Koc, denounced cooperation 'with Greek businessmen in protest of the aid Greece offered to the Kurdish leader' (*Naftemporiki*, 25 February 1999). This reaction was framed by the climate created after Öcalan's arrest in Turkey, a climate marked by fierce polemics in the Turkish media against Greece. The devastating earthquake that occurred in August 1999 put this initiative back on track.

2.2.4 International Peace Research Institutes

Several recognised international academic and research institutes were involved in the reconciliation efforts between Greece and Turkey between 1996 and 1999. Among them we find the well-known names of the Carnegie Endowment, the Royal

[22] Interview with Jenny Katsarea, publisher of the local newspaper, *Komotini Paratiritis*, Komotini, 01 November 2001.

[23] Interview with Ambassador Costas Zeppos, Athens, 14 September 2001.

United Services Institute for Defence Studies (RUSI) and the Norwegian Peace Research Institute of Oslo (PRIO) in a joint project, Harvard University, the Fletcher School of Law and Diplomacy, the Conflict Research Group at Yale, the Konrad Adenauer Foundation and the Search for Common Ground Foundation. Some of them organised conferences and workshops with Greeks and Turks on a regular basis. At times these kinds of projects were implemented in cooperation with Greek and Turkish academic institutes and think tanks. At other times, professionals from the above institutes were invited to attend and/or facilitate meetings organised by Greek and Turkish civil society organisations.[24]

Undertaking these initiatives requires an idea developed into a proposal for a conflict resolution programme and funds to enable its realisation. The main sources of financing are international governmental and non-governmental organisations and individuals such as Greek and Turkish business people.[25] These initiatives emerged through structural couplings among various social systems like the system of science, organisations specialised in conflict resolution, the systems of economics, politics etc. The paper will present the details of a joint programme, organised by RUSI and PRIO, which gave birth to the Greek–Turkish FORUM, a civil society initiative that has a special place in the Greek–Turkish process of reconciliation.

The Greek–Turkish Forum

The Greek–Turkish Forum was born out of an initiative undertaken by the Director of the Roberts Center, James Bruce Lockhart.[26] Lockhart initially proposed the project to the RUSI. Later, the PRIO was also invited to participate in the project (Tsardanidis, 2000).[27] RUSI initially hosted a meeting of some 30 opinion leaders from the two countries. Most of them had been involved in the conflict because of their past or present professional positions as journalists, academics, ex-politicians, ex-diplomats and ex-military officers. The first meeting was held in 1997 at Wilton Park in London.

Two years later and after several transformations, the Political Analysis Group (PAG) with 15 members emerged out of this large group of people. The PAG has discussed complex issues of the conflict such as the demarcation of the continental shelf in the Aegean Sea, and it has managed to come up with elaborate proposals for its resolution.[28]

---

[24] The yearly summer conference of the Hellenic Foundation for European and Foreign Policy (ELIAMEP) in Chalki was facilitated by a professional from George Mason University. Interview with Kemal Kirişci, Istanbul, 3 October 2001.

[25] Interview with Theodore Couloumbis, Professor of International Relations and Director of ELIAMEP, Athens, 3 September 2001. Interview with Dan Smith, PRIO's Director for 8 years and currently Senior Adviser of PRIO, Istanbul, 14 October 2001.

[26] Interview with Dan Smith, Istanbul, 14 October 2001.

[27] Interview with Dan Smith, Istanbul, 14 October 2001.

[28] See the paper the Forum produced on its web page, http://www.greekturkishforum.org/.

For James Lockhart, a British Foreign & Commonwealth Office (FCO) diplomat who became director of the Roberts Center after his retirement, the stimulus was the crisis of 1996. He conceived the initial idea, which he proposed to RUSI, and also found the sponsor for its realisation, the British FCO. For Great Britain, the prevention of an open conflict in the Aegean between two NATO allies was important. The crisis of 1996 was perceived as an alarm signal. After the end of the Cold War, there was no longer a common enemy to bind Greece and Turkey together under NATO's umbrella. In this new international environment, a Greek–Turkish war appeared to be possible.[29]

Furthermore, according to Dan Smith,

> [t]he goal of the first meeting was simply to find ways of building bridges between Greece and Turkey. The feeling or the analysis of that moment was that the situation was so bad that any contact was better than the existing situation.[30]

After the first meeting, PRIO was invited to join the project and offer its experience in facilitating PSWs. Norway then undertook the burden of financing this project. The rationale for Norway was twofold. On one hand, the motive was simply altruistic. On the other, it matched the profile Norway had been developing over the years as an important actor promoting peaceful conflict resolution in the world.[31]

This presentation demonstrates the multiple causality involved in the emergence of this process. From the point of view of its development, the Greek–Turkish Forum managed to get over the obstacles thrown in its way from the time of its inception in 1997 until the earthquakes in 1999. The Öcalan crisis was a turning point for the group, which, however, reinforced its bonds of trust and solidarity. At the first meeting after the crisis, they decided they should meet more often. The Greek members of the Forum and the facilitator, Dan Smith, agree on the important role played by Turkish members of the Forum, especially by Ambassador Ilter

[29] This is how members of the forum, as well as Dan Smith, perceive the involvement of the British Foreign Office in this initiative.

[30] Interview with Dan Smith, Istanbul, 14 October 2001.

[31] Norway became known for promoting peace and conflict resolution facilitation after the back channel communication it provided between two old enemies, the Israelis and Palestinians, in 1993. However, at that time, Norway's role was neither perceived nor planned as such. The Oslo process was more the result of the personal initiatives of individuals than due to a governmental decision. It was only later that Norway decided to capitalise on this success. Three factors played an important role in this decision: the first was the publicity the Oslo process gained as a successful peace initiative and thus the prestige Norway gained. The second factor was the negative result in the referendum on Norway's membership in the EU. It is important to note here that Norway, which has a particular national interest in energy matters, found itself outside of the Ministerial Council of the EU on energy, in 1995. This was a traumatic experience, which pushed it to seek for a new place in the international community. This led to investment in and further institutionalisation of the peaceful conflict resolution section. Last, but not least important, peaceful conflict resolution fits Norway's self-image, which is characterised by a low and dialectic profile. Interview with Dan Smith, Istanbul, 14 October 2001.

Turkmen, the coordinator of the Turkish section of the Forum. Ambassador Turkmen's stance was determined by two main factors.[32] One was his previous professional experience of Greek–Turkish crises from within the Turkish Ministry of Foreign Affairs. These experiences had formed his firm belief that, even at the most critical times, communication should be sustained. Another factor was that the Forum, and thus its Turkish members, had not been exposed to publicity. That helped them to continue their work quietly, without risking accusations, in Turkey, of cooperation with the 'enemy'.

3 Analysis: Introducing New Perspectives

The focus of conventional analyses of peace processes is primarily the interaction among state representatives or, if the discussion concerns PSWs, the interaction among the participants in the workshop. This approach reduces the analysis of peace processes to a static description of the process isolated from its environment.

Modern Systems Theory demands that we probe into the complexity that defines the emergence and determines the development of peace processes, taking into account the system/environment relationship that is constitutive of the system. The above description sought to illustrate the multiple causality involved in peace processes by pointing to many functionally equivalent causes that cannot be reduced to either actions or individuals. Neither was there one motive – for example, the improvement of Greek–Turkish relations or the value of peace as such – that enabled their emergence. This conclusion would be an over-simplification of the complexity involved in every peace initiative.

The development of peace processes depends not on social structures, as discourse analysis would probably argue, but on the coincidental structural, that is, unintended, couplings among various interdependent social systems. Institutionalised practices of conflict resolution, interests of organisations and programmes of action/goals became points of connection that guided the choices of different social systems towards cooperation.

And yet, it is the simultaneity of the system/environment relationship and its complexity that determined the emergence of peace processes as combined selectivity.

An important aspect pointed out here was also that *time* is a functional equivalent to social structures. Different time frames structurally coupled with each other increased contingency and constrained complexity. Time frames constrained the domain of communicative possibilities for further connections of the emerging peace processes.

For the political system, time was structured by elections, for the press, by the next edition and for a peace initiative by dates that had been set. The change in the Turkish Premiership doomed Yilmaz's peace initiative to failure, the Gavdos crisis

---

[32] Interview with Ambassador Ilter Turkmen, Istanbul, 13 November 2001.

undermined the process that had been initiated by the two governments, the Kosovo crisis offered the occasion for cooperation. The Öcalan crisis affected the activities of civil society organisations.

This new perspective leads to a new definition of peace processes as *temporalised complexity*. The dynamics of peace processes are found in the dynamics of communication; that is, in the connectivity and selectivity of communication in a society. Thus, the instrumental view of peace processes is replaced here by the more productive description of a peace process as 'a field of experimentation' in a functionally differentiated society. The development of peace processes is part of the broader process of society's autopoiesis. They are constituted through the normal operations of social systems that fulfil their functions according to their own rationale, aims and programmes of action/goals.

This perspective illuminates the constitution of peace processes as morphogenetic. The various peace processes came into being through autocatalytic deviation, amplifying mutual causal processes of communication. The cooperation/conflict difference that emerged after the crisis of 1996 was amplified through multiple connections among existing social systems on the side of cooperation. The paradoxical nature of these processes is further exposed if we remember that their stimulus, the crisis of 1996, was not a necessary development.[33]

4 Conclusion

The relevant literature on Greek–Turkish relations, following an intuitionist analysis, argues that the crisis of 1996 led to deteriorating Greek–Turkish relations. Furthermore, when it comes to conflict resolution, it mostly focuses on bargaining processes guided by an instrumental rationality.

This chapter showed instead that the crisis triggered a number of peace processes that were undertaken by governmental and non-governmental agents. The emergence of the peace processes described above was not imposed by any necessity or any kind of objective historical law. Moreover, their development did not follow one rationale such as the rationale of peace. Rather, the increase in complexity and the need for its reduction led to the emergence of the various initiatives in a highly complex, multi-centred modern society as *temporalised complexity*. The examples of the Greek–Turkish peace processes clearly illustrate that these processes were independent and autonomous from one social system or a particular rationale.

The system/environment perspective of modern systems theory employed here emphasises that selection is part of the dynamics of peace processes, which further means that these are contingent emerging orders.

Luhmann's theory explains that the process of connecting the various initiatives is self-referential and every change is self-change. The institutionalised aims of the

[33] For more on the Imia/Kardak crisis, see Vathakou (2003).

EU and NATO, institutionalised Greek–Turkish economic interests, a culture of an active civil society and women's movements were points of connection along the cooperation–conflict continuum on the side of cooperation. The modelling of the complexity within complexity in interactions like PSWs and conferences hastened structural couplings and enabled the emergence of new social structures.

This perspective enables us to see that there are multiple paths to peace depending on the interconnection of a system's complexity, contingencies and sensitivity to information. These cannot be identified and mapped out as conventional analysis has attempted to do. Furthermore, the same analysis touched upon another aspect of the autopoiesis of Greek–Turkish relations; namely, that there are multiple paths to conflict, too, not just the one involving the protection of national interests. Every time that a peace process was hindered, the recursive processes of communication about the conflict won the day.

Finally, to connect this chapter with the major theme of the book, if the evolution of Greek–Turkish relations depends on the complexity and contingency of their environment and the connectability of the themes of conflict or cooperation, the process of European integration on one hand has increased the complexity of the environment of the Greek–Turkish conflict, creating structures such as themes, roles and institutions, which guide the operations of different social systems in the direction of peace. On the other hand, however, examples like the ones discussed here demonstrate that there is also the potential for the emergence of chains of multiple connections among existing social systems on the side of conflict.

References

Athanassopoulou, E. (1997). Blessing in disguise? The Imia crisis and Turkish–Greek relations. *Mediterranean Politics, 2*(3), 76–101.

Syrigos, A. M. (1998). *The status of the Aegean Sea according to international law*. Athens: Sakkoulas/Bruylant.

Tsardanidis, C. (2000). The Greek-Turkish economic relations, 1999–2000. In *Review of defense and foreign Policy*. Athens. ELIAMEP, 407–419 [in Greek].

Vathakou, E. (2003). *International crisis and peace processes as autopoietic systems in world society: Examples from Greek-Turkish relations*. PhD. Thesis, University of Kent at Canterbury.

Turkey and the Identity of Europe: Contemporary Identity Politics on the European Frontier

Dimitris Keridis

1 The Debate: Turkey's Europeanness in Question

According to the 1957 Treaty of Rome, the founding document of the European Economic Community, for a state to join, it must be European.[1] That treaty and subsequent EU treaties have avoided defining the term 'European'. In the language of Brussels, this is euphemistically termed 'creative ambiguity', according to which the costs of defining who is European exceed the benefits. Thus, while it is generally accepted that enlargement is a finite process, the exact limits of Europe, especially towards the east, have remained open-ended. Practically, the question arises in the case of Turkey and Russia. Whereas Russia has, for the time being, shown no interest in joining the EU and its case might arise only in the distant future, Turkey has been an associate EU member since 1963 and becoming a full member is its top foreign policy priority.[2]

The question of Turkey's Europeanness, a precondition for entering the European Union, is constantly under discussion. In principle, the matter was settled at the EU Summit in Helsinki in December 1999, when Turkey was accepted as a legitimate

[1] According to Article 237, 'Any European State may apply to become a member of the Community. It shall address its application to the Council which, after obtaining the opinion of the Commission, shall act by means of a unanimous vote. The conditions of admission and the amendments to this Treaty necessitated thereby shall be the subject of an agreement between the Member States and the applicant State. Such agreement shall be submitted to all the contracting States for ratification in accordance with their respective constitutional rules' (Treaty Establishing the European Economic Community, 1957). In the same way, Article 1 of the European Constitutional Treaty drafted in 2003 stated that 'The Union shall be open to all European States which respect its values and are committed to promoting them together' (Treaty Establishing a Constitution for Europe, 2004).

[2] The official website of the Ministry of Foreign Affairs of the Republic of Turkey states that 'The first goal is to make Turkey an integral part of the European Union', http://www.mfa.gov.tr/synopsis/.

C. Arvanitopoulos (Ed.), *Turkey's Accession to the European Union*

candidate state.[3] 'Helsinki shifted the question from essentialist considerations of Turkey's Europeanness to functionalist considerations of Turkey's preparedness' (Nicolaidis, 2004). Then and there, European leaders, regardless of European public opinion, agreed that Turkey is a European nation, at least in the sense of the Treaty of Rome, and that it has every right to become a full member, provided it complies with the *acquis communautaire*. In that sense, Turkey is no different from other candidate countries like Croatia. It would be foolish, however, to think that this is so.

No matter what the official policy statements are, Turkey's candidacy is intimately intertwined with Europe's current identity politics, as former French President Giscard d'Estaing (2002) made famously and plainly clear. This is a matter that should not be ignored but be dealt with openly and honestly. Otherwise it is bound to poison Euro–Turkish relations and accession negotiations.

2 The Politics of Identity

It is often said that we live in an era of identity politics. It is true that with the collapse of the Soviet empire and the global Left after 1989, ethnic, religious and cultural identities have become the focus of much attention and provided the explanatory framework for many conflicts in today's world. Traditionally, identity was an analytical category favoured by anthropology. Political science, being historically more positivist and materialist, has been a late convert.

The term itself and its applications remain fairly elusive. Identity is often confused with culture. Frequently, it is left ill-defined, open-ended and all-inclusive. In this sense, identity has been allowed to dominate political thinking in an unprecedented and often risky way. The problem is that if identity explains everything, it risks explaining nothing. Thus, identity should be acknowledged but also contextualised. It should be connected with other categories, such as class and material interests, and their interdependence and dialectic interaction properly analysed.

Identity is part of the world of ideas. The division of reality into matter and ideas is as old as Plato and beyond. Many have studied the interaction of matter and ideas, including, first and foremost, Karl Marx himself.[4] For Marx, ideas and the ideational universe of individuals were simply dependent on the material relationships provided by the modes of production. Later, beginning with Antonio Gramsci, thinkers of the Marxist tradition attempted to invest ideas with some autonomy in defining social reality beyond or even in opposition to material interests. The intent

[3] According to Conclusion 1.12 of the Presidency of the Helsinki European Council of 10 and 11 December 1999, 'The European Council welcomes recent positive developments in Turkey as noted in the Commission's progress report, as well as its intention to continue its reforms towards complying with the Copenhagen criteria. Turkey is a candidate State destined to join the Union on the basis of the same criteria as applied to the other candidate States'. See European Council (1999).

[4] For a good introduction to the question of the role of ideas in foreign policy making and international relations, see Goldstein and Keohane (1993).

was to explain some of the paradoxes of twentieth-century politics, including the widespread popular support for fascism in interwar Europe and, more broadly, the failure of political democracy to turn into economic democracy or the fact that the universal franchise did not lead to massive economic redistribution, as was initially expected and feared.

But identity is more than an 'idea'. It is a widely shared system of beliefs and values that creates a community and the sense of belonging among many individuals. More than its content per se, an identity creates a collective 'we' in opposition to 'them'. This function of identity in forming communities is most crucial. Because humans are social beings, they look to join a wider grouping. In today's atomised and alienating world, in which traditional identities are often in crisis, this need is even more pronounced. Often, people do not care much about the ideas of the group they have joined, as long as their need for belonging is satisfied. A teenager who registers with a communist youth organisation knows little and understands even less of Marxist philosophy – nevertheless, he does register, often mostly for the feeling of camaraderie.

While ideas are fairly abstract and work at an intellectual or elitist level, identities have to do with the masses; it is only in that sphere that an idea becomes politically powerful. Very few ideas have the potential to bridge the elite level and the masses: in the past, the religious, the national and the communist idea did. The European idea has not yet reached that potential but many would like it to, and it has already made some progress towards that goal, despite occasional reversals.

Thus, while identity originates in the ideational world, it has real material consequences and produces distinct political results. Moreover, identities are historically constructed and socially conditioned. In other words, identities might be slow to form, but they evolve over time, as history and their social context gradually change. It would be a mistake to see them as static and inalterable. In this way, national identities emerged in eighteenth- and nineteenth-century Europe and, during the twentieth century, in much of the rest of the world. Finally, identities overlap and amalgamate into all sorts of combinations. Today, European identity coexists, sometimes happily, sometimes not, with national and/or regional and local identities.

3 Europe's Identity

Is there a European identity? If there is, in what does it consist? And who belongs to the European community created by European identity? Since identities create communities and communities are defined in opposition to the rest of the world, these are questions with serious political implications.

Let us try to be clear: in the past, there was much talk about 'Europe' and a common European civilisation. This sense of Europeanness was reinforced in the eighteenth century by the Enlightenment and made its way first to Eastern Europe, the lands east of Prussia – mainly Russia (Wolff, 2001) – and then to the Orient, starting with the Ottoman Near East and later the colonised Third World. In this long historical process of the emergence of a common European historical consciousness, World War II was the cataclysm that brought about a new Europe.

Europe's identity was radically transformed by World War II and its consequences. The war unleashed unprecedented levels of violence and, in the process, resulted in the massive redefinition of Europe's self-image, role and position in the world. This was, after all, first and foremost Europe's civil war. The destruction caused led to the questioning of many aspects of European modernity. It delegitimised not only fascism and its authoritarian excesses, but the very idea of the moral superiority of Europe vis-à-vis the rest of the world. Without that moral superiority, there was no basis for the continuation of colonialism other than naked force, of which post-war Europe was in short supply. For the first time in memory, Europe was no longer the master not just of the world but even of its own destiny, as it was divided by and dependent on the two superpowers.

Defeated, traumatised, morally, politically and economically bankrupt, withdrawn from the world and virtually consumed by the demands for reconstruction, post-war Europe embraced a new identity in opposition to both its past and its powerful contemporaries, the United States and the Soviet Union. With few exceptions, this new Europe no longer had global ambitions but was introverted and self-absorbed. It was a Europe in which the use of force, militarism and extreme nationalism had no place in inter-state relations. This was a departure from Europe's historical past, which had been dominated by antagonistic and authoritarian states.

It is also a Europe where human rights take precedence over state rights and democracy is the only game in town. Determined to leave behind old and destructive polarisations, this new Europe has geared public policy towards smoothing social tensions and promoting social solidarity and cohesion, practised thorough-going income redistribution and valued equality almost as much as freedom. While nations have not withered away, a certain Kantian transformation has taken hold, in favour of trade, cooperation and interdependence. This transformation is nowhere more pronounced than in Germany. It is in this way that this new Europe resolved its old German question. If a German Europe was defeated in war, a European Germany would prevail in peace.

While the United States played a crucial role in both the defeat of fascism and the fostering of a new Europeanness through the defence of liberalism, the introduction of an activist New Deal state, the generous aid of the Marshall Plan and the security umbrella it has provided to Western Europeans, this new Europe has become increasingly defined in opposition to America and American culture and identity.

The two sides of the Atlantic practise a different kind of capitalist free market politics; in Europe the levels of taxation, regulation, environmentalism, social protection and unemployment are all much higher than in America. Furthermore, a historical reversal occurred: whereas America started as a mercantile republic with a miniscule standing army and limited foreign ambitions or colonial impulses, after World War II it built a robust military-industrial complex, according to the famous warning of US President Dwight Eisenhower (1960). If the 'war party' was defeated and politically marginalised in Europe after World War II, in the United States it established its political hegemony during and after the Cold War. The two sides look at international relations differently: Europe instinctively wants to project its own successful Kantian experience onto the rest of the world. Thus it supports the deepening institutionalisation of interstate relations, while the United States remains loyal to a more Hobbesian (or Clausewitzian) paradigm that trusts force and its use as the main 'currency' and the ultimate arbitrator in international politics (Kagan, 2004).

During the Cold War, the presence of a common Soviet threat helped paper over these differences and both sides had no interest in making too much out of them. With the collapse of the Soviet Union and Cold War antagonism and the emergence of the United States as the sole superpower, the differences between the two sides of the Atlantic community were bound to become more pronounced. As their politics have diverged – especially with the emergence of a radical new right in the United States (Keridis, 2008) – away from the old common post-war liberal consensus, there are many in Europe who seek a common bond in opposition to the all-too-powerful United States. For them, to be European is to be anti-American.

As for the Soviet Union, for all the heroic and often attractive and popular narrative of the European Left, while it existed, this new, post-war Europe of the Stalinist east was very distinct. This was true even in European countries such as Austria and Finland where the Soviets had some influence. The European *modus operandi*, for all the activism of the European post-war state, remained fundamentally different from that of the Soviet Union. This was felt by all when the Berlin Wall fell in 1989.

4 Turkey and European Identity

The fundamental argument of this essay is that Turkey's Europeanness can be questioned mainly because the country did not participate in World War II. Contrary to what is often claimed – that Turkey is not European because it is a Muslim country or geographically lies largely outside Europe – most important is its non-participation in Europe's defining moment, in the birth convulsions of the new Europe, which has had a number of important consequences, both in regard to Turkey's international image and self-image and in regard to its political development.

Turkey participated in World War I and at Gallipoli one can see the graves of Turks, fallen in the battles of 1915–1916, buried side by side with Englishmen and other fellow Europeans. Blood bonds; Turkey did participate as a European nation in the fundamentally European war of World War I. But it did not participate in World War II. If World War II made the United States a European power, it broke Turkey's long association with the European inter-state system. By choosing to stay on the sidelines, Turkey came to be regarded by fellow Europeans as an alien, Asiatic country geared more towards the Middle East than the Balkans and Europe. One could say the same for Spain, but the Spanish Civil War is justifiably claimed as the prelude to World War II and, in that sense, Spain did participate in the great conflict, both physically and ideologically.

It is quite ironic that what was thought back then as a blessing and a diplomatic triumph of President Inönü, keeping the country safely out of the war and its repercussions, has come back to haunt Turkey. Why is that?

Since the establishment of the Turkish Republic in 1923 after the fall of the Ottoman Empire, Turkey has been ruled by a hybrid and eclectic ideology, widely referred to as Kemalism after its founding father Mustafa Kemal Atatürk. Kemalism has been many things and has proved quite adaptive over time. Its basic premisses continue to define Turkish politics and be forcefully applied by the Turkish military, judiciary and, more broadly, the state bureaucracy. Thus, understanding Kemalism is a necessary introduction to the politics and current political realities of Turkey.

One way to analyse Kemalism is to view it as a continuation and reformulation of Ottoman reformism that was initiated with the Tanzimat movement in 1839 and was reinvigorated with the revolution of the Young Turks in 1908 (Lewis, 2001; Zurcher, 2004). It is a modernist and nationalist program that asked for the emancipation of the Turkish nation from foreign influences and, in that sense, predated the post-World War II anti-colonial movements.

But the most important fact about Kemalism is that it came into being in the interwar period and was naturally influenced by the historical conditions prevalent at the time of its birth. In the interwar period, democracy, liberalism and parliamentism went through a deep crisis and collapsed in most of Europe. Authoritarianism and totalitarianism were popular and fascism and communism were thought by many to be the way of the future. The creators of the Turkish Republic were military officers schooled in the discipline, the hierarchical order and the obedience of the army and were unaccustomed, if not openly hostile, to liberal ideals and free thinking. When they looked around Europe for models and examples to follow, they saw Mussolini, Hitler and Stalin.

All these infused Kemalism with a deep-rooted authoritarian streak that has survived to the present day. By not participating in World War II, authoritarian Kemalism was not defeated nor was it delegitimised. It remained vibrant and dominant, an interwar ideology in a post-war world. Moreover, even if Turkey had been among the victors, if it had sided with Britain, its mere association with the liberal democracies of the West would have forced a clean break with the past and the full democratisation of the Turkish Republic after the war.

In reality, Turkey did somehow adapt. In search of a post-war alliance with the West against a threatening Soviet Union to the north, Turkey had to acquire a certain democratic façade. Competitive elections were introduced in 1950 and 2 years later Turkey was admitted into the North Atlantic Treaty Organization (NATO). But here is the catch: democratisation was never completed and Turkish democracy has remained unconsolidated. As far as democratic transitions go, Turkey's is one of the longest: it started in 1950 and still continues (Huntington, 1993). As a result, a perennially unstable, hybrid polity has come about in which elections take place and freedom of expression is, to a great extent, permitted, but popular sovereignty is not the sole foundation of the regime as it is in every other normal western democracy. Next to the people there are a few self-proclaimed guardians of the

Republic and its Kemalist ethos. They include mainly the military and the judiciary. They have intervened several times in the past in the democratic process and forcefully rebalanced Turkish politics.

More recently, 57 years after the first election of 1950, the Kemalist guardians or the so-called deep state struck again. In the spring of 2007, the military openly opposed the candidacy of Abdulah Gül for the Presidency of the Republic. The ruling AKP persisted, won the elections with an increased share of the popular vote and imposed the mildly Islamist Gül on the office first held by Atatürk himself. A year later, in the spring of 2008, the constitutional court of Turkey initiated a case against the ruling party and 71 of its members, including Prime Minister Tayyip Erdoğan and President Gül. It was widely believed that the court would ban the party and its leaders from politics. Although the process was provided for by Turkey's current constitution, which was drafted by the military regime of Kenan Evren back in 1982, it would have been without a doubt undemocratic to topple a recently elected and popular government, under the exaggerated, if not wholly fabricated, charge that it aimed to introduce Islamic sharia law to Turkey.

What these episodes make plain is that despite all the progress achieved so far and the constitutional changes introduced since Helsinki in 1999, Turkey's state structures suffer from a persistent democratic deficit that cannot be ignored nor wished away. This is the most anti-European feature of contemporary Turkey. Until the dualism in Turkey's polity is resolved and popular sovereignty is restored and respected as the sole source of authority, Turkey will be unable to share in full the common European identity.

5 The Promise Ahead

This essay has been careful to define Europe's identity in civic and political rather than in historical and essentialist terms. History matters, but recent history matters more. The argument here is that there is nothing divine, unalterable or primordial about the basic content of Europe's identity. This identity is the product of specific historical processes. In analysing these processes one should start from the recent past and then go back in time. It is ahistorical to ignore recent events, circumvent long time periods and focus exclusively on distant history in order to explain current conditions. Before talking about Christianity, the Renaissance, Protestantism or the Enlightenment, one should start with the twentieth century and mainly World War II, which, in Eastern Europe in some respects did not completely end until 1989, as the historical turning point for our Continent.

Everything matters but, overall, what is recent matters more. Popular perceptions and journalistic accounts continue to be dominated by essentialist arguments that equate Europe with a static understanding of a Roman, Greco-Roman or Judeo-Christian civilisation or, simply, Western Christianity. But it should be remembered that European leaders avoided introducing a reference to Europe's Christian roots in the preamble of the Constitutional Treaty in 2004.[5] This is not only because Europe is today culturally very secular and much of European politics in the past was strongly anti-clerical and opposed to the Catholic Church, it is also because it makes political sense.

It is worth remembering that there are both indigenous and immigrant Muslim communities in Europe today. The former are found mainly in Bosnia, Kosovo, Albania, Bulgaria, Greece and Cyprus. The latter are spread all over Western Europe: from the Indian subcontinent in Britain, from the Maghreb in France, Turks and Kurds from Turkey in Germany.

It is also worth noting that Islamic traditions vary in tenacity and, compared with some of these traditions, Turkish Islam has historically been extremely moderate, pragmatic, accommodating and adaptive. Even under the Ottomans, who thought of themselves as pious Muslims and derived legitimacy from Islam, secular law was widespread – the sultans were great legislators themselves and systematically made their own laws beyond the sharia.

The Ottoman Empire was built on and reinvigorated the imperial legacy and traditions of Byzantium (Iorga, 2000). In addition, beginning in early modern times Ottoman Turkey was a player in the European diplomatic game, allied with Catholic France against the Habsburgs and later with Protestant Britain against Orthodox Russia. In World War I, the Young Turks miscalculated colossally and allied Turkey with Germany against its former protector, Britain, causing the destruction of the empire. What is important is the very fact that Turkey was a part of the European world, the European balance of power and the European system of alliances. As has been said, Turkey was 'the sick man of Europe', but of Europe nevertheless.

By avoiding the essentialist argument about Europe's identity, one builds on the legacy of Europe's founding fathers in the 1950s: a vision of a post-national Europe, open and inclusive rather than defensive and xenophobic. This is an important policy choice given the current pace of globalisation and the changes it brings. If Europe wants to be a global player with an influence beyond its borders, it has to find a way

[5] The preamble reads: 'DRAWING INSPIRATION from the cultural, religious and humanist inheritance of Europe, from which have developed the universal values of the inviolable and inalienable rights of the human person, freedom, democracy, equality and the rule of law, BELIEVING that Europe, reunited after bitter experiences, intends to continue along the path of civilization, progress and prosperity, for the good of all its inhabitants, including the weakest and most deprived; that it wishes to remain a continent open to culture, learning and social progress; and that it wishes to deepen the democratic and transparent nature of its public life, and to strive for peace, justice and solidarity throughout the world, CONVINCED that, while remaining proud of their own national identities and history, the peoples of Europe are determined to transcend their former divisions and, united ever more closely, to forge a common destiny, CONVINCED that, thus "United in diversity", Europe offers them the best chance of pursuing, with due regard for the rights of each individual and in awareness of their responsibilities towards future generations and the Earth, the great venture which makes of it a special area of human hope, DETERMINED to continue the work accomplished within the framework of the Treaties establishing the European Communities and the Treaty on European Union, by ensuring the continuity of the Community acquis' (Treaty Establishing a Constitution for Europe, 2004).

to integrate a variety of traditions including, first and foremost, moderate Islam as best represented by Turkey.

In other words, Turkey's accession is a great strategic gamble that will, to a great extent, determine the future of Europe. In the meantime, it is worth remembering that no EU enlargement has been popular; public instinct has often favoured avoiding the mental changes and discomfort that the newcomers bring. Neither the Greeks in 1981 nor the Poles in 2004 were particularly welcomed. And yet enlargement has been Europe's most successful policy for the transformation of the continent into a model of cooperation, democracy and prosperity. If that was the case with southern Europe in the 1970s and Eastern Europe in the 2000s, it can be so with Turkey in the 2020s. It is precisely because the EU is more than free trade, it is such a great historical, transformational and political project, that Turkey's accession is necessary. With Turkey as a member in her own right, Europe will be more than a white, Christian, inward-looking club. It will be able to project a powerful positive influence on the Muslim world and beyond.

Because Europe's common identity is recent and was forged in World War II, it is also evolving and adoptable. So is Turkey's. Turkey might never become Protestant, although deep down some Kemalist fundamentalists might have wanted that, but it can become democratic. In other words, identity talk should not be avoided. Nor should it be ignored in the vain hope that it will somehow go away by itself. After all, we live in an age in which there is constant talk about identities of all kinds – religious, cultural, ethnic, gender, sexual and so on. Identity is part and parcel of politics and of our contemporary understanding of politics. But there is a right and a wrong way of talking about identity. The latter is often a cover for racist arguments that are based on an understanding of identity as something set in stone and inalterable over time. While we recognise our own ability to change and evolve, we deny this ability to others. Europe lost any claim to its own civilisational superiority long ago, above all during World War II. If Europe can change, so can Turkey.

6 Setting the Agenda Straight: Democratising the Republic

Identity is often an all-encompassing analytical category and a political refuge for all those who like simple and comforting truths. In the case of Turkey, identity has been used to deny its Europeanness and thus its entrance into the EU. Recognising Turkey's strategic importance and long association with Europe, opponents of Turkey like French President Nicolas Sarkozy propose a special relationship between Turkey and the EU as an alternative to full membership (Deutsche Welle, 25 May 2007; *Turkish Daily News*, 3 February 2007). This is empty talk at its worst. The reason is simple: Turkey already has a very special relationship with the EU. It cannot become more special than it already is. Turkey has been an associate EU member since 1963, a customs union with the EU has been in place since 1996 and Turkey is a regular participant in EU summits, albeit without voting rights. Neither Sarkozy nor others have made the effort to define in detail how they envision this proposed special relationship.

Turkey's identity is not fully European, not because Europe's identity is primordial and doesn't change, but because it is recent and has changed so much since World War II. The Kemalist project was European both in inspiration and orientation. For Atatürk, Turkey needed to westernise as much and as fast as possible, but since his time, the West and subsequently Europe has reinvented itself. The tragedy of Kemalism has been that it aspires to a Europe that no longer exists. This Europe of unyielding state sovereignty, authoritarian modernisation, national homogenisation and Jacobinian anti-clericalism was largely swept away with the bombs and the blood of World War II.

If Turkey is to remain European in orientation and aspiration, then Kemalism needs to reinvent itself. Guarding against Islamism is legitimate but the diehard Kemalists' suspicion of Erdoğan and his associates seems to have more to do with their anxiety about losing their power and privileges than any sincere interest in the health of Turkish democracy. After all, in the past the military had no problem cooperating with unreconstructed Islamists in its fight against the Turkish Left in the early 1980s or Kurdish nationalists after 1984. Too often, the military and its friends have engaged in a deliberate escalation of crises in order to polarise politics and derail the democratic process. But Turkey is no longer a patriarchal, agrarian and illiterate society, as was largely the case before the 1980s. Turkey has successfully modernised and, in the process, pluralised. Social and political controls are much harder to impose today than in the past. In a sense, Kemalism is the victim of its own success. It helped change Turkey but has not itself changed sufficiently and is increasingly becoming a straightjacket that Turkish society can ill afford.

A starting point for the convergence of Turkey with Europe is the drastic revision of the 1982 Constitution. Constitutional changes so far have been significant, but the basic spirit of the document continues to impose restrictions on a free, liberal and democratic society. It is a pity that Erdoğan did not use his landslide victory in July 2007 and his enhanced power thereafter to push courageously for the full democratisation of the Turkish Constitution. It is also true that, so far, his record has proved him to be a Europeanist out of convenience rather than conviction. But all politics everywhere is about what is feasible and involves imperfect compromises. The ruling AKP, albeit far from perfect, has already proved more liberal and more efficient in government than its secular predecessors. For this reason, Europe has been endorsing Erdoğan. It should continue to welcome Turkey, even after Erdoğan, if it wants to retain its influence in Turkish politics.

Furthermore, the generals and their allies should realise that turning back the clock is not an option. Turkish society is too restive and too integrated into the world to be controlled and restrained in the good old ways. The generals risk destroying Turkey's European aspirations at the very least and possibly a civil war. Banning the Kurdish party and the AKP that together represented 85% of the popular vote in Turkey's southeast (in the elections of 22 July 2007) would open the way to taking politics outside of parliament and straight into the mountains, renewing guerrilla warfare. In the meantime, the economy, more sensitive than ever to the volatile trust of investors, would undoubtedly suffer. All these factors mean that interference by the military would be a massive miscalculation and greatly detrimental.

There is still time to find a way out of the present impasse. But it will take a lot of courage and vision from all sides. Europe can provide an anchor and a framework within which all the players can feel safe. This is what Europe did during the Iberian, the Greek and the East European transitions to democracy. In Turkey's case, Europe can reassure the Kemalists that a democratic Turkey does not have to be an Islamic Turkey, while, at the same time, acknowledging and respecting the rights and cultural choices of Islamists and liberals.

Greece's role can be crucial and far above what its size might imply. The reason is that, due to past history, Greece's acceptance of Turkey carries unique symbolic significance. Simply put, if Greece can welcome Turkey as a partner within the broader European family, then everybody can and should. After all, Greece is a country that was founded in opposition to Turkey,[6] has fought numerous wars against Turkey and has had a rivalry since 1955 with Turkey over Cyprus and, later, over the Aegean.

Greek foreign policy should avoid falling victim to popular anti-Turkish perceptions. Sarkozy's position is not just anti-Turkish but should be viewed as anti-Greek. The reason is that, without Europe the normalisation of the Greek-Turkish relationship is infinitely more complicated. Ultimately, accepting Turkey requires a healthy redefinition of Greek identity (also by Turkey), a process that has already tentatively begun. Officially, Greek policy remains committed to Turkey's EU accession. This is positive. At the unofficial level, the rapprochement, with increased business, culture and social contacts, is proceeding at a great pace. At this time of crisis for Turkey and its relations with Europe, Greece should step in and use its influence and past 'anti-Turkish credentials' in Brussels to argue in favour of further engaging Turkey.

In conclusion: identity politics matter, especially in today's post-Cold War world. They heavily influence the debate over Turkey in Europe. They should be dealt with honestly and directly. Unfortunately, they have often provided a convenient cover for xenophobic populists who view any EU enlargement with distaste. However, identity politics should be put in their proper context and their historicity and evolutionary potential acknowledged. In particular, if the current European identity has been largely the product of World War II, without which there would not be a process of voluntary, democratically based European integration, then it is a more open and inclusive identity than many anti-Turks in Europe might want to admit. Turkey has a lot of homework to do in reforming and adapting its interwar Kemalism to the present European realities. This is both feasible and desirable. It needs proper management. But that is how today's Europe was created. At every step there were obstacles and popular resistance. Nothing was predetermined and it took a great deal of visionary leadership[7] to arrive at today's united Europe of peace and prosperity.

---

[6] This holds true for the Turkish Republic as well – it was established in the aftermath of the Turkish victory against the Greeks in 1922. In fact, Greece and Turkey are the two nations in the world that have fought their wars of independence against each other.

[7] For example, there should be no doubt that had it not been for Constantine Karamanlis, Greece would not have joined the EU in 1981 and might have had to wait until 1995, 2004 or 2007.

References

Eisenhower, D. D. (1960). Military-industrial complex speech, 1961. In *Public papers of the presidents, Dwight D. Eisenhower,* 1035–1040, http://coursesa.matrix.msu.edu/~hst306/documents/indust.html/.

European Council. (1999). *Helsinki European Council: Presidency conclusions,* SN 300/99, 10–11 December.

Giscard d'Estaing, V. (2002). Pour ou contre l'adhésion de la Turquie à l'Union européenne. *Le Monde*, 11 January.

Goldstein, J., & Keohane, R. O. (Eds.). (1993). *Ideas and foreign policy: Beliefs, institutions and political change*. Ithaca, NY: Cornell University Press.

Huntington, S. P. (1993). *The third wave: Democratization in the late twentieth century*. Oklahoma City: Oklahoma University Press.

Iorga, N. (2000). *Byzantium after Byzantium*. Bucharest: Center for Romanian Studies.

Kagan, R. (2004). *Of paradise and power: America and Europe in the new world order*. New York: Vintage.

Keridis, D. (2008). *The US foreign policy and the conservative counter-revolution*. Athens: I. Sideris [in Greek].

Lewis, B. (2001). *The emergence of modern Turkey*. Oxford: Oxford University Press.

Nicolaidis, K. (2004). Turkey is European … for Europe's sake. In *Turkey and the European Union: From association to accession*. The Netherlands: Ministry of Foreign Affairs, http://www.sant.ox.ac.uk/ext/knicolaidis/sortedpubs.htm#EUenlargement/.

Treaty Establishing a Constitution for Europe. (2004). *Official Journal of the European Union*, C310, 16 December, http://eur-lex.europa.eu/JOHtml.do?uri = OJ:C:2004:310:SOM:EN:HTML.

Treaty Establishing the European Economic Community. (1957). Rome, 25 March, http://eur-lex.europa.eu/en/treaties/dat/11957E/tif/TRAITES_1957_CEE_1_EN_0001.tif.

Wolff, L. (2001). *The Enlightenment and the Orthodox world*. Athens: Institute for Neohellenic Research, National Hellenic Research Foundation.

Zurcher, E. (2004). *Turkey: A modern history*. London: I. B. Tauris.

The Debate's Impact on Europe

Ranier Fsadni

1 A Neglected Vision of Europe and Turkey

It is said that the past is a foreign country: so discontinuous with what is taken for granted that to understand it one needs cultural translation. The precept is usually applied, however, to the distant past, not to a mere half-century ago. And when it comes to the origins and initial impulse behind the European project out of which the European Union has emerged, it is continuity of purpose and vision that is usually emphasised.

Yet when one turns to what Alcide De Gasperi, one of the founders of contemporary Europe, had to say about Europe and Turkey, an acute need arises for the services of a cultural anthropologist. For nothing in the contemporary debate prepares one for what De Gasperi (2004, p. 184; author's translation) said in his address to the Conference of the Round Table of Rome on 13 October 1953: 'In Europe there is not only Rome. How can one neglect or set aside the Near Eastern element, the Greek element, the African coastal element of the Mediterranean, the Germanic element, the Slav element?'

Although Turkey is not mentioned by name, it is clearly referred to in the phrase 'Near East', here distinguished from the Middle East. It is to be noted that he is not referring to an area that lies 'near' Europe – what today would be called the immediate neighbourhood – but 'in' Europe. He speaks of 'elements' rather than countries, but in a context where elsewhere he makes it clear that he does not think Europe can be limited to a physical geographic expression.

As if anticipating debates on the limits of enlargement, on the same occasion he also stated (2004, p. 182) that 'It is dishonest to accuse us of excluding the rest of humanity ... the family which we are creating excludes nothing.'

These are not words that belong to the same lineage of European thought that today argues for Turkey's membership in the EU on the grounds that 'people with different languages, cultures and religious beliefs can form a community, provided they subscribe to the same fundamental rules. That is why Turkey belongs in Europe' – to cite Bernard Bot (2004), the Dutch Minister of Foreign Affairs when the Netherlands occupied the EU Presidency in the second half of 2004. De Gasperi attached great importance to Europe's Christian identity (2004, p. 185); he was a

C. Arvanitopoulos (Ed.), *Turkey's Accession to the European Union*

major figure in Christian Democrat politics. But he was struck by the overlap between Christianity and Islam, especially when compared with other civilisations – such as those of the Far East. Europe and North Africa and the Near East share a heritage of monotheism and Roman law; for De Gasperi, salient factors shaping their respective identities.

So De Gasperi cannot be easily categorised in terms of today's European debate on Turkey (and Islam). He would certainly have been disappointed by the lack of explicit reference to Christianity's contribution to European identity in the constitutional treaty drafted by the Convention on the Future of Europe. Yet clearly, unlike many (though by no means all) Europeans who today would still like Christianity's historic contribution to the formation of Europe to be explicitly recognised, he did not take his preference to imply an objection to Turkey's membership.

If De Gasperi's position elicits any surprise, it is a marker of how much that position has been largely forgotten. Is this because the speech is marginal to his thought? No: the speech is to be found in the posthumous edition of his discourses on Europe, painstakingly collected by his daughter, Maria Romana De Gasperi, and published for the first time on the twenty-fifth anniversary of his death and reprinted on the fiftieth anniversary.

He clearly was not thinking just of the past, as his comment on the European project – that it 'excludes nothing' – indicates. In this he was at one with the other founders of Europe, who thought of their project as an intermediate experiment that would eventually lead to a form of governance in which all humanity would participate. Indeed, his thinking is of a piece with the Association Agreement that was signed with Turkey only 10 years after his speech.

2 Debate and Political Vision

That agreement, of course, was signed with a view to opening negotiations on membership. In the present writer's personal experience, it has not been easy to meet many Europeans ready to say, in an informal tête-à-tête conversation, that in 1963 this prospect was offered in full political seriousness. Otherwise astute and informed observers of European politics somehow explain it as an offer made in a moment of political glibness: 'They thought the moment would never really come', etc. Perhaps the glibness lies in this kind of explanation.

Glib explanations, made informally, do not carry political weight; but their cultural weight is more significant. The fact that few people seem capable today of explaining *why* the offer was made – that is, why it made sense to *those* political leaders with *those* political and cultural beliefs *then* – is a sure sign of how much the contemporary European cultural imagination has changed from those times: so much so, that the debate on Turkey makes little allowance for a vision like that of De Gasperi. Either the offer cannot be imagined to have been a serious one, or else it is justified in terms that make sense in the context of twenty-first century political and cultural beliefs, but which do not necessarily make sense of the actions of the European leaders *then*, in terms of what they thought they were doing and achieving by giving their commitment.

Over the last 50 years, the world has changed for Europeans in a way that has conspired both to obscure and to pre-empt certain options on Turkey from being canvassed. One set of changes has to do with Europe's institutional arrangements. Paradoxically, the shift to increasing global governance that the European founders looked forward to has placed in question 'the European model' that the same founders did so much to establish. De Gasperi was thinking of and debating European civilisation in self-confident terms; today, debate takes place during, and as part of, a European identity crisis. Indeed, if today there is something that may be called 'the politics of identity', not current in 1953, it is because today identity and authenticity seem to be precarious, provisional achievements. The historian Perry Anderson (1992, pp. 266–270), reviewing Fernand Braudel's *The Identity of France*, shows how the prevalent concern with 'national identity' has much to do with structural and cultural anxieties; and the same might be said about concerns with European identity.

Another set of changes has to do with what De Gasperi called the African coast of the Mediterranean and the Near East. In 1953, the State of Israel had just been founded and the first Arab–Israeli war had been fought. But the regional and international crises caused by Suez (1956), the Six Day War (1967), the Yom Kippur War (1973), the Israeli invasion of Lebanon (1982), the Palestinian intifadas (the first beginning in 1988) and the two Gulf wars (1991 and 2003–?) had yet to happen. There were still sizeable Christian communities in the region, apart from the Lebanon; not just in the Palestinian territories and in the still-colonised Maghreb, but also in newly independent Libya (1951) and the new Republic of Egypt (1952), in both of which there were several significant European settler communities. Thinking of 'Europe' as spilling over a bounded physical geography became more difficult when these communities were almost entirely effaced from the region. In addition, De Gasperi made his address when the reformist movement known as 'Islamic modernism' still exercised a strong influence: an impetus behind independence movements in North Africa and elsewhere, it had an open, inquiring attitude towards Western modernity. However, decades after independence, when the promise of Arab national liberation came to be widely considered bankrupt, a different kind of political Islam, 'Islamism', dominated the political-cultural landscape.

The point behind this thumbnail sketch is not simply to recall how much the sense of political possibility is shaped by the broad circumstances in which debate takes place. As historians of political thought like Quentin Skinner (2002) have shown, the terms of debate also shape those circumstances. The same point was a major theme of the late, great English political journalist, Hugo Young (1999), whose study of the United Kingdom's fraught relationship with the European project shows how the very terms in which the debate was conducted, from Churchill to Blair, served to illuminate or obscure, open up or pre-empt, possible courses of action.

One does not need, however, to stray from the subject at hand to illustrate the point. News reports have sometimes reported on the impact of the debate on membership on Turkish politics, how it feeds back into the political process and constrains what Turkish politicians may do. Should one not consider that the debate may also be constraining and shaping the European political process?

In one sense, this is obviously the case. Because of the controversy over Turkey, President Jacques Chirac promised French voters a referendum on the subject – a promise that may not strictly bind his successors, but which will certainly affect what they say and do. In other member states, Turkey's case is dialectically related to the identity politics concerning, for example, immigration and cultural policy.

The rest of this chapter, however, will focus on the less immediately obvious ways in which the debate itself is shaping European politics. (The impact on Turkey will not be explored.) Those in favour of Turkish membership speak of how Turkey will facilitate greater access – to energy sources, labour and Middle Eastern and Muslim counterparts; those against, of how Turkish membership would make Europe's current burdens heavier – straining an already limited budget, taxing an already troubled cultural identity further. How are these arguments about the future affecting the present?

The focus will be on two areas that seem to be the most important. One raises questions of cultural identity and policy – both that of Europe and of some of its immediate neighbours. The other concerns external relations.

The intention is not to arbitrate the debate. Indeed, it will be argued that on some significant points the two opposing sides share important assumptions, which the debate, by letting these assumptions go without saying, reinforces. More than that, some of these assumptions are obscuring or pre-empting European options.

First, however, something needs briefly to be said about the present writer's assumptions. Although no argument is made or implied either for or against Turkey's membership, the article is written by someone in favour of Turkey's membership if the Copenhagen political criteria are fulfilled. What would effect a change of mind would be if Turkey's membership were accompanied by a redefinition of the democratic arrangements of the EU, such that these arrangements discard the original European principle of according equal formal status, and votes, to all member states irrespective of their size, and become wholly biased in favour of population size. (At the Convention on the Future of Europe, the Turkish participants argued along these lines, and similar arguments are made independently in some European quarters.)

This concern, like some of what follows, shows how much the standpoint informing this chapter is rooted in a particular part of Europe: Malta, the smallest member state, situated on Europe's southern frontier, in latitude marginally below the northern tips of Morocco and Tunisia. But a perspective with a particular slant cannot be avoided.

3 Impact on Identity and Cultural Dialogue

Modern politics, ranging from the interpersonal to the international, is saturated with discourses about identity. The discourses are an outcome of economic and cultural conditions that disturb fixed images and narratives of the self and community.

'As an unfolding story', the sociologist Richard Sennett (2001, pp. 176–177) notes, 'an identity originates precisely in the conflict between how others see you and how you see yourself. The two seldom fit....' Sennett is interested in how the globalised economy has disturbed identities based on work and place ('home'); other writers, of widely different persuasions, have sought to explain both the increasing concern with identity ('the politics of recognition', to use Charles Taylor's [1994] sympathetic phrase) and to spell out its consequences for politics, culture, ethics and the management of global relationships (see, e.g., Appiah, 2006; Sen, 2006).

The political evaluations may be different, but there is broad consensus that cultural relations have begun to affect the dynamic of contemporary societies in important ways (e.g., Taylor, 1991; Touraine, 2005). It will demand not only theoretical understanding but also adequate cultural policies to address social relations within societies and between them. Like earlier discourses about, say, class struggle, discourses about identity can peddle myths as well as truth; but myths have political consequences too. Since, as Sennett points out, identity originates in conflict, identity talk is necessarily argumentative, political and, perhaps, partisan; it can create political conditions as much as reflect them; but this does not mean that it cannot be measured against some standard of plausibility in the light of what is best known about contemporary cultural life.

Given these considerations, how do the 'identity arguments' about Turkey's membership measure up? Do they illuminate real questions and point to plausible (however partisan) political solutions?

The overarching argument of what follows is that both sides of the debate tend to cover up more of the relevant issues than they illuminate.

3.1 *Arguments for Turkey's Membership*

The explicit arguments boil down to three: from countries like Spain and Turkey itself we hear that Turkey in the EU would mean that an 'alliance of civilisations' has been forged. For the second argument, we can borrow from former British Foreign Secretary Jack Straw (2007): 'By welcoming Turkey into Europe, we will prove how two cultures can not only exist together, but thrive together, as partners in the modern world. Accession means a more pluralist, tolerant and inclusive Turkey – and a more pluralist, tolerant and inclusive Europe.' The third argument was made succinctly by Bernard Bot (2004), then Dutch Foreign Minister: 'It demonstrates that Western nations have no insuperable prejudice against Islam. It will confirm Turkey's role as a nation whose Muslim heritage is fully compatible with democracy.'

The first two arguments will be discussed in a later subsection (see Self-Reinforcing Misunderstandings and Impact on External Policy, below). The third raises an obvious question: Who needs to learn that Islam is 'fully compatible' with democracy.

Bot suggests that it is Muslims themselves: he writes about a 'Europe that shows leadership and confidently promotes democracy and the rule of law in the Islamic world....' Yet surely the many activists for democracy in the Arab world already know this; they have repeatedly asked Europe to show more leadership by standing up to the undemocratic governments they oppose.

In addition, there is something odd about stating that one has no prejudice against Islam while presuming to lecture Muslims about their own religion. The patronising tone may be unintended but it is surely noted and felt by Muslims. The outcome for Europe's cultural dialogue with Muslim third countries may well be the opposite of what Turkey's membership is meant to achieve.

If, on the other hand, it is Europeans who need to learn that Islam is compatible with democracy, it is not clear that Turkey's membership would resolve the concerns that electorates like those of the Netherlands and France have shown. Such concerns need to be addressed by specific cultural and social policies for one's own society, not by pointing to another society elsewhere.

3.2 Arguments against Turkey's Membership

Just as the pro-Turkey membership arguments do not survive closer scrutiny, neither do the standard anti-Turkey arguments on identity. They boil down to two. First, that 'Islamic culture' is alien to Europe and the values that shape it; second, that opening the EU to Muslim nations will lead to political demands that will erode the cultural underpinnings of established European forms of life.

Admittedly, this summary brings together arguments that are clearly bigoted with others that are not; arguments based on crude caricatures of Europe and of Islam, and others informed by wide learning. However, even the sophisticated arguments of, say, Larry Siedentop (2000, pp. 189–214) and Pope Benedict XVI do not fit the best that is known about either the historic relationship between Europe and Islam or the various currents within Muslim thought and culture.

To show this would require very detailed argument and here one can only gesture at what such an argument would look like.

On Europe and Islam, the anthropologist Jack Goody (2004) has summarised the arguments: for better and for worse, Europe has been decisively shaped by its encounter with Islam and Muslims; popular culture, the arts, the landscape, the history of science and technology would not have been the same in Europe. Unlike Samuel Huntington (1998), whose thesis about the clash of civilisations effectively claims that Islamic civilisation has more in common with the civilisation of China than with Europe, Goody shows what a great deal is shared by Islamic civilisation and Europe, not least because of the common roots of Islam, Christianity and Judaism. Goody concludes (2004, p. 160): 'Both in the past and in the present Islam cannot be construed simply as the Other. Even in Asia, Muslim traditions are close to Christian and Jewish traditions. Muslims are very much part of the European scene.'

Some of the shared aspects of culture are also apparent in detailed ethnographic studies. It is difficult to read a recent collection on popular culture in Turkey (Kandiyoti & Saktanber, 2002) without being struck not only by the heterogeneity, but also by how much religion, as a factor, jostles alongside class, gender and secular means of communication. It is far from obvious that religion is the dominant factor in each case.

3.3 Self-Reinforcing Misunderstandings

Pointing out how the cultural arguments, for and against, fail to measure up to the conclusions of scholarship is not an end in itself. The aim is to spell out the consequences for politics and policy. These consequences will be seen more clearly after an examination of the assumptions about culture that are shared by the two sides of the Turkey debate.

Essentially, they share four. First, in Muslim countries religion always dominates culture. Second, the relationship between Islam and the West is dominated by the radical differences. Third, cultures are entities that can live 'side by side' – in harmony or in tension, but the point is that they have clear boundaries and coherent 'interiors'. Fourth, 'civilisations' are entities that can clash or make alliances.

The differences between the two sides of the debate concern their pessimism or optimism about what one can do in the circumstances, given the assumptions. Anti-Turkey arguments are not confident that, given the differences, having cultures living 'side by side' would be harmonious. Jack Straw (2007), on the other hand, is optimistic precisely because he sees the symbolic importance if this is achieved: 'By welcoming Turkey into Europe, we will prove how two cultures can not only exist together....' And he quotes Turkey's Prime Minister, who also shows that he believes that Europe needs a cultural bridge to the Islamic world: 'What do you gain by adding 99 percent Muslim Turkey to the EU? You gain a bridge between the EU and the 1.5 billion-strong Islamic world'.

These assumptions are important precisely because they are mistaken. Cultures are not the kind of entities that have tight boundaries. Islam does not always dominate the culture of Muslim countries. The differences between Europe and 'Islam' are not such that a 'bridge' does not yet exist. Without challenging the assumptions, the 'transnational' identities of Europe's Muslim citizens would not make sense; one would not understand why they enjoy the comic-strips (Douglas & Malti-Douglas, 1994) and popular music (Gross, McMurray, & Swedenburg, 1997), for example, that they do. Nor would one understand some of the cultural identities and dilemmas that some scholars (Kandiyoti & Saktanber, 2002) have claimed to find celebrated and debated within Turkey – identities and dilemmas, one should add, that tend to show how much Turkey already shares with Europe. Intensive cultural exchange is already taking place on the ground in Europe and in its immediate Muslim neighbourhood.

The irony is that Europeans and Turks should even be conducting the debate in these terms. The apparent contrast between cultures can be misleading, as the novelist Orhan Pamuk (2004) has imaginatively shown in his novel *Snow*. Ostensibly about the clash between Kemalist secularism and Islamism, what the novel shows is how the two ideologies share the same cultural style of thought – paranoid and authoritarian. The Cypriot anthropologist Yiannis Papadakis (2005) has similarly explored the unexpected, sometimes shocking cultural similarities between opposing sides of the Cyprus debate.

But it is not mere irony. The assumptions, unchallenged, unchecked and reinforced, subvert the possibility of conducting a proper policy debate on Europe, Islam and culture. There are real questions that need to be addressed concerning sustainable inclusion and pluralism within both Europe and Muslim countries. While the answers depend a great deal on one's political preferences, they also depend on understanding how cultural exchange and crisis should be analysed. The writings of scholars like Olivier Roy (2007), Tariq Modood (2007) and Ulrich Beck and Edgar Grande (2007) provide examples of the questions that are crying out for policy engagement and debate but which the current form of the debate on Turkey unfortunately obscures.

4 Impact on External Policy

Whereas the arguments about cultural identity tend to obscure real questions needing attention, the arguments concerning external policy tend to pre-empt options. There is another difference: arguments against Turkish membership tend not to focus much on external policy, although it will be seen that they share an important assumption with those who champion Turkey's membership.

One argument in favour of membership tends to be made only by Spain (at least under the last Aznar government) and Turkey: namely, that it would represent an 'alliance of civilisations'; an argument that has an external policy dimension. But in a world dominated by states, civilisations are not the kind of entity between which an alliance can be declared, even if it is for the best of motives. Not to mention that it is odd to have a declaration of an alliance in the name of democracy, without any democratic authorisation from the peoples Spain and Turkey respectively claim to represent.

A similar argument looks at the other side of the coin. If Turkey is refused after all these years, a 'clash of civilisations' might be the price to pay. One can certainly imagine a far less friendly Turkey, but again, in a world dominated by raison d'état, and fragmentation within the regional and international system of Muslim states, is it likely that Turkey could mobilise a significant number of Muslim states against the EU because of its individual grievance?

A sharper argument is one that indicates that Turkey would increase the EU's weighting in Middle East affairs – provide a bridge. There is no doubt that in recent years Turkey has moved closer to many Arab states, after years of being rather closer to Israel; a fact noted and resented by Arabs, some of whom consider the Ottoman period to have been one of colonial rule.

But Turkey's greater even-handedness in recent years coincides with the Erdoğan government. Surely, in a democracy, this government will one day lose power and, possibly, be replaced by one that reverts to the previous foreign policy, or even another that irks its neighbours rather than provides a communications link to them. Is it reasonable to decide membership on the basis of a governing party's foreign policy?

What is important in this criticism is that all these arguments, by assuming that dialogue is best carried on by governments whose members share the same faith (even if they leave their faith out of politics), make assumptions about international relations that would be queried by foreign policy experts. Moreover, they pre-empt the possibility of developing a cultural diplomacy that is far more energetic than what has been done so far (even taking the Anna Lindh Foundation for the Dialogue of Cultures into consideration).

One final important pro-Turkey argument is a negative one. Some politicians, opposed to Turkey's membership, have mooted the idea of offering a 'partnership' instead. Turkey has angrily dismissed this as second-class status. And – here is the important point – pro-Turkey European politicians have endorsed this evaluation. The lack of protest by anti-Turkey politicians suggests they too agree.

Such agreement is troubling from a Maltese perspective, even one, like that of the present writer and the government of Malta, that favours Turkey's membership. And it should trouble all EU members. For characterising partnership as second-class membership has grave consequences for the EU's external policy. Might the Union not want to offer its southern neighbours a partnership, especially since full membership will not be offered in the foreseeable future? Might the Union not develop a specific European partnership for the joint governance of certain resources (such as those of the sea, as the Commission's Blue Paper on maritime affairs has indicated)? But could it credibly offer such options if the status of partnership were already stigmatised as second-class?

Once again, the terms on which the debate is conducted actually compromise the policies that the EU may want to pursue. And it compromises them in part by pre-empting certain possibilities from even being considered.

This is not just a matter of the future. It poisons the well in the present. The Euro-Mediterranean Partnership has for many years been undermined by Arab resentment, even if diplomatically couched, of what they perceive as their second-class status. And although only Muammar Gaddafi criticised the Union for the Mediterranean in these terms, he was voicing the privately expressed thoughts of diplomats of several other Arab states, including some who publicly praised the initiative.

5 Conclusion

This chapter has throughout alluded to options that are obscured and foreclosed by the way the debate is conducted. What these options might be has, however, been beyond the scope of the argument. Yet the discussion of Alcide De Gasperi's vision does suggest, in outline, some options. His ability to embrace the Near Eastern and

North African 'elements' as part of European identity suggests that he thought of identity not as a kind of shield but as a dialogic process. His self-confidence in pronouncing that the European project excludes no one suggests he could conceive of a Europe whose instruments of external relations include not just enlargement but also participation with third countries in regional institutions of governance.

Whatever one makes of a vision such as De Gasperi's, it is clearly a European vision, in the sense that it tackles specifically European challenges using specifically European strengths and ideas. This is a characteristic worth noting. For it is one of the paradoxes of the debate on Turkey's membership that, while what is at stake is Europe's identity and future, the terms in which it is conducted highlight the increasing Americanisation of European politics. Is it a coincidence that the main ideas about identity and culture are derived from Samuel P. Huntington? Is it just an over-fertile imagination that detects Francis Fukuyama's thesis about 'the end of history' lurking in the belief that any alternative to enlargement can only be its pale shadow? Perhaps, if Europeans can revise some of the terms of the debate on Turkey, they can also revitalise the Union's capacity to manage global relationships with the institutional creativity that marked its origins.

References

Anderson, P. (1992). *A zone of engagement*. London: Verso.

Appiah, K. A. (2006). *Cosmopolitanism: Ethics in a world of strangers*. London: Allen Lane.

Beck, U., & Grande, E. (2007). *Cosmopolitan Europe*. Cambridge, Malden, MA: Polity, 26 December.

Bot, B. (2004). Turkey belongs to Europe. *Washington Times*, 26 December.

Douglas, A., & Malti-Douglas, F. (1994). *Arab comic strips: Politics of an emerging mass culture*. Bloomington, Indiana: Indiana University Press.

De Gasperi, A. (2004). *L'Europa: Scritti e discorsi*. A cura di Maria Romana De Gasperi. Brescia: Morcelliana.

Goody, J. (2004). *Islam in Europe*. Cambridge, Malden, MA: Polity.

Gross, J., McMurray, D., & Swedenburg, T. (1997). Rai, Rap, and Ramadan nights: Franco - Maghribi cultural identities. In J. Beinin & J. Stork (Eds.), *Political Islam: Essays from Middle East report* (pp. 257–268). Berkeley, Los Angeles: University of California Press.

Huntington, S. P. (1998). *The clash of civilizations and the remaking of the world order*. New York: Simon and Schuster.

Kandiyoti, D., & Saktanber, A. (Eds.). (2002). *Fragments of culture: The everyday of modern Turkey*. New Brunswick: Rutgers University Press.

Modood, T. (2007). *Multiculturalism*. Cambridge, Malden, MA: Polity.

Pamuk, O. (2004). *Snow*. London: Faber and Faber.

Papadakis, Y. (2005). *Echoes from the dead zone: Across the Cyprus divide*. London: IB Tauris.

Roy, O. (2007). *Secularism confronts Islam*. Translated by George Holoch. New York: Columbia University Press.

Sen, A. (2006). *Identity and violence: The illusion of destiny*. London: Allen Lane.

Sennett, R. (2001). Street and office: Two sources of identity. In W. Hutton & A. Giddens (Eds.), *On the edge: Living with global capitalism* (pp. 175–190). London: Vintage.

Siedentop, L. (2000). *Democracy in Europe*. London: Allen Lane.

Skinner, Q. (2002). *Visions of politics vol I: Regarding method*. Cambridge: Cambridge University Press.

Straw, J. (2007). *Turkey and Europe: A partnership in security and prosperity*. Speech given at Bosphorus University, 23 November, http://www.justice.gov.uk/news/sp291107a.htm/.
Taylor, C. (1991). *The ethics of authenticity*. Cambridge, MA: Harvard University Press.
Taylor, C. (1994). The politics of recognition. In A. Gutman (Ed.), *Multiculturalism: Examining the politics of recognition*. Princeton: Princeton University Press.
Touraine, A. (2005). *Un nouveau paradigme pour comprendre le monde aujourd'hui*. Paris: Fayard.
Young, H. (1999). *This blessed plot: Britain and Europe from Churchill to Blair*. London: Macmillan.

Imagining the EU in the Turkish Mirror

Ali Ihsan Aydin

Turkey's EU membership seems very likely to be one of the most historic and decisive events in the construction of Europe. It is widely accepted now that Turkey is not a candidate like the others. Centuries after the Ottoman invasions, today Turkey is challenging Europe once again, this time not as an adversary but with the desire to be part of Europe. Ironically, this challenge is as much cultural as political for a Europe preoccupied more and more with its identity, borders and future. The opening of membership negotiations has unsettled Europeans, provoking passionate and unprecedented debates. Muslim Turks, on the threshold of the EU, are again being imagined as the 'Other', through allusions to history and memory. EU membership is a priori a political affair. But in Turkey's case the debates show that it goes beyond politics. Europeans seem to have rediscovered in Turkey a mirror of the cultural and religious heritage of Europe; this has provoked an existential reflection about nature and identity. With their close interest and active presence on the national and European level, the European Christian churches are among the actors most engaged in these debates. In a highly secularised Europe, where religion should have nothing to do with politics, what kind of stance or role should the churches assume? Is religion back in the new Europe? This chapter aims to look at how 'Christian Europe', which historically had led the hostile response to Muslim Turks, is now positioning itself vis-à-vis the integration of Muslim Turkey into the EU.

1 A Candidate Not Like Others

Turkey's bonds with Europe date back centuries, and with the European Union, half a century. Still, it seems that membership will not come about soon. All parties, including Turkey, are now convinced that the negotiation process with Ankara is not and will not be the same as with previous or present enlargements. Even though the road leading to Brussels is in principle the same for all, seemingly minor incidents show that Turkey's path is full of pitfalls and in these unsettled times the end of the road is not at all clear.

The requisite conditions to start negotiations and become a member of the Union are defined clearly in European agreements. These conditions are set out in a series

C. Arvanitopoulos (Ed.), *Turkey's Accession to the European Union*

of political and economic criteria. But we have seen the emergence of a new criterion, not formally set out, since Europe was plunged into the issue of Turkey's candidacy: *européanité*. This has never been a criterion for other candidate countries. When Brussels and Turkey began taking their half-century-long relationship one stage further, Europeans, for their part, began hotly to question the Europeanness of Turkey. The debates often take a cultural tone in many member states. The fact that the opening of the negotiations coincided with Europe's own interrogation of its identity and future, especially during the constitutional process, meant that there was fertile ground for judging Turkey's accession on cultural and religious grounds. The declarations of some major European public figures on Turkey's *europeanité* also contributed to inflaming the debates in public opinion.

One of the first to set the cat among the pigeons was the President of the European Convention, Valery Giscard D'Estaing, who announced in 2002 that Turkey's entry into the EU would be 'the end of Europe' because it was 'not a European country' (*Le Monde*, 9 November 2002). In the same vein, former EU Commissioner Frits Bolkestein sparked controversy by declaring that if Turkey joins the EU, '[t]he liberation of Vienna in 1683 would have been in vain' (*Financial Times*, 8 November 2004). Additional examples abound. The harsh opposition to Turkey in Europe of President Nicolas Sarkozy of France, who relentlessly claims that Turks are not Europeans, is mostly based on cultural rhetoric. Today, although negotiations have started, the debates about Turkey still revolve around cultural and civilisational issues.

Why has Turkey provoked such a fanatical debate about the nature and future of Europe, unseen during recent enlargements (e.g., Bulgaria or Romania)? Is this a question of geography? Is it the fact that Turkey is situated mainly on the wrong side of the Bosporus? Why, then, was there no debate about Cyprus? Of course, there may be a combination of different factors to explain European scepticism about Turkey. But the differences in culture and religion consistently dominate the debates and serve to construct Muslim Turks as the Other of Europe when Europeans try to define what is to be European. Turkey has become 'a catalyst and the Other for self definition of what it was to be defined as European' (Nilüfer, 2006). In this perspective Turkey serves as a 'mirror' for a Europe 'for its identity, its project, its essence' – in search of a 'collective consciousness' to invent a feeling of European belonging (Kastoryano, 2006).

Muslim Turks have epitomised the figure of the Other for Europe in different ways through the centuries, from the Middle Ages to the twentieth century. In the Middle Ages, the Muslim Saracens and Turks represented the infidel Other of Christendom, as it defined itself then, rather than of Europe, which is a later invention. The enmity, fed by the Crusades, against the Muslim Orient played an important part in the formation of the collective identity or consciousness of Christendom (Delanty, 1995). After Christendom, European perceptions of the Muslim Orient as religiously Other were replaced by secular markers generally based on the rhetoric of civilisation that became dominant during the time of the European Renaissance and Enlightenment. Unbelievers and infidel Turks became the non-civilised and barbarian Turks (Neumann, 1999). In the eyes of Enlightenment Europe, the East was regarded as incapable of progress and as uncivilised, despotic and backward (Delanty). Later, in the age of imperialism, this idea of the superiority of the 'European civilisation' served as an ideological tool justifying colonisation.

However, it would be inadequate to view Europe as one unified bloc throughout all history as the enemy of Turks. The Ottoman Empire, whose frontiers stretched out beyond the Balkans, was also within Europe; the traces of its presence are still visible today in many countries. As a result of their long presence in Europe, the Ottomans, who were always inclined to the West from the first days of *Beylik*, entered into economic and political alliances with Europeans, sometimes against other Europeans, and were involved in the making of the political and social landscape of Europe. One of the most widely remembered episodes is the alliance between the French King Francis I and the Ottoman Sultan Kanuni against the Hapsburgs. Interestingly, this policy of Francis I was regarded in Europe as a betrayal of Christendom (Yapp, 1992).

In fact, from the seventeenth and eighteenth centuries till today, the nature of the relations between the Turks and Europe has continued to be a matter of discussion. In the late seventeenth century, William Penn argued that Ottomans Turks could be included in his plan for a European association of states if they renounced Islam and converted to Christianity (Neumann, 1999). Current arguments about Turkey's Europeanness, with all the associated historical and cultural connotations of that notion, proves that this idea of cultural or religious prerequisites to entry has been perpetuated to the present day. In 1856, the Treaty of Paris marked the official entry of the Ottoman state into the Concert of Europe and 'the law between Christian nations' was replaced with 'the law between civilisations' (Delanty, 1995). This change was granted in order to convince Turkey to side against Russia. The Ottomans were then officially recognised as part of Europe. But this decision was not acceptable to the natural law theorist James Lorimer; for him the Turks had not reached 'the standard of civilisation' and only limited membership in the 'family of nations' was conceivable. Cultural and religious differences have continued to frame the representations of Muslim Turks in Europe despite the secularisation of European societies (Neumann). Today we see the manifestations of this mentality in the recurrent evocation of historical events like the siege of Vienna or the fall of Constantinople in 1453 whenever Turkey's membership is discussed.

It seems a paradox that it is in France, probably the most secular member of the EU, which formed alliances with Turks in the past and, unlike the Viennese, did not experience a Turkish assault, that the *europeanité* of the Turks is questioned on the basis of cultural and civilisational arguments.

2 Is Europe Still Christian?

Those who oppose Turkey's EU membership with cultural and identity-related arguments associate Europe's identity and roots with a Judeo-Christian background. It is not within the scope of this chapter to discuss the identity or roots of Europe.

Nonetheless, it is worth noting some points. Today, anyone looking at a European city can see the dominant influence of Christianity everywhere. The organisation of time and space in Europe (from the holidays to the architecture) is sharply marked by the cultural infrastructure of Christianity. No one can ignore this. However, to assert that Europe is exclusively Christian would be a selective and partial reading of European history. It is even a matter of controversy between different Christian denominations. Catholics, for example, tend to concentrate on the first millennium when talking about European history whereas Protestants prefer to highlight the second millennium, and from time to time criticise Catholics for their selective reading of history (Willaime, 2004). This may partly explain the difference of vision between Christian confessions with respect to mentioning the Christian roots of Europe in the preamble to the European constitution. While the Catholic Church mobilised and used all its institutions to apply pressure to have a Christian reference in the Constitution, the Protestants were not that keen to defend this cause. If Turkey is 'otherised' on the basis of the notion that Europe is exclusively Christian – thus dissociating Islam from Europe – it would be necessary to brush aside Andalusia and the centuries of Ottoman presence in Eastern Europe, the traces of these that survive and also the actual Muslim population in Europe. It would also mean ignoring the deep roots of Christianity in Anatolia.

On the other hand, it can be asked: To what extent is Europe still Christian today? As a result of the long process of secularisation in Europe, religion has lost its influence and its capacity to frame political and social orientations in Europe. Although this process has been experienced in varying degrees, depending on the specific national and historical contexts of the various European countries, religion today is far from its historic role as a decisive social and political actor. Despite the emergence of new forms of religiosity, this situation is particularly a reality in Europe, which, moreover, constitutes an exceptional case in the world according to major social scientists (Davie, 2006).

Having said this, however, we are still far removed from a situation in which religion has completely disappeared because of the rapid pace of secularisation, as theorists of secularism once expected would happen. Grace Davie, who thinks Europeans were ill-prepared for the revived prominence of religion in public debates, analyses the religiosity in Europe by using the concepts of 'believing without belonging', 'belonging without believing' and 'vicarious religious' (Davie, 2006; Hervieu-Léger & Davie, 1996). This particularity of Europe in terms of the patterns of religion is being challenged by the growing presence of Islam, voluntarist Christian minorities and the integration of some Eastern European countries (Davie, 2006).

Despite the fact that churches have lost most of their impact on society, current events show that religion has not, for all that, receded into the private sphere without any impact on public space. Indeed, religion has made a remarkable comeback into the social debate. According to the French sociologist Jean Paul Willaime, we have moved into a new era of 'ultramodernity' in which we see the return of religion as a political problem and as a media subject. In ultramodernity, considered as a sort of a disenchanted modernity,

> [w]e are in a time when religion, far from being obsolete, appears as a possible symbolic resource that can contribute to preventing the political from becoming a simple matter of management… It allows for a kind of comeback for religion, but this does not call into question the process of autonomy of modern societies. (Willaime, 2007)

This was seen during the controversy about the reference to Christianity in the European Constitution, the crisis surrounding the cartoon caricatures of the Prophet Muhammad and the new debates over *laicité* in France. In the debates about European identity and memory, the question of Turkey revealed very clearly how religion may assume a symbolic function and be a political resource in European public opinion, especially when it is able to serve as a tool of 'demarcation' (Schlesinger & Foret, 2006). On the other hand, the proponents of the clash of civilisations thesis, which gained widespread visibility in the period following the 9/11 attacks, favour the inclusion of cultural dimensions in political questions. The debates around the Turkish candidacy, based on cultural or religious arguments, should be viewed within this larger perspective.

3 The Churches and the Construction of Europe

Although this is not always stated openly, religion occupies just as important a place in Europe's reflection about its identity as it does in the debates about Turkey's membership. In this context, what are the attitudes and the opinions of the churches, which from the very beginning have been keenly interested in the construction of Europe and which have asserted more strongly their presence in the European public sphere over the past few years? Do they also view Turkey as the Other and, consequently, oppose its aspirations for EU membership? The rest of the chapter focuses on the position of the churches vis-à-vis the European project and the Turkish question.

From the very beginning the Catholic Church has closely followed the European project. After World War II, the two primary preoccupations of the Church were the integration of a defeated Germany into the European family and the defence of European civilisation against totalitarian communism, which was considered to be a danger threatening the future of Christian civilisation (Chenaux, 1990). For the Holy See, the re-unification of a ruined Europe constituted the only way to salvation. To that end, popes did not hesitate to become actively engaged by taking initiatives and intervening in the discussions on the possibilities of European unity. Pius XII (1939–1958), who had always dreamt of a unified federal Europe, followed with great attention even the minutest technical details of the construction of Europe and interfered regularly, whether through his sermons or through the Christian Democrat politicians in power at the time. Such an active engagement of the Catholic Church in a post-war Europe governed predominantly by Christian Democrats led to some negative reactions and raised suspicions about the restoration of a 'Catholic Europe' in some countries (Hours, 1953; Willaime, 2004).

For the Catholic Church, the realisation of European unity could not be achieved without Christian spiritual and moral bases. This idea is recurrently stressed in the interventions of popes from Pius XII to John Paul II. For Pius XII, without Christianity, 'Europe does not have the internal force to preserve its ideals, its material and territorial independence' (*Documentation Catholique*, 1953). For him, the bond between Europe and Christianity was hereditary:

> [A] son can deny his mother, but he still remains biologically and spiritually part of her. Just as, far from their fathers' home, from which they became strangers, the sons [European nations] still hear – always – without perhaps even being aware, like the call of blood, the echo of this Christian heritage.

As for John Paul II, it was Christianity that had shaped Europe, and without it European civilisation and identity would be 'meaningless' (*L'Europe unie dans l'enseignement des papes*, 1981). However, linking the fate of Europe to Christian faith does not imply, according to the first Slavic pope in history, 'a will to conquest or the restoration' of Catholic Europe or that the Holy See wishes to turn Europe into a confessional state (*Documentation Catholique*, 1982; *L'Europe de demain*, 1990). What the Church wants, according to papal discourses on Europe, is rather to promote a Christian conception of European identity and civilisation and to remind Europe, which is now considered as a land of mission, of its Christian roots and values.

Until the 1990s, European Protestants were not as greatly interested in the construction of Europe as were Catholics. Compared to Catholics, Protestants remained relatively indifferent to the European project. J. P. Willaime, an expert on Protestantism, explains that Protestants perceived European unity as a Catholic project (Willaime, 2004). Indeed, due to its plural and diverse structure, Protestantism is far from adopting a homogeneous position vis-à-vis the European Union. The position taken may vary according to the national or regional contexts in which a Protestant church finds itself. However, it is possible to talk about a common Protestant stance concerning the Christianity of Europe. Protestants, in contrast to Catholics, emphasise the multiple cultural and religious legacies of Europe, opposing the restoration of an exclusive Christian Europe. They insist that the Reformation and other religious or philosophical traditions also belong to the European heritage and should be taken into account.

As for the Orthodox, for historical reasons they have only recently become interested in the construction of Europe. Except for Greece, the Orthodox nations of Eastern Europe remained under the yoke of the Soviets – the enemy bloc of Western Europe where the European project was born and developed. Besides, in Orthodox societies, there is wariness over Western Europe, nourished by the long-established opposition between Catholicism and Orthodoxy. Makrides (1993), for example, points to the role played by the Orthodox churches, and especially the radical bishops, in the formation of the anti-European and anti-Western feeling in Greek society that has existed for centuries. So much so that the EEC was considered a danger, even an enemy, for Greece and Greek culture by religious nationalists. The latter feared that Greece might lose its Orthodox identity if it joined the Union. In recent decades, however, attitudes towards the European Union in the Orthodox world have become more positive. The impact of ecumenical dialogue between Christian confessions cannot be underestimated. The EU has now become an important concern for Orthodox churches too.

Today, the European Union mobilises not only Catholics but also other churches and religions present in Europe. It has become an important issue for churches to take part and assert their role in. Opening representative offices in Brussels, churches have adopted new strategies and created new structures and inter-Christian organisations to adapt themselves to the institutional structure of the European space. The activities of the churches' representations in Brussels, like COMECE (the Commission of the Bishops' Conferences of the European Community) or KEK (the Conference of European Churches), are not limited to defending the interests of churches or lobbying for Christian references. They participate actively in European politics in all domains, from agriculture to questions of human rights. The desire and the efforts of the churches to contribute to the construction of Europe have not gone without reciprocation from the European Union. A forum for dialogue and cooperation between religious organisations and European institutions was established during the European Commission Presidency of Jacques Delors. The Forward Studies Unit, created in 1989 with the objective of promoting dialogue between religious or philosophic organisations and the European Union, has resulted in a programme called 'Soul of Europe'. The churches were especially invited by the former president of Commission, Jacques Santer, 'to give an interpretation of and meaning to the construction of Europe' (Willaime, 2004). The relationship between the EU and religious institutions has evolved and takes place now within new formal and informal structures. With the Lisbon Treaty, religious and philosophical groups prepare to entertain closer relations and to strengthen cooperation.

4 'Christian Europe' vis-à-vis Turkey's EU Candidacy

In Europe, even though the religion-state-society relation varies according to the historical specificities of every society, churches do not participate, at least directly, in political life. However, the separation is not as clear-cut in every European country as it is in France. In many EU member states, particularly in some Eastern countries, religion still plays an important role in society. Religious actors do not stand apart from the political, social and economic preoccupations of their societies. At a global level, we have observed in recent years how the stances and declarations of religious actors may have an impact on public opinion, in what Willaime calls the 'ultra-modern' world of today. European churches are not indifferent to the Turkish question that has provoked Europeans to question their identity, culture and civilisation, which are *par excellence* subjects dear to the churches. They have not hesitated to express their views in the debates.

In the thought of the post-war popes, Turkey represents a bridge between the East and the West. This image of 'bridge' is a recurrent theme in the discourse of popes like Paul VI or John Paul II regarding Turkey. At the same time, Turkey is seen as 'having greatly contributed to the development of Christianity' and is regarded as an important place for Christians because their 'common origins' are there. Antioch, Ephesus, Smyrna and Nicaea were the places where the Christian faith was defined. John Paul II (2001) has described Turkey as follows:

> Turkey is geographically and culturally situated between the Orient and the West, and that is the first reason why it can be an important bridge. It is an overwhelmingly Muslim society, deeply marked by the religious and cultural heritage that was transmitted in the first centuries of the Seljuk and Ottoman periods. But Turkey turns towards the West also because of her Christian roots, and because there are Turkish migrant communities in many European countries, just as there are Christian communities in Turkey.

John Paul II was very active in European debates and struggled hard to have Christianity mentioned in the European Constitution. The re-evangelisation of Europe was one of the main preoccupations of his papacy. Despite his insistence on the mention of Christianity in the preamble to the EU Constitution, he did not adopt a negative position, at least publicly, on Turkey's EU membership. Indeed, the position of the Catholic Church on the question of Turkey was revealed in the declarations of Cardinal Ratzinger, then Prefect of the Congregation for the Doctrine of the Faith, now Pope Benedict XVI. In response to the question of a French journalist whether Turkey's membership would lead to 'a clash or an enrichment of cultures', Cardinal Ratzinger answered by saying that it would be a 'mistake' to identify Turkey with Europe. Defining Europe as a 'culture', Ratzinger claimed that Turkey belonged to another continent, by mentioning events like the wars against Byzantium, the fall of Constantinople and the siege of Vienna (*Le Figaro Magazine*, 8 September 2004).

These words provoked hot debates in the media and public opinion, at a time when Brussels was discussing whether to open negotiations with Turkey. There is no doubt that these statements take on added significance with the enthroning of Ratzinger as Pope Benedict XVI. His speech at the University of Regensburg in Germany again sparked some tensions, but he later visited Turkey in November 2007 and calmed the controversies about his attitude to the Turkish bid to join the EU. Afterwards the Holy See affirmed, through its Secretary of State, Cardinal Tarcisio Bertone, that the Catholic Church was favourable to the integration of Turkey into Europe (*Le Figaro*, 31 May 2007).

On the other hand, the very active COMECE, the EU representation of the Catholic churches in EU countries, declared that 'Religion does not constitute an obstacle for a country such as Turkey, with a majority Muslim population, from becoming a member of the EU', in a statement before the 6–17 December 2004 meeting of the European Council. Discussing the Turkish candidacy in internal and external meetings, the COMECE asked the EU to make the opening of negotiations conditional on the improvement of religious freedom and the legal status of Christian minorities. COMECE has a permanent working group studying the legal, political and social issues raised by the integration of Muslims into Europe (COMECE, 2004).

Apart from the Catholic COMECE, the KEK, representing the Protestant and Orthodox Churches of Europe, got involved in the debate about Turkey's accession through its Church and Society Commission. The Conference issued a public statement following extensive consultations among its members in 2004. It stated that

> [f]or the Churches in Europe the issue of religious difference is not an obstacle to continuing the improvement of the relationship between Turkey and the EU and even for Turkey's eventual membership in the Union. For the Churches the accession of Turkey to the EU is, in other words, not a question of religious differences. Turkey's eventual membership in the Union may even have potentially good effects on the positive development of the relationship between religions and cultures in Europe and may become a foundation stone in a bridge between the Christian and Muslim worlds. (CEC-KEK, 2004)

Yet, in the same statement, the KEK drew attention to the 'far-reaching consequences for the future existence of the Union' and 'the risk that taking this substantial political decision without sufficient support from the Union's citizens may lead to increasing the distance between the EU and its citizens'. Moreover, the Conference urged the Union to encourage the reflection on European identity by pointing out that '[e]thnic, cultural and religious factors' constitute 'its essential components'.

Churches, through their representations in Brussels, have publicly pronounced that they do not oppose Turkey's membership in EU for religious reasons. Nevertheless it is difficult to say that they openly and heartily support it. This is not the case with churches in Turkey, which are very willing to see Turkey in the EU and even lobby for it in Europe. At the time of the opening of the negotiations, the Orthodox Patriarchate of Constantinople, the Armenian Church and even the Catholic Church expressed publicly their desire to see Turkey in the EU. The Christian churches in Turkey no doubt consider that their problems would be more easily solved within a Turkey in the EU.

However, the public statement of the KEK in Brussels does not imply that all member churches endorse exactly the same position. For example, the previous head of the Orthodox Church of Greece, Archbishop Christodoulos, who died in 2008, was a fervent opponent of Turkey, in contrast to the Greek government, and made his opposition public. The very popular and influential Patriarch warned Europe, just before the official opening of accession negotiations, about the danger of the 'Turkisation of Europe'.[1] However, the situation seems to have changed now with the new Archbishop. The Director of the Representative Office of the Church of Greece to the European Union, Bishop Athanasios of Achaïa, acting in tune with the Greek government, gave assurances that the Church of Greece supported Turkey's membership.[2]

On the Protestant side, every national or regional church may adopt its own stance. The EKD (Evangelische Kirche in Deutschland), which has its own representation in Brussels and is one of the most active in European affairs, has expressed

---

[1] He warned, 'let us not believe that the Turks will supposedly become Europeanised. I am afraid, on the contrary, that it is Europe which will be turkised' (AFP, 10 October 2005).

[2] Interview in Brussels with Bishop Athanasios of Achaïa, 6 March 2008.

certain reservations about the Turkish candidacy. In a public statement, the EKD voiced doubts as to whether Turkish Islam would be able to Europeanise. The President of the Council of Evangelical Churches, Wolfgang Huber, has also called for a referendum on the accession of Turkey. In Germany, it is clear that the problems experienced with the integration of almost three million Turks seem to be transferred into the debates about Turkey's EU membership.

Protestants do not believe that the roots of Europe are exclusively Christian and stress the pluralist character of Europe. Europe is seen as a 'multi-cultural community of peoples and societies, in which Christians, Muslims, Jews and people of other religions co-exist and tolerate one another' (CEC-KEK, 2004). Yet, despite this approach, some European Protestants in countries with an significant Muslim minority, such as in Germany, may react very conservatively about the place of Islam in Europe. The negative reactions, for example, to the construction of mosques in Germany clearly illustrate the extent to which tensions can arise from the Muslim presence. Even in the uncompromisingly laicist France, the construction of mosques does not cause such anxiety among church members. On the contrary, even right-wing politicians may fight for a mosque, as was seen recently in the city of Marseilles with its mayor, Senator Jean-Claude Gaudin.

5 To Conclude

The churches of Europe, which from the very beginning have been closely following the evolution of the European project, do not consider, at least on the level of discourse, that the religion and the culture of Turks constitute an obstacle for the integration of Turkey into the EU. But this does not mean that the churches are enthusiastic about Turkey joining the Union. Indeed, it is not unusual to hear representatives of the different churches voice, directly or sometimes indirectly, their scepticism about the candidacy of Turkey. However, the opposition to Turkey in Europe on religious grounds is primarily a political strategy of far-right parties, rather than the attitude of the churches. Some churches have even responded vehemently to this kind of argumentation.

The debate on Turkey's membership will more than likely continue on the grounds of culture, as well as in a political framework. The debate is related above all to Europe's deep questioning of its identity and nature. In this context, Turkey, which for a large part of its history has been constructed as the religious and cultural Other, represents a historic and crucial challenge for Europe. On the other hand, as Casanova put it quite appropriately, Muslims do not challenge Europe only by their religious otherness as non-Christian and non-European, but also and more importantly by their very religiousness as the Other of secular Europe (Casanova, 2007).

The constitutional process has intensified the reflection about European identity. As Europe moves further in its political and social integration towards a political community, it is more and more looking for a common basis, the glue that will bind it together. In this search for identity, history and collective memory reveal themselves to be the primary symbolic resources. Europeans are trying to define what they are now by looking at what Europe was not in the past. This is construction by way of exclusion, not inclusion. Muslim Turks, on the threshold of the Union, the infidel or Oriental Other of yesterday, could not have come at a better time.

The history of Europe is full of images of internal or external Others. Those who oppose Turkey on cultural or civilisational grounds demonise just one of them: the Turks. But Europeans seem to have forgotten that today's European unity was born out of a project of reconciliation, not confrontation, with the overcoming of many historical Others. It is sufficient to look at the history of the construction of Europe. If the founders of Europe had looked at the differences and the conflicts, rather than focussing on reconciliation, they would not have needed to go as far back in history as some Europeans do now with Turks. The European Union was a peace and reconciliation project: between France and Germany, between Eastern and Western Europe, between Catholics and Orthodox and between many other internal and external Others. Who can assert that the confrontation between Catholics and Orthodox was milder and less historic than the one between Muslims and Christians?

If the EU is still a compromise project, why not now seize the occasion for a historic reconciliation between Muslims and Christians in a time when the two are constructed more and more against one another, as incompatible and as enemies? In this respect, and also to see how much the universal humanist values and norms identified with Europe really matter to Europeans, Turkey's membership will most probably serve as a litmus test for the EU. Will Europe transform itself into a fortress or continue as a project?

References

Casanova, J. (2007). Religion, European secular identities, and European integration. In T. A. Byrnes & P. J. Katzenstein (Eds.), *Religion in an expanding Europe*. Cambridge: Cambridge University Press.

CEC-KEK. (2004). The relationship of the EU to Turkey. *Conference of European Churches*. Public statement, 5 October, http://www.cec-kek.org/content/integration.shtml/.

Chenaux, P. (1990). *Une Europe Vaticane: Entre le Plan Marshall et les Traités de Rome*. Brussels: Editions Ciaco.

COMECE. (2004). EU Bishops: Europe's priority should be its people. *Commissio Episcopatuum Communitatis Europensis*. Press Release, http://www.comece.org/comece.taf?_function = church&_sub = &id = 2&language = en/, 19 November.

Davie, G. (2006). Religion in Europe in the 21st century: The factors to take into account. *European Journal of Sociology, 47*(2), 271–296.

Delanty, G. (1995). *Inventing Europe: Idea, identity, reality*. New York: St Martin's Press.

Documentation Catholique. (1953). Paris, Bayard.

Documentation Catholique. (1982). Paris, Bayard.

L'Europe de demain. (1990). Speeches of John Paul II on Europe. Paris: Fayard.

L'Europe unie dans l'enseignement des papes. (1981). Solesmes.

Hervieu-Léger, D., & Davie, G. (Eds.). (1996). *Les identités religieuses en Europe*. Paris: La Découverte.

Hours, J. (1953). L'idée Européenne et l'idéal du Saint-Empire. *L'année politique et économique,* 111–112, 1–15.

John Paul II (2001). *Discours au nouvel ambassadeur de Turquie près le saint-siège lors de la présentation des lettres créance*. 7 December, http://www.Vatican.va/.
Kastoryano, R. (2006). Turkey/Europe: Space-border-identity. *Constellations, 13*(2), 275–285.
Makrides, V. (1993). Le role de l'Orthodoxie dans la formation de l'antieuropéanisme et l'antioccidentalisme Grecs. In G. Vincent & J. P. Willaime (Eds.), *Religions et transformations de l'Europe*. Strasbourg: Presses Universitaires de Strasbourg.
Neumann, I. B. (1999). *Uses of the other: "The East" in European identity formation*. Manchester: Manchester University Press.
Nilüfer, G. (2006). Europe's encounter with Islam: What future?. *Constellations, 13*(2), 248–262.
Schlesinger, P., & Foret, F. (2006). Political roof and sacred canopy: Religion and the EU constitution. *European Journal of Social Theory, 9*(59), 59–81.
Willaime, J. P. (2004). *Europe et religions: Les enjeux du XXIe siècle*. Paris: Fayard.
Willaime, J. P. (2007). Les reconfigurations ultramodernes du religieux en Europe. In F. Foret (Ed.), *L'espace public Européen à l'épreuve du religieux*. Brussels: Edition de l'Université de Bruxelles.
Yapp, M. E. (1992). Europe in the Turkish mirror. *Past and Present, 137*(1), 134–155 .

What Makes Turkish Islam Unique?

Mustafa Akyol

For many Westerners, Turkey is the shining star of the Muslim world. It is a secular democracy, a NATO member and a US ally. It challenges, therefore, the more radical interpretations of Islam as a theocratic political system with an anti-Western standpoint. Turks themselves note and appreciate the fact that they are different from other Muslims nations, especially their neighbours in the Middle East.

But why is Turkey exceptional? The official Turkish history, into which virtually all Turks have been educated, answers this question by referring to the perceived clean break with the Ottoman (i.e., Islamic) heritage by the modern Turkish Republic, which was founded by Mustafa Kemal Atatürk in 1923. 'We were in darkness', my primary-school textbooks reiterated, 'but then came Atatürk who shone on us like the sun'. Consequently, many Turks believe they would have lived under something like the Taliban regime in Afghanistan had they not been saved by the authoritarian and secularist modernisation project of the Kemalist regime. In other words, to the question 'Why is Turkey the most advanced democracy in the Islamic world?', the standard answer is 'Because Atatürk created it ex nihilo'.

Historians who examine the origin of Turkey with a more critical eye, however, find reasons to think that the creation story should be reversed. It seems that it was in fact the Ottoman legacy that gave rise to both Atatürk and modern Turkey.[1] The Kemalist period was undoubtedly a leap forward in several respects, but it was preceded and made possible by a rich heritage of Ottoman modernisation.

1 Ottoman Modernisation Revisited

To see how this is so, one should first examine the Turks' experience with Islam. Compared with the Arabs, the Turks were latecomers to the Muslim faith. The former were politically and intellectually more advanced until the thirteenth century, when the brilliant civilisation of the Arabs was nearly destroyed by one of the most devastating

---

[1] For a detailed study of the Ottoman political and social heritage of modern Turkey, see Karpat (2001).

C. Arvanitopoulos (Ed.), *Turkey's Accession to the European Union*

conquests ever, the Mongol catastrophe. The shift in world trade routes, from ancient roads through the Middle East and the Levant to the oceans, was an additional misfortune that would steadily impoverish the Arab world, which owed much of its wealth to trade. The long-term result was the stagnation of the Arab peoples.

Meanwhile, the leadership of Islam was passing to the Turks, who created powerful states under the Seljuk dynasty and especially the subsequent Ottoman dynasty. The Ottoman state extended its borders both towards the West and the East and, in the sixteenth and much of the seventeenth centuries, acted as the world's foremost superpower.

The political power of the Turks, and their continual interaction with the West, led them to an important insight: they were facing the rise of modernity. The Ottoman elite had to rule an empire, make practical decisions, adopt new technologies and reform existing structures – all of which allowed them to understand and cope with secular realities. Sociologist Şerif Mardin defines the consequent praxis as 'Ottoman secularity' and gives examples of Ottoman bureaucrats who started to discover 'Western ways' more than two centuries before the Turkish Republic:

> It is quite clear that the eighteenth century brought about a number of cumulative changes that promoted the 'secularist' aspect of the discourse of Ottoman bureaucracy. One of these changes was the creation of a new bureau (*Amedî Odası*) through which flowed all communication with Western states. The employees of this bureau were now increasingly exposed to information about the major European states. Antedating this change already in the 1730s there had been an increase in the number of bureaucrats who were sent to various European capitals to observe Western 'ways'. An innovation of the same years was the practice of these envoys to write reports about their missions upon their return. What is striking about these reports is the 'materiality' of their content. The reports did not contrast the religious or political institutions they found in the West with their Ottoman equivalents, but focused on the material elements of life. They detailed technological advances such as the construction of stone buildings, both military and civilian, and they described the splendor of Versailles, its organisation of leisure activities and in particular the theatre. The precision of the tables of astronomical observatories also impressed them. (Mardin, 2005, pp. 149–150)

According to Mardin, such practices helped in the formation of 'Turkish–Islamic exceptionalism', which is overlooked by most contemporary Western scholars on Islam because of their 'concentration on Arab or Salafi Islam'. Mardin adds that the exceptionalism is not solely a product of the Turkish Republic, as is often thought, but was built on a long process of historical evolution thanks to milestones such as 'the earlier rise of a Turkish bureaucratic class (circa 1780) … the type of institution building policy that goes back to the reign of Sultan Abdulhamid II (r. 1876–1909) and the type of synthesis between Islam and modernity that was promoted by an intellectual elite between 1908 and 1923' (Mardin, 2005, p. 145).

2 Tanzimat and Equal Citizenship

The eighteenth-century discovery of Europe by Ottoman bureaucrats resulted in the famous 'Imperial Gulhane Decree of 1839', also known as the *Tanzimat* Edict, which introduced the idea of the supremacy of law and modern citizenship to the empire.

In a second substantive reform edict, in 1856, the *dhimmi* ('protected') status was abolished, and Jews and Christians gained equal citizenship rights.

That *dhimmi* status that Islamic states have traditionally given to Jews and Christians – and adherents of any other traditional faith but not Arab idolaters – has been the subject of much criticism recently. There are writers who present it as a kind of slavery that Islam imposes on non-Muslims (Ye'or, 2002). Although it is true that the *dhimma* was an unequal status that grew out of and should remain in pre-modern times, it was actually quite generous according to the norms of that period. One interesting fact that supports this conclusion is that many non-Muslims of the Ottoman State were actually content with the *dhimma* and resisted its abolition. According to historian Roderic H. Davison,

> The program of equality between Christian and Muslim in the empire remained largely unrealized not because of bad faith on the part of leading Ottoman statesmen but because many of the Christians wanted it to fail ... The ecclesiastical hierarchies that ruled the Christian millets also opposed equality. *Osmanlilik* [Ottomanhod] would both decrease their authority and lighten their purses. This was especially true of the Greek Orthodox hierarchy, which had the most extensive prerogatives and by far the largest flock. When the *Hatt-i Sherif* [*Tanzimat* Edict] was solemnly read in 1839 and then put back into its red satin pouch it is reported that the Greek Orthodox patriarch, who was present among the notables, said, 'Inshallah-God grant that it not be taken out of this bag again'. In short, the doctrine of equality faced formidable opposition from Christians of the empire who were leaders in the churches and the nationalist movements (Davison, 1954, pp. 844–864).

Davidson also notes that

> [b]oth in 1839 and 1856 the sultan proclaimed that his Christian subjects should be equally privileged to serve in the armed forces along with the Muslims, instead of paying an exemption tax as they had previously done. It soon became obvious that the Christians would rather continue to pay than serve, despite the step toward equality which military service might mean. (Davison, 1954)

In the nineteenth century, the Ottoman state also started to accept the principle of religious freedom. As early as May 1844, an official Ottoman edict read, 'No subject of the Sublime [Ottoman] State shall be forced by anyone to convert to Islam against their wishes' (Deringil, 2000, pp. 547–575). In the Reform Edict of 1856 the Sultan proclaimed, 'All forms of religion are and shall be freely professed in my dominions. No subject of my empire shall be hindered in the exercise of the religion that he professes' (Deringil, 2000). The Ottoman Constitution of 1876 established a limited monarchy all of whose subjects were considered '*Osmanli* (Ottoman), whatever religion or creed they hold.' The constitution further affirmed that 'all *Osmanli* are equal before the law ... without distinction as to religion' (Deringil, 2000).

What is striking about these events is the fact that the Ottoman Empire – an Islamic state which many Muslims around the world still respect – gave full citizenship rights to Jews and Christians. This would create a precedent for the ecumenical approach towards Jews and Christians that would be articulated in Turkey's Republican era by scholars like Said Nursi and Fethullah Gülen.

It is a crucial point that the Ottoman Empire was not abandoning Islam by reforming the sharia laws. It was, rather, modernising itself from within the tradition.

The Qur'anic verse 'There is no compulsion in religion' was stressed by the Ottoman religious elite to justify the reforms (Deringil, 2000). Under the auspices of Sultan Abdulhamid II, Ahmet Cevdet Pasha, an Ottoman bureaucrat and an Islamic scholar, prepared the *Mecelle*, a new legal code that was based on traditional Islamic law but which also included many important modifications, with the goal of updating the sharia according to 'the requirements of the time' (Karpat, 2001, p. 189).

The Ottoman project of Islamic modernisation ended with the demise of the empire in the First World War. From its ruins arose what we now call the Middle East – with a legacy that doomed it from the start. All of the post-Ottoman states, except Turkey and Saudi Arabia, were colonised by European powers, a phenomenon that would soon breed anti-colonialism and anti-Westernism throughout the entire region. This was one of the causes of the end of what Albert Hourani, the great historian of the Middle East, called the 'liberal age' of the Arab world (Hourani, 1983) – which was, basically, the Arab counterpart of Ottoman modernisation.

3 The Two Trends

The Ottoman reforms were articulated and carried out by the intellectual elite of the empire. Most of these men – and some women – spoke English and French and were very well versed in European thought, not to mention the Islamic tradition. There were differences among them, but it is possible to generalise and speak of two main camps. One of these was what one can call the 'modernisation within the tradition' camp. Its proponents realised that reforms were needed, but hoped to bring these about without abandoning traditional values, especially religious values.

The second could be called the 'modernisation despite the tradition' camp, which found its most extreme expression among some radical Young Turks such as Abdullah Cevdet. 'The Young Turk *Weltanschauung*, as it developed between 1889 and 1902', according to historian Şükrü Hanioğlu, 'was vehemently antireligious, viewing religion as the greatest obstacle to human progress' (Hanioğlu, 2001, p. 305). In later years, the Young Turks played down their secularist views for political purposes, but the *Weltanschauung* remained intact.

During Turkey's War of Liberation (1919–1922), both of these intellectual camps – and all other segments of the society, which included Islamic clerics, Kurdish leaders and local notables – were united against the occupying powers under the umbrella of the Turkish Parliament. But even during those years, the two different political lines became evident within Parliament. The first group consisted of the enthusiastic supporters of Mustafa Kemal, the leader of the War of Liberation who was also a follower of the secularist and revolutionary line of thinking. The second group, on the other hand, included those who had reservations about Mustafa Kemal's increasing political power.

4 The Fate of Terakkiperver Firka

When the war was won and the Republic was proclaimed in 1923, the First Group turned into the People's Party (Halk Firkasi), which was directed by Mustafa Kemal (Atatürk) and his closest ally, İsmet İnönü. About a year later, the Second Group established the Progressive Party (Terakkiperver Firka), whose leaders were also war heroes such as Kazim Karabekir, Refet Bele and Rauf Orbay.

There were three main differences between the conservative Progressive Party and the revolutionary People's Party:

1. The Progressive Party believed in free markets and individual entrepreneurship, an idea that had been advanced by Prince Sabahattin, a nephew of the late Sultan Abdulhamid II. The People's Party, on the other hand, promoted a more 'statist' approach towards the economy, which would carry corporatist overtones in the 1930s.
2. The Progressive Party was sympathetic to religion. Its founding document included the famous Article 6, 'We are respectful of religious ideas and sentiments'.
3. On political issues such as the fate of the Kurds, the Progressive Party was tolerant and liberal. Kazim Karabekir, its leader, prepared a detailed report arguing that Kurds needed to be integrated gradually into Turkish society by encouraging agriculture and trade and by promoting the spirit of common Muslim values. The People's Party, on the other hand, believed in what its leader Ismet Inönü called the 'Turkification' of the Kurds, by using authoritarian methods such as banning their language and destroying their culture.

Yet the disagreement between the parties would not last long. On 5 June 1925 the Progressive Party was closed down by the regime. The party had survived for only 6 months and 2 weeks. Then, not only was it destroyed, but also its leaders were excluded from politics. Its most important figure, Kazim Karabekir, lived under house arrest for many years. All of his works were collected and burned on the orders of the government.

The announced reason was Article 6 of its programme: the clause 'We are respectful of religious ideas and sentiments'. For the new regime, this was a statement that encouraged 'backward minded thought and action' and could not be tolerated.

5 The Post-1925 Trauma

From 1925 to 1950, Turkey lived under a 'single party regime', which was characterised by its self-styled secularism. Unlike the separation of church and state, which is the American version of secularism, the Kemalist model was 'based on the radical Jacobin laicism that aimed to transform society through the power of the state and eliminate religion from the public sphere' (Yavuz & Esposito, 2003, p. xvi).

This had the negative effect of establishing the perception that religion and modernity were incompatible. Turkey's practicing Muslims felt themselves forced to abandon the former for the sake of the latter. The authoritarian secularist effort also drove Turkey into an acute version of the problem that Richard John Neuhaus has identified: the vacuum created by absent religion was filled by ersatz religion (Neuhaus, 1984, pp. 80–84). In just a decade, Islam was replaced by a new public faith based on Turkishness and the cult of personality created around Mustafa Kemal Atatürk. 'Let the Ka'aba be for the Arabs', wrote the poet Kemalettin Kamu, 'for us, Çankaya is enough.' That new shrine was Atatürk's residence.

The people who bought into this new faith became known as the 'secular elite'. They were a small minority in a very traditional society. That is why they decided that they had no time to waste on democracy. The people needed not to be represented and served but to be ruled and indoctrinated. Unlike the American Republic, which celebrates itself as a 'government of the people, by the people, for the people', the Turkish Republic, in its early decades, adopted a definition of government as 'for the people, in spite of the people'.

The two main segments of the society that the Republic governed 'in spite of' were practicing Muslims and Kurds. Both groups were suppressed. The former had their religious institutions destroyed, the latter saw their language and identity banned. Not surprisingly, both of these alienated groups had a hard time accepting this undemocratic Republic and instead hoped for a democracy through which they could realise their longing for freedom. In Turkey's first free and fair elections, in 1950, they elected the Democrat Party, whose motto was, 'Enough! The nation has the word.' The first acts of the DP were to legalise the Muslim call to prayer (the daily 'ezan') and to ease the burden in Kurdish areas. It also brought some suppressed Kurdish leaders to the parliament. Moreover, it took Turkey into NATO, accepted the Marshall Plan and brought in Western capital, which many 'Republicans', who had socialist views, saw as imperialism.

The democratic honeymoon did not last long, however. In 1960 the military staged a coup, disbanded the DP and, after a controversial show trial, executed Prime Minister Adnan Menderes and two of his ministers.

6 Said Nursi and His Heritage

The iron hand of the Republic led some Kurds to initiate a terrorist war against it (carried out by the bloody PKK and its forerunners), but the reaction of practicing Muslims has been peaceful. After all, Turkey does not have a tradition of Islamist violence and there is a synthesis of Islam and democracy that goes back to the Ottoman Empire.

Thus, instead of fighting against the Republic, practicing Muslims have preferred to vote for conservative parties that would soften its autocratic nature. Some of them hoped to bring in Islamic rule via elections, while others only demanded democratic rule that would respect their religious freedom. A very prominent name in the latter camp is Said Nursi (1878–1960), whose treatises on Islamic faith and morality are founding texts for Turkey's most important Islamist movement.

The Turkish scholar Yasin Aktay describes Nursi as a 'very apolitical, other-worldly and loyal character', referring to his allegiance to Republican Turkey. Unlike Sheik Said, another Kurdish Islamic leader who led a popular but unsuccessful revolt against the secular Turkish Republic in 1925, Nursi rejected political radicalism and focused his energy on articulating a religious worldview and moral code compatible with the modern world. According to Aktay (1997), Nursi, in his books, developed 'a very elective and appropriate combination of the elements of the popular culture, mystical discourses, orthodox Islam and science and rationality'.

In his thought, Nursi was closer to someone like C. S. Lewis – the Oxford professor who is widely regarded as one of the most important Christian apologists of the twentieth century – than to Muslim contemporaries such as Hassan al-Banna, the founder of Egypt's Muslim Brotherhood. His enemies were not Zionism or Western imperialism but materialist philosophy and communist ideology, and he saw the Christian West as an ally against both. In 1951, Nursi sent one of his books to the Vatican, along with a letter in which he called for an Islamo–Christian alliance against atheism. During the Korean War, which Turkey joined as an American ally, Nursi encouraged his followers to enlist in the army to fight against the communists.

Nursi's millions of followers, who constituted the Nur ('Light') movement, have always steered away from Islamist political parties and voted for centre-right parties that promised not sharia but religious freedom. According to Hakan Yavuz (2003, p. 11), Nursi, unlike the Young Turks and Kemalists who praised the state, 'treated the state as the servant of the people and argued for a neutral state without any ideology'. Moreover, he was very much in favour of modernising Turkey and the Islamic world in general by importing Western science and technology.

But even that modernist Islam was too much for the secularist establishment. 'In spite of all [their] compatibility with the modernisation process, Said Nursi and his movements have been prosecuted by the state,' notes Yasin Aktay. 'Because ... in order to constitute themselves as Western, Kemalists had to deny and repress any traces of the Orient' (Aktay, 1997).

7 The Rise of the Gülen Movement

After the death of Nursi in 1960, his followers ('nurcus') divided into several camps with differing views on how to interpret his legacy and engage with politics. In the 1970s a cleric in Izmir, who had been influenced by some of Nursi's ideas but also had new approaches of his own, started to attract attention and a following. He was Fethullah Gülen, whose popularity and influence would soon exceed those of all other Islamist movements in Turkey. According to Aktay,

> Fethullah Hoca, as a preacher famed in İzmir, following the same path of the Nurcu movement in that sense, seems to have been discovered by the state at least since the mid-eighties. He left the mainstream Nurcu movement at the early seventies and began to

> publish a monthly named *Sizinti*. The underlying idea of the name implies that it represents the leakage of the essence of the absolute truth, of the revelation. The major themes in the journal turn around catching the dispatches from the God which is embodied through a striking and mysterious order of the world. Undoubtedly a relevant discourse analysis of the journal may clarify various aspects of the community in terms of also the constitution of the self-identity in relation with the nature, religion and the political body. After leaving the mainstream movement he found an alternative community which depended on his personal charisma achieved by his strong ability in preaching and organising, and of course, on his deep intelligence. (Aktay, 1997)

Gülen had a vision that would take him and his followers to a place that no other Islamist group in Turkey had ever dreamed of reaching. Instead of simply trying to create a limited living space for itself in public life, like many other Islamist groups did, the Gülen movement decided to engage with society and create publications and institutions that would appeal to people from all walks of life. Their newspapers and TV channels, such as *Zaman* or *STV*, are not in-house community organs but speak to the whole of society. Their schools, which are famed for their high quality of education and moral integrity, have students with diverse backgrounds. Their initiatives, such as the Abant Platform or the Intercultural Dialogue Platform – which are both supported by the Journalists and Writers Foundation, whose honorary president is Fethullah Gülen – address not sectarian issues but deal with virtually all of the social problems of Turkey.

Moreover, since the mid-1990s the Gülen movement has become a global phenomenon. They began by opening schools in former Soviet republics, which proved to be a very successful enterprise. Soon the schools spread to the four corners of the world, from South Africa to Mongolia, from Australia to Denmark. Gülen's move to the United States in the late 1990s also contributed to the globalism of the movement. And while the movement was hoping to help change the world for the better with all these activities, they were also being changed by the world for the better: their engagement with different cultures and especially with that of the West helped Gülen's followers to develop a more liberal and cosmopolitan mindset and discourse.

8 Incorporating Capitalism

Today the 'Muslimhood' of Turkey is increasing – to use the term the sociologist Jenny B. White defines as an alternative to Islamism (White, 2005). This Muslimhood is in favour of democracy, secularity, pluralism and even capitalism – something that many modern Muslims perceive as alien to Islam.

Some striking examples of the latter phenomenon have emerged in Turkey in the past two decades. Turkey is not the richest country in the Islamic world but it is arguably the most developed. The richest are the oil-rich Arab nations, most of which, despite their petrodollars, remain socially premodern and tribal. Regrettably, oil brings wealth but it does not modernise. Modernisation comes through rationality, which can be achieved only through organisation, order, exchange and risk-taking in pursuit of goals. The late Turgut Özal, one of Turkey's wiser Presidents, once said, 'We are lucky that we don't have oil; we have to work hard to make money'.

Özal was a pro-Western politician and a Muslim believer. His revolutionary, Reaganesque reforms during the 1980s transformed the Turkish economy by giving up import subsidisation in favour of free markets. In this new setting the conservative Muslim masses of Anatolia have found fertile ground for a socio-economic boom. Thanks to their astounding successes in business, they have been called 'Anatolian tigers'. They constitute a new class that rivals the long-established, privileged, highly secularised and utterly condescending 'Istanbul bourgeoisie'.

The European Stability Initiative (ESI), a Berlin-based think tank, conducted an extensive study of the Anatolian tigers in 2005. ESI researchers interviewed hundreds of conservative businessmen in the central Anatolian city of Kayseri. They discovered that 'individualistic, pro-business currents have become prominent within Turkish Islam', and a 'quiet Islamic Reformation' was taking place among Muslim entrepreneurs. The term they used to define these religious capitalists was also the title of their report: 'Islamic Calvinists' (ESI, 2005).

This amalgamation of Islamic values with the practical rationality of the free market indeed reminds one of the spirit of the original Calvinists, who, according to sociologist Max Weber, spearheaded the rise of capitalism in the West. Interestingly, Weber was not very hopeful for Islam in this regard. For him Islam was an obstacle to capitalist development, for it could foster only aggressive militancy (jihad) or contemplative austerity. However, one of the greatest Turkish sociologists, Sabri F. Ülgener – both a student and a critic of Weber – argued that Weber, despite his genius in analysing the origins of capitalism in the West, misjudged Islam and overlooked its inherent compatibility with a 'liberal market system' (Ülgener, 2006, pp. 57–64).

The rise of an Islamic entrepreneurial class is a remarkable phenomenon, because it marks the beginning a whole new era for Islamic civilisation. People understand religion on the basis of not only its textual teachings but also their social environment. For Islam, this environment has been feudal, imperial or bureaucratic in the past. But now, in Turkey and in a few other Muslim counties such as Malaysia, Islam is being transformed into a religion of the middle class with its rational, independent individuals.

9 The Rediscovery of the West

A related aspect of the new Muslimhood in Turkey is its growing advocacy of Western-style democracy. One reason for this phenomenon is the significant discovery that Turkey's observant Muslims – especially those who have had the opportunity to come to know the West, such as the leadership of the AKP – have made in the past quarter century: that the West is better than the Westernisers.

What this means is that they recognise that Western democracies give their citizens all of the religious freedoms that Turkey has withheld from its own. In fact, no country in the free world has a form of secularism as illiberal as Turkey's self-styled *laicité*. Any society or club that has an Islamic name or purpose is illegal and religious education is very limited. A woman wearing a Muslim headscarf has no opportunity to pursue education of any kind in Turkey, whether in public or private schools. There is also the bitter language used by the secular elite towards observant Muslims.

For many decades, devout Muslims in Turkey have perceived this secular fundamentalism as a product of the West, and hoped that de-Westernisation would end their feeling of being 'a pariah in their own land', as the late Islamic poet Necip Fazil once put it. Yet, the more they learned about the West, the more they realised that the problem was in Ankara – not in Washington, London or Brussels. In Europe and North America, one can establish Islamic centres, Sufi clubs and independent mosques, none of which are allowed in their homeland. It is possible to attend American or European universities with the headscarf, while it is banned in Turkey.

All these facts have transformed the way Turkish Muslims perceive the West. Having realised that the real West is preferable to the caricature of it they have at home, they have reoriented their search for freedom. Instead of trying to Islamise the state, they have decided to liberalise it.

Hence the pro-EU and liberal stance of the AKP, which came to power in 2002 and has been governing Turkey ever since. The successive AKP governments have brought many reforms to Turkey, which have boosted the economy and brought in many new freedoms. This also explains the remarkable alliance in today's Turkey between Muslim conservatives and the secular liberals. Their coalition is in favour of democratisation and the bid to join the EU, whereas the nationalist front – which includes diehard secular Kemalists, ultra-right-wing Turkish nationalists and hardline Islamists – abhors both of those objectives.

10 Conclusion

The experience of Turkish Islam also hints at how the much-sought renaissance of the Islamic world will come about: through the flourishing of democracy, freedom and economic opportunity. Only these social dynamics create individuals and communities that are willing to adapt to modernity. On the other hand, if Muslim societies are forced to accept modernity – through, say, secularist tyrannies or Western military interventions – they will simply react against it, and the backlash will fuel radicalism.

It is a fact that Christianity overcame its Dark Ages thanks to its religious – not secular – reformers. Islamic civilisation needs to follow a similar path to accomplish its renewal. The Turkish experience suggests that there are reasons to be hopeful.

References

Aktay, Y. (1997). *Body, text, identity: The Islamist discourse of authenticity in modern Turkey*. PhD. Thesis. Ankara: The Graduate School of Social Sciences of the Middle East Technical University.

Davison, R. H. (1954). Turkish attitudes concerning Christian–Muslim equality in the nineteenth century. *American Historical Review, 59*(4), 844–864.

Deringil, S. (2000). 'There is no compulsion in religion': On conversion and apostasy in the late Ottoman Empire: 1839–1856. *Comparative Studies in Society and History, 42*(3), 547–575.

ESI. (2005). *Islamic Calvinists: Change and conservatism in central Anatolia*. European Stability Initiative. Available at http://www.esiweb.org/pdf/esi_document_id_69.pdf/, September 19

Hanioğlu, Ş. (2001). *Preparation for a revolution: The Young Turks, 1902–1908*. Oxford: Oxford University Press.

Hourani, A. (1983). *Arabic thought in the liberal age, 1798–1939*. Cambridge: Cambridge University Press.

Karpat, K. H. (2001). *The politicization of Islam: Reconstructing identity, state, faith, and community in the late Ottoman state*. New York: Oxford University Press.

Mardin, Ş. (2005). Turkish Islamic exceptionalism yesterday and today: Continuity, rupture and reconstruction in operational codes. *Turkish Studies, 6*(2), 145–165.

Neuhaus, R. J. (1984). *The naked public square: Religion and democracy in America*. Grand Rapids, MI: William B. Eerdmans.

Ülgener, S. F. (2006). *Zihniyet ve Din İslam, Tasavvuf ve Çözülme Devri İktisat Ahlaki*. Istanbul: Derin Yayınları.

White, J. B. (2005). The end of Islamism? Turkey's Muslimhood model. In R. Hefner (Ed.), *Modern Muslim politics* (pp. 87–111). Princeton, NJ: Princeton University Press.

Yavuz, M. H. (2003). Islam in the public square: The case of the Nur movement. In M. H. Yavuz & J. L. Esposito (Eds.), *Turkish Islam and the secular state* (pp. 1–18). Syracuse, NY: Syracuse University Press.

Yavuz, M. H., & Esposito, J. L. (2003). Islam in Turkey: Retreat from the secular path? In M. H. Yavuz & J. L. Esposito (Eds.), *Turkish Islam and the secular state* (pp. xiii–xxxiii). Syracuse, NY: Syracuse University Press.

Ye'or, B. (2002). *Islam and dhimmitude: Where civilizations collide*. Translated by M. Kochan & D. Littman. Cranbury, NJ: Associated University Press.

The Political Economy of Turkey's Accession to the EU: A Comparative Analysis

Pantelis Sklias

1 Introduction

This chapter is an attempt to address issues concerning the political economy of Turkey's accession to the European Union. The prospect of Turkey becoming a full member of the EU has triggered intense debates and attracted a lot of controversy concerning the future of the EU. The question whether Turkey should and, in fact, can achieve full membership status has many ramifications, touching upon all aspects of the EU enlargement process. In this chapter, however, we will focus on one of them, namely, what distinguishes Turkey's case from that of the CEECs that either joined the EU in the 2004 and 2007 enlargements or are currently in the process of conducting accession negotiations.

The purpose of this chapter is not to conduct an in-depth analysis of all issues concerning Turkey's accession or to give an extensive account of the political economy of the matter. The object of this chapter is, rather, to point out some fundamental elements that make Turkey's case unique, especially when compared to the case of the CEECs.

In conducting our analysis we will present, first, the status of the negotiation process as it stands today, since the 'freezing' of the accession chapters relating to the *acquis communautaire*. For this purpose we will take into account the opinions expressed by Commissioner Joaquin Almunia, as well as those of the World Economic Forum (WEF). Next we concentrate on four basic features that we believe distinguish and, to a large extent, define Turkey's accession to the EU. These are: advanced trade integration, low human capital, demographic dynamism and migration. Each one of those factors, as well as their impact on Turkey's potential, is assessed separately. We then move on to some concluding remarks and, in particular, assess the prospects for full membership and its implications, as well as other possible scenarios.

The purpose of our analysis is to inform the reader of the current status and the repercussions of one of the most debated issues concerning EU enlargement. By the end of this chapter, it should be clear that Turkey's accession could yield many

C. Arvanitopoulos (Ed.), *Turkey's Accession to the European Union*

benefits to the Union but also that, as things stand today, Turkey has to overcome important difficulties that hinder its prospects for full membership.

2 The European Union Today: The Current Situation of Turkish Accession

The EU is currently dealing with the great challenges of managing the enlargement that recently took place as well as the forthcoming ones, which from every point of view constitute a test for the Union. The enlargement from 15 to 25 and 27 member states, the bringing together of old and new members and the economic dimensions that differentiate them put a new complexion on EU general facts.

It is obvious that, at the moment, concepts such as enlargement and integration are in a conflictual relationship with each other. The possibility of ongoing enlargement and border drift has considerable consequences. That is, it can alter the nature of the EU from an international organization of integration and completion into an international organization of cooperation. An EU with a large number of member states has neither decision-making ability nor the ability to compel adherence to already existing rules, but confines itself to the effort of balancing conflicting interests. Despite all of this, the procedure of aggregation and completion still has the dynamic it had in the past, even if today there are 27 member states.

The query that concerns us at this point, taking into consideration the situation described above, is how a prospective Turkish accession to the EU could benefit not only Turkey but also the EU. Under what conditions could this eventuality contribute towards EU integration and prosperity for the member states? Is it possible that Turkey, characterised by unemployment, migration, economic stagnation and insecurity could fit into the EU, taking into account the institutional problems that the EU faces today?

The challenge is obvious. However, integrating a Muslim country into EU structures will definitely bridge the gap between Europe and the Islamic world, as well as bring a dynamic economy into the EU. Turkey is a country of great geopolitical importance with a population of 72.6 million people (World Bank, 2006) and there is no doubt that it would make a great addition to any organisation. At the same time, Turkey is also characterised by considerable disparities in every social, cultural and political measure.

The issue of whether Turkey belongs or not to the EU family is wide-ranging as well as vague. In this chapter, we attempt to address the political-economic aspect, taking into consideration the current state of the process of Turkish accession to the EU. The accession negotiations have already begun and the only thing that remains unresolved, on the way to full membership, is Turkey's compliance with the *acquis communautaire*. What exactly is, however, the current situation?

As things stand today, accession negotiations are becoming increasingly problematic for Turkey, especially after the December 2006 European Council decisions (European Council, 2006). The Foreign Ministers of the member states of the EU, after taking into account an earlier suggestion of the Commission, decided on the partial suspension of the accession negotiations with Turkey, due to the latter's refusal to adopt the Protocol of the Customs Union with the Republic of Cyprus and to allow – as a result – the free use of its airports and ports to Cypriot aircraft and ships (BBC News, 29 March 2007). This decision of the Council of the EU (the Council of Foreign Ministers), later adopted by the European Council on 14 December 2006, consists of freezing 8 out of 35 accession chapters under negotiation, specifically those related to transportation and trade (BBC News, 29 March 2007; EUPolitix.com, 29 March 2007). After this decision there was some progress on other chapters of the *acquis*, since in March and December 2007 the chapters on Enterprise and Industrial Regulations (EUPolitix.com, 29 March 2007), on Health and Consumer Protection and on Trans-European Transport were opened (*Zaman*, 20 December 2007), but this was still not enough to change Turkey's status after the freezing of the eight chapters. In June 2007 the chapters on Statistics and Financial Control were opened, but the opening of the chapter on Economic and Monetary Policy was blocked by French President Nicholas Sarkozy (*New York Times*, 25 June 2007).

Joaquin Almunia, the EU Commissioner in charge of economic and monetary policy, stated, in the framework of the WEF, that he was satisfied with the progress made by the Turkish economy during the previous five years (WEF, 2006/2007). It had achieved a significant rate of development and seen a parallel decrease in inflation and the public deficit, close to the requirements of the Maastricht Agreement. Nevertheless, he pointed to the necessity for further reforms with regard to public revenue and the simplification of the tax system, so that companies that operate at a European level could profitably operate in Turkey. He referred, finally, to the challenges ahead, such as the balance of payments on the current account and the high interest rates relative to those of the European Union.

The WEF (2006/2007), in its semi-annual report that concentrates on the evaluation of the progress made towards targets established by the European Council of Lisbon in 2000, mentions that Turkey has succeeded in achieving important progress in relation to the opening of the economy, on the one hand, and to the unification of financial services supporting entrepreneurial initiative, on the other. Turkey appears to be doing better than some members of the EU (Bulgaria, Poland and Romania) (Turkish Statistical Institute, 2006), based on the quality of economic reforms and, more specifically, judging from the benefits coming from productivity gains and competitiveness. On the other hand, there are concerns about the low productivity of the Turkish agricultural sector, fiscal fluctuations and high inflation, problems that the Turkish government should solve in order to take further steps towards European membership.

In the 51 years of the EU's political life there has been no accession of a new member that has caused so much reaction. It is obvious that Turkey's accession negotiations present exceptional obstacles that, for the time being, may hinder the country's progress towards full membership. In the following section, we will focus on the economic aspects that distinguish Turkey's accession from that of other countries.

3 The Four Features that Distinguish the Accession of Turkey to the EU from that of the CEECs

3.1 Some Basic Comparative Statistics

Table 1 shows some basic data on the Turkish economy and makes possible a comparison with the CEECs and the EU (Flam, 2004).

The most important fact about Turkey is its size; in terms of population it would be the second-largest member of an enlarged EU. Moreover, the demographics are such that Turkey is likely to surpass Germany and become the largest country in about 2020 (World Bank, 2005).

Turkey is among the poorest candidate countries and has about the same income per capita, adjusted for purchasing power parity, as Bulgaria and Romania (OECD, 2005). It should be added that the income disparities within Turkey are great, with the population in the southeast having less than half the average national income and the large rural population generally being much poorer than the urban population.

Turkey's relatively low level of development is clear from the percentage of the labour force involved in agriculture and related industries. Only Bulgaria and Romania have a similar dependence on agriculture.

As mentioned above, in the 51 years of the EU's history, no other potential accession has triggered so much controversy. Certainly, if we were to analyse Turkey's accession from the political point of view we would conclude that the challenges are many and widely known. In the EU, however, attention tends to focus on economic issues.

Turkey is still a poor country in terms of per capita income (OECD, 2008). Income levels are substantially lower than those of Western Europe countries, for example. Expressed in terms of purchasing power parity (PPP), per capita consumption is only $5,500 and per capita GDP is about $3,000. This is far below the poorest current members of the EU (World Bank, 2007).

A large part of the economy remains agricultural. The proportion of Turkey's workforce engaged in agriculture is no longer above 50%, as it was in 1989, but it is over 40% (compared with around 2% in the United Kingdom). This rural workforce of over 15 million people is larger than the population of several EU member states, and its levels of income are far below the average, even for Turkey (European Commission, 2008). Transforming it from an economy based on traditional agriculture into a modern economy will require enormous and prolonged structural reforms.

There are also severe regional imbalances. Istanbul and western Turkey now enjoy something close to the prosperity of an industrialised European country. In much of central and eastern Turkey, however, incomes are far lower and the economy is still overwhelmingly agricultural.

The focus of this chapter, however, is to ascertain and list the challenges in relation to the political economy of Turkish accession and especially the challenges that distinguish the accession of Turkey to the EU from that of the CEECs. When it

Table 1 Comparison between EU-15, CEEC-10 and Turkey, 2000

				Agriculture		Export shares to	
	Population (million)	GNI, PPP (current billion euro)	Per capita GNI PPP (current billion euro)	Value added, per cent of GDP	Employment, per cent of total employment	Turkey (%)	EU (%)
Bulgaria	8.2	45	5,530	15.8	11.2	10.3	51.7
Czech Republic	10.3	140	13,610	3.4	5.3	0.6	68.8
Estonia	1.4	13	9,050	5.7	7.0	0.2	68.5
Hungary	10.0	121	12,060	3.9	7.2	0.7	75.2
Latvia	2.4	17	6,960	3.9	14.4	0.0	64.7
Lithuania	3.7	26	6,960	2.5	18.4	1.8	47.9
Poland	38.7	349	9,030	2.9	18.7	0.4	70.1
Romania	22.4	143	6,380	11.4	45.2	6.1	64.0
Slovak Republic	5.4	59	11,000	2.7	7.5	0.4	59.1
Slovenia	2.0	35	17,390	4.3	9.6	0.8	63.9
Total CEEC-10	104.5	948	9,068	5.1	21.5	2.0	67.6
Austria	8.1	213	26,310	1.2	6.1	0.7	61.6
Belgium	10.3	282	27,50	1.1	1.9	1.0	74.9
Denmark	5.3	145	27,120	2.0	3.7	0.4	67.3
Finland	5.2	128	24,610	0.9	6.2	1.3	55.3
France	58.9	1,440	24,470	2.3	4.2	1.1	61.4
Germany	82.2	2,054	25,010	0.9	2.6	1.4	56.5
Greece	10.6	179	16,940	6.8	17.0	5.1	43.6
Ireland	3.8	97	25,470	2.6	7.9	0.5	60.0
Italy	57.7	1,348	23,370	2.4	5.2	1.8	54.9
Luxembourg	0.4	20	45,420	0.6	2.4	0.5	84.0
Netherlands	15.9	417	26,170	2.2	3.3	0.8	78.8
Portugal	10.0	169	16,880	2.4	12.5	0.4	79.5
Spain	39.4	757	19,180	3.7	6.9	1.7	69.1
Sweden	8.9	211	23,770	0.7	2.9	1.2	55.0
United Kingdom	59.7	1,407	23,550	0.7	1.5	1.0	56.9
EU-15	376.3	8,865	23,557	1.7	4.3	1.2	62.1
Turkey	65.3	459	7,030	14.2	32.7	–	52.3

Sources: Flam (2004, p. 178); The first three columns are from World Development Indicators Online, World Bank. Agricultural value added and agricultural employment data are from European Commission, Directorate General for Agriculture. Trade data are from IMF, Direction of Trade Statistics CD-ROM

comes to political economy, there are four specific issues that are widely considered to be the key factors related to Turkish accession: advanced trade integration; low human capital; demographic dynamism and migration. These four challenges create enormous barriers, capable of freezing the accession process of a candidate country. This very fact is what differentiates to a large extent the accession of Turkey to the EU from that of the CEECs. These factors are listed and analyzed below.

3.1.1 Advanced Trade Integration (Customs Union)

There is a debate on whether a special relationship should be offered instead of full membership, but taking into consideration that the EU and Turkey have been linked by a Customs Union since 31 December 1995, it seems that a special relationship already exists, at least in the economic field.

Through the Customs Union agreement, Turkey today enjoys a far more integrated status than did the CEECs before they became full members. Although the customs union does not cover essential economic areas such as agriculture, services and public procurement, what is of great significance is the fact that the EU is by far the number one source of Turkey's imports and the top destination for its exports, while Turkey ranks seventh among the EU's top import sources and fifth among its export markets.[1]

In addition, at the December 2002 Copenhagen Council meetings, the EU member states endorsed the Commission's objective of extending and deepening the customs union. The Council has agreed on negotiating guidelines for the liberalisation of services and public procurement. Several rounds of negotiations have so far taken place.

Obviously, advanced trade integration through the customs union is a fact that distinguishes, to a great extent, the accession of Turkey to the EU from that of the CEECs. This special relation is of great importance, considering that it provides Turkey with privileges in strategic economic sectors. There was no case of trade integration between a CEEC and the EU prior to the accession of the CEECs, and, where there was, it was not established to the same extent as that of Turkey. Trade integration gives the relationship between Turkey and the EU a degree of reliability and dependability and brings the accession process to a higher level.

3.1.2 Low Human Capital

Another point that differentiates, to a great extent, the accession of Turkey from that of the CEECs is Turkey's low level of human capital. Human capital consists of education, skills and culture. According to the new growth theories, human capital is one of the fundamental sources of economic growth. The contribution of human capital to economic development is of cardinal importance, and this alone makes it a factor worthy of consideration. Human capital is one of the determinants of productivity; it raises a nation's ability to produce goods and services and is a crucial factor of production (Mankiw, 2007, p. 556).

In terms of indicators of human capital, the CEECs are close to the EU average. Turkey clearly lags behind, with potentially important consequences for its growth prospects. The human potential (capital) of the Turkish economy determines the development possibilities of several other sectors, which makes the low human capital in Turkey an issue of great importance. The quality of a country's

[1] For more details, see http://ec.europa.eu/trade/issues/bilateral/countries/turkey/index_en.htm/.

workforce, in terms of human capital, determines, to a considerable extent, its economic potential and development. As is obvious from Table 2, Turkey invests relatively little in education, less than most EU member states. In comparison with the other countries, excluding Portugal, Turkey lags behind in its total expenditure on education and the proportion of the adult population with upper secondary education. The literacy rate in Turkey is 81% whereas in western and northern European countries it is 95–100%. The consequences of low human capital will have an impact not only on Turkey's economic growth but will also slow down EU-wide development, as more money and effort will be needed for Turkey to adapt to EU standards.

3.1.3 Demographic Dynamism

Turkey is characterised by demographic dynamism (Gros, 2005). Turkey's labour force will continue to experience growth rates of more than 1% per annum for at least one more generation (World Bank, 2005). By contrast, the labour force is currently shrinking in many CEECs. An expanding population provides economic opportunity only if employment increases as well. This, however, does not seem to have been the case for Turkey, so far. This fact is a matter of great importance, as it can have a potentially negative impact, both socially and economically. Turkish public policy should emphasise this issue if Turkey wants to find a way to make its demographic bonus more profitable.

3.1.4 Migration

Given the positive demographic profile of Turkey, particularly compared to the aging population and problematic demographics of the EU, potential migration from Turkey to the Union should constitute one of the positive economic impacts of Turkish accession. At the same time, as has been seen with the enlargement of the ten new member states, migration is a sensitive political issue in most of the EU-15 member states, with public opinion easily stirred against it. In the case of

Table 2 Total expenditure on education and adult population with upper secondary education

	Total expenditure on education as % of GDP	Adult population with upper secondary education (%)
Turkey	3.91	24.3
Poland	5.31	45.9
Portugal	5.69	19.8
Greece	3.86	51.4
Hungary	5.15	70.2

Source: OECD, quoted by Gros (2005, p. 6)

the 2004 enlargement, these political issues were dealt with by allowing a flexible transition period of up to seven years.

A key difference in Turkey's accession compared with the 2004 and 2007 enlargements is that a large number of Turkish citizens have been firmly established for some time in the EU, concentrated in one country in particular, Germany. A corollary of this is the fact that (given existing regulations in Germany on family reunification) a substantial net flow of migrants is taking place even at present (with no formal mobility for workers).

Since the early 1960s, more than three million Turkish workers have migrated for employment purposes to more than 30 countries. Turkish labour emigration to Western Europe occurred in three phases: (a) European employers recruited Turkish workers during the 1960s and early 1970s; (b) Turkish emigration to European nations changed in the mid-1970s from comprising mostly workers to being made up largely of the spouses and dependents of workers; and (c) today, as is clear from Table 3, two million Turks have apparently settled permanently in Western Europe.

4 Concluding Remarks: The Alternatives and the Challenges Ahead

4.1 *The Prospects for Full Membership*

After the customary stage of pre-entrance negotiations for Turkey's accession to the EU, on 4 October 2005 Turkey was invited to fulfil the requirements of the EU's negotiating framework. As a matter of course, the Foreign Ministers of the member states of EU, after taking into account an earlier suggestion of the Commission, later decided on the partial suspension of accession negotiations with Turkey, but this decision appears to be temporary. Given the determination with which Turkey has pursued the goal of EU membership, it is likely that sooner or later Turkey will succeed in meeting the criteria that are required for full membership.

Table 3 Turkish population in selected EU countries 2000

Country	Thousands	As % of total foreign population
Germany	1998.5	27.4
France	208.0	6.4
Austria	134.5	17.7
Netherlands	100.8	15.1
United Kingdom	58.0	2.2
Belgium	56.2	6.5
Denmark	35.2	13.6

Source: OECD – Not including those of Turkish origin who have taken on citizenship of the country of residence. Quoted by Yasar Yakis (2005, p. 118)

Pacta sunt servanda has been one of the EU's fundamental principles since its establishment. Therefore, given the clarity of the membership criteria, it falls upon Turkey itself to prove its commitment to the negotiation process. However distant this process seems to be at present, it should necessarily come to an end, at which point, if Turkey complies with all the criteria, it will inevitably become a full member.

Assuming that Turkey does, after all, become a full member of the Union, there are some interesting matters we should take into consideration, such as the following: How much will Turkish membership cost and what would be the impact of this cost? How will the human potential of the Turkish economy determine the whole process? Will demographic dynamism be another obstacle to progress after accession? It is expected that should Turkey ever become a full member of the EU, one third of the community funds will be needed in order to support Turkish development. Moreover, the EU's decision-making system, which is based on the population of each country, will give Turkey great power; a fact that could potentially be a matter of controversy among member states and perhaps lead to a new crisis within the EU.[2]

It should be clear to the reader at this point that Turkey's accession negotiations warrant an analysis of issues that did not arise in the previous enlargements.

4.2 The Challenges Ahead: Other Scenarios

Negotiations were officially launched, after intense bargaining, on 4 October 2005, and Turkey was invited to conform to the EU's negotiating framework. A first possible scenario would be that Turkey, after many delays, finally enters a period of transformation and begins to adapt to European standards. The second scenario is that persistent frictions and tensions with the EU will freeze accession negotiations, and Turkey's European perspective will lead de facto to a still undefined special partnership.

Certainly, those who are pessimistic about Turkey's full EU integration believe that Ankara, supported by the American–British axis and counting on the favourable stance that Europe has shown in the past, might attempt to interpret, in its own way, its obligations towards the EU, namely to implement, for itself, a special kind of EU membership.

Turkey, as the Ottoman Empire did in the past, is trying to find the ideal balance between East and West. Yet its European adventure compels Turkey to attach more importance to the West. This action has brought about a series of major alterations and reforms, which in turn have caused intense turbulence in the country's internal political and social system.

---

[2] For a start, Turkey will necessarily be allocated significant voting power in the Council of the EU as well as in the European Parliament. This fact, although not a problem in itself, may lead to the creation of a new pole within the EU, thus potentially rendering the decision-making process even more complicated.

Ankara has responded in various ways to the challenges mentioned above: first, moderate voices are urging Turkey not to abandon its efforts to become a member of the EU; progress made so far – any progress – should not be disregarded. On the other hand, extremist political forces, and opponents of the EU, when they do not refer to 'a closed Christian club', speak darkly that there are those who are planning to divide their country.

Nevertheless, following Turkey's most recent evolution, some believe that the country has entered an era of political instability. On the whole, a general sentiment of increased Euroscepticism has been observed. It takes the form of a common belief shared by all parties and impels political leaders to adopt a more unyielding position on issues of Euro-Turkish relations. Of course, Euroscepticism (Yılmaz, 2005a, 2005b) is enhanced by unfavourable messages coming from European capitals concerning the future of Euro-Turkish relations.

Most analysts are interested in analysing Turkey's eventual EU membership. However, it would be more realistic to analyse the possibility of failure in the accession process. We must bear in mind that despite enormous efforts made by Turkey to adopt the *acquis communautaire*, the current situation is not in its favour. Scepticism about Turkey's eventual EU membership is widespread in Europe, especially after the election of Sarkozy in France, while, as mentioned above, the domestic situation in Turkey is quite volatile.

The first question that arises is this: What will happen to the reform process if Turkey fails to become a full EU member? Everybody agrees that the reforms promote Turkish prosperity and will always constitute a major objective, regardless of whether they lead to EU accession or not. Turkish officials have often declared that the Copenhagen criteria are part of their policy and should be implemented in any case.

The second question is whether the customs union constitutes the ideal solution. Apparently, even if the EU and Turkey maintain excellent relations in the economic or commercial field, the problem lies in further incorporation. In case Turkey does not become a full EU member, how worthwhile would any efforts towards further incorporation be? In other words, the customs union does not constitute a solution, but is only an instrument for avoiding total rupture and establishing a special status between full membership and a customs union.

Some claim that there will be further convergence between the United States and Turkey if the latter does not manage to become an EU member. It is, however, important to note that the United States needs a Turkey fully integrated into EU and that the two countries are major allies within NATO. Consequently, it is obvious that relations between those two countries will remain at the same level.

Turkey may turn to the enhancement of its bilateral relations with individual countries within the EU and with other countries (in the Middle East, for example) in all areas. We can confidently predict that Turkey's progress towards EU membership might last for many years and cause much debate and controversy. We cannot come to any safe conclusions, however, since many changes may take place in the coming years.

The path to membership will be long and rough. It is true, however, that a Turkey with a European perspective, enjoying political stability, democratic values and economic prosperity, would bring immediate benefits to Europe. It remains only to observe the means and the sacrifices that Turkey will choose, in its turn, in order to attain its European ambition.

Appendixes

Table 1 Total population: Various EU member states and candidates, and total EU-25, EU-27 and EU-28; UN estimates 2003–2050

	Population (in thousands)			
	2003	2015	2025	2050
Austria	8,116	8,058	7,979	7,376
Belgum	10,318	10,470	10,516	10,221
Bulgaria	7,897	7,167	6,609	5,255
Czech Republic	10,236	10,076	9,806	8,553
Denmark	5,364	5,447	5,469	5,273
Finland	5,207	5,284	5,289	4,941
France	60,144	62,841	64,165	64,230
Germany	82,476	82,497	81,959	79,145
Greece	10,976	10,944	10,707	9,814
Hungary	9,877	9,324	8,865	7,589
Italy	57,423	55,507	52,939	44,875
Netherlands	16,149	16,791	17,123	16,954
Poland	38,587	38,173	37,337	33,004
Portugal	10,062	10,030	9,834	9,027
Romania	22,334	21,649	20,806	18,063
Slovakia	5,402	5,441	5,897	4,048
Spain	41,060	41,167	40,669	37,338
Sweden	8,876	8,983	9,055	8,700
UK	59,251	61,275	63,287	66,166
Turkey	**71,325**	**82,150**	**89,995**	**97,759**
Total EU-25	**454,187**	**456,876**	**454,422**	**431,241**
Total EU-27	**484,418**	**485,692**	**481,837**	**454,559**
Total EU-28 (including Turkey)	**555,743**	**567,842**	**570,832**	**552,318**
Turkey as % of EU-28	**12.8%**	**14.4%**	**15.5%**	**17.7%**

Source: UN World Population Division, *World Population Prospects* (the 2002 revision); quoted by Hughes (2004, p. 9).

Table 2 Turkey: Major economic indicators

							ECFIN forecast		200602	200603	200604	200610	200611	200612
		2002	2003	2004	2005	2006	2007	2008	Q2	Q3	Q4	Oct	Nov	Dec
1. Output and demand														
Industrial confidence[1.1]	Balance	102.0	104.1	106.8	102.8				104.2	102.8	:	100.4	100.7	
Industrial production[1.2]	Ann. % ch	9.4	8.7	9.8	5.4				9.3	5.6	:	2.5	:	
Gross domestic product[1.3]	Ann. % ch	7.9	5.8	9.0	7.4	6.0 f	6.4	6.3	7.8	3.4	:	N.A.	N.A.	N.A.
Consumer confidence[1.4]	Balance	N.A.	N.A.	106.7	100.1	:			98.2	90.5	:	91.6	93.4	:
Private consumption[1.5]	Ann. % ch	2.1	6.6	10.1	8.8	7.8 f	7.0	5.5	10.4	1.3	:	N.A.	N.A.	N.A.
Gross fixed capital formation[1.6]	Ann. % ch	–1.1	10.0	32.4	24.0	11.3 f	10.3	8.1	11.5	9.4	:	N.A.	N.A.	N.A.
Change in stocks[1.7]	% of GDP	4.7	7.3	7.9	5.2	:			4.5	3.6	:	N.A.	N.A.	N.A.
2. Labour market														
Unemployment[2.1]	%	10.4	10.5	10.3	10.2	9.8 f	9.1	8.9	8.8	9.1	:	:	:	:
Employment[2.2]	Ann. % ch	–0.3	–0.8	2.0	1.7	1.6 f	1.9	1.4	0.6	1.9	:	:	:	:
Wages[2.3]	Ann. % ch	37.2	23.0	13.4	12.2	16.7 f	14.1	12.3	11.4	10.8	:	:	:	:
3. International transactions														
Exports of goods[3.1]	Ann. % ch	16.7	27.6	30.9	14.8	:			18.8	16.4	:	–0.1	:	:
Imports of goods[3.2]	Ann. % ch	24.5	34.5	40.7	19.7	:			23.1	17.9	:	11.8		
Trade balance[3.3]	% of GDP	–4.0	–5.8	–7.9	–9.1	–10.4 f	–10.2	–10.0	–10.1	–10.6	:	N.A.	N.A.	N.A.
Exports goods and services[3.4]	% of GDP	29.2	27.4	28.9	27.4	5.2 f	5.9	5.2	27.1	27.6	:	N.A.	N.A.	N.A.
Imports goods and services[3.5]	% of GDP	30.7	30.7	34.7	34.0	6.4 f	6.0	5.5	35.1	35.8	:	N.A.	N.A.	N.A.
Current account balance[3.6]	% of GDP	–0.8	–3.3	–5.2	–6.4	–6.5 f	–7.2	–7.2	–7.6	–8.5	:	N.A.	N.A.	N.A.
Direct investment (FDI.net)[3.7]	% of GDP	0.5	0.5	0.7	2.4				4.4	4.7	:	N.A.	N.A.	N.A.

4. Prices														
CPI[4.1]	Ann. % ch	45.0	21.6	8.6	8.2	9.6	8.6	6.1	9.6	10.8	:	10.0	9.9	9.7
GDP deflator[4.2]	Ann. % ch	44.3	22.5	9.8	5.4	6.5 f	8.0	5.0	9.5	14.2	:	:	:	:
Producer prices[4.3]	Ann. % ch	50.1	22.7	14.6	5.9	9.3			8.4	12.6	:	10.9	11.7	:
Import prices[4.4]	Ann. % ch	:	:	:	:	:			:	:	:	:	:	:
5. Monetary and financial indicators														
Interest rate (3 months)[5.1]	% p.a.	50.49	37.68	24.26	20.40	:			19.42	23.80	:	23.91	23.91	:
Bond yield[5.2]	% p.a.	:	:	:	:	:			:	:	:	:	:	:
Stock markets[5.3]	Index	11,013	12,312	19,899	29,353	39,867			39,805	36,572	38,809	38,487	38,929	39,011
M4[5.4]	Ann. % ch	36.5	31.9	40.9	30.9				41.1	20.2	:	24.8	22.6	:
Exchange rate TRY/EUR[5.5]	Value	1.43	1.69	1.77	1.67	1.80			1.83	1.91	1.87	1.86	1.88	1.89
Nominal eff. exchange rate[5.6]	Index	31.05	27.47	26.72	28.04	:			25.79	24.62	:	:	:	:
6. Government balance and debt														
General government balance[6.1]	% of GDP	−12.9	−11.3	−5.7	−1.2	−3.6 f	−4.0	−3.3	:	:	:	:	:	:
General government debt[6.2]	% of GDP	93.0	85.2	76.9	69.6	69.4 f	66.1	63.3	:	:	:	:	:	:

[a] Interim HICP is not available for Turkey

ECFIN forecast autumn 2006

Source: European Commission (2005a, p. 16)

Table 3 Main economic trends (as of 7 October 2005)

		2000	2001	2002	2003	2004		2005
Gross domestic product	Ann. % ch	7.3	–7.5	7.9	5.8	9.0	4.5	1st half
Private consumption	Ann. % ch	6.2	–9.2	2.1	6.6	10.1	4.2	1st half
Gross fixed capital formation	Ann. % ch	16.9	–31.5	–1.1	10.0	32.4	12.4	1st half
Unemployment[a]	%	6.6	8.5	10.4	10.5	10.3	10.5	1st half
Employment[a]	Ann. % ch	:	0.0	–0.3	–0.8	2.0	3.6	1st half
Wages	Ann. % ch	55.8	31.8	37.2	23.0	13.4	12.5	1st half
Current account balance	% of GDP	–5.0	2.4	–0.8	–3.3	–5.2	–5.7	1st half
Direct investment (FDI, net)	% of GDP	0.1	1.9	0.5	0.5	0.7	0.7	1st half
CPI	Ann. % ch	54.9	54.4	45.0	21.6	8.6	8.0	Jan–Sep
Interest rate (3 months)	%p.a.	47.2	74.7	50.5	37.7	24.3	20.4	Jan–Aug
Bond yield	%p.a.	N.A.	N.A.	N.A.	N.A.	N.A.	N.A.	
Stock markets	Index	14,458	10,127	11,013	12,312	19,899	27,366	Jan–Sep
Exchange rate TRY/EUR	Value	0.58	1.09	1.43	1.69	1.77	1.69	Jan–Sep
Nominal eff. exchange rate	Index	74.2	41.5	31.1	27.5	26.8	28.0	Jan–July
General government balance[b]	% of GDP	–6.1	–29.8	–12.3	–9.7	–3.9	:	
General government debt[b]	% of GDP	57.4	105.2	94.3	87.2	80.1	:	

Source: Eurostat, ECOWIN, national sources
[a] LFS data
[b] ESA 95 data

References

European Commission. (2005a). *Candidate countries economies quarterly*. Brussels: Directorate General, Economic and Financial Affairs, April.

European Commission. (2005b). *Turkey 2005 progress report*. SEC 1426. Brussels, 9 November.

European Commission. (2008). *Turkey – Agriculture and enlargement*. Available at http://ec.europa.eu/agriculture/enlargement/countries/turkey/profile_en.pdf

European Council. (2006). *Brussels European council: Presidency conclusions (14–15 December 2006)*, 16879/06. Brussels.

Flam, H. (2004). Turkey and the EU: Politics and Economics of Accession. *Cesifo Economic Studies*. 50(1), pp 171–210.

Gros, D. (2005). *Economic aspects of Turkey's quest for EU membership*. CEPS Policy Brief No. 69. Brussels: Center for European Policy Studies, April.

Hughes, K. (2004). *Turkey and the European Union: Just another enlargement? Exploring the implications of Turkish accession*. Brussels: Friends of Europe Working Paper, June.

Mankiw, N. G. (2007). *Principles of economics* (4th Ed.). Mason, OH: Thomson/South-Western.

OECD. (2005). *New GDP comparisons based on purchasing power parities for the year 2002*. Paris, 11 January.

OECD. (2008). *Fact book*. Paris.
Turkish Statistical Institute. (2006). *GNP and GDP as of September 2006 (DOC)*. Ankara, 12 November.
WEF. (2006/2007). *Annual report*. Geneva: http://www.weforum.org/pdf/annualreport/2007/annual_report.pdf/.
World Bank. (2005). *Data and statistics for Turkey*. Washington, DC: World Bank.
World Bank. (2006). *Turkey at a glance*. Washington, DC: World Bank, 13 August, http://devdata.worldbank.org/AAG/tur_aag.pdf/.
World Bank. (2007). *Global economic prospects managing the next wave of globalization*. Washington DC: The World Bank.
Yakis, Y. (2005). Turkey-EU relations. In *Harvard Black Sea security programme* (p. 110). Available at http://www.harvard-bssp.org/static/files/26/bulletin.pdf/.
Yilmaz, H. (2005a). Indicators of euroskepticism in the Turkish public opinion by the end of 2003: Basic findings of a survey. In H. Yilmaz (Ed.), *Placing Turkey on the map of Europe* (pp. 182–186). İstanbul: Boğaziçi University Press.
Yilmaz, H. (2005b). Swinging between eurosupportiveness and euroskepticism: Turkish public's general attitudes towards the European union. In H. Yilmaz (Ed.), *Placing Turkey on the map of Europe*. (pp. 152–181). İstanbul: Boğaziçi University Press.

Index

Printing: Krips bv, Meppel, The Netherlands
Binding: Stürtz, Würzburg, Germany